Democracy Promotion as Foreign Policy

This book looks at democracy promotion as a form of foreign policy. Elliott asks why *democracy* was seen to be the answer to the 7/7 bombings in London, and why it should be promoted not in Britain, but in Pakistan. The book provides a detailed answer to these questions, examining the logic and the modes of thinking that made such a response possible through analysis of the stories we tell about ourselves: stories about time, history, development, civilisation and the ineluctable spread of democracy.

Elliott argues that these narratives have become a key tool in enabling practices that differentiate selves from others, friends from enemies, the domestic from the foreign, civilisation from the barbarian. They operate with a particular conception of time and constitute a British, democratic, national identity by positing an "other" that is barbaric, alien, despotic, violent and backward. Such understandings are useful in the wake of disaster, because they leave us with something to *do*: danger can be managed by bringing certain people and places up-to-date. However, this book shows that there are other stories to be told, and that it is possible to read stories about history against the grain, and author alternative, less oppressive versions.

Providing a genealogy drawing on material from colonial and postcolonial Britain and Pakistan, including legislation, political discourse, popular culture and government projects, this book will be of interest to scholars and students focusing on democracy promotion, genealogy, critical border studies, poststructural international relations, postcolonial politics, discourse analysis, identity/subjectivity, and the "war on terror".

Cathy Elliott is a Senior Teaching Fellow at the School of Public Policy, University College London. She previously worked as a development manager in Pakistan. Her research interests include poststructural international relations; time, temporality and history; politics and aesthetics; and feminism and gender.

Interventions

Edited by: Jenny Edkins, Aberystwyth University and Nick Vaughan-Williams, University of Warwick

The Series provides a forum for innovative and interdisciplinary work that engages with alternative critical, post-structural, feminist, postcolonial, psychoanalytic and cultural approaches to international relations and global politics. In our first 5 years we have published 60 volumes.

We aim to advance understanding of the key areas in which scholars working within broad critical post-structural traditions have chosen to make their interventions, and to present innovative analyses of important topics. Titles in the series engage with critical thinkers in philosophy, sociology, politics and other disciplines and provide situated historical, empirical and textual studies in international politics.

For a full list of available titles please visit https://www.routledge.com/series/INT.

The most recent titles in this series are:

Refugees in Extended Exile
Living on the edge
Jennifer Hyndman and Wenona Giles

Security Without Weapons
Rethinking violence, nonviolent actions, and civilian protection
M. S. Wallace

Disorienting Democracy
Politics of emancipation
Clare Woodford

Democracy Promotion as Foreign Policy
Temporal othering in International Relations
Cathy Elliott

Asylum Seekers, Sovereignty, and the Senses of the International
A politico-corporeal struggle
Eeva Puumala

Global Powers of Horror
Security, politics, and the body in pieces
François Debrix

Democracy Promotion as Foreign Policy

Temporal othering in international relations

Cathy Elliott

LONDON AND NEW YORK

First published 2017
by Routledge
2 Park Square, Milton Park, Abingdon, Oxon OX14 4RN

and by Routledge
711 Third Avenue, New York, NY 10017

Routledge is an imprint of the Taylor & Francis Group, an informa business

© 2017 Cathy Elliott

The right of Cathy Elliott to be identified as author of this work has been asserted by her in accordance with sections 77 and 78 of the Copyright, Designs and Patents Act 1988.

All rights reserved. No part of this book may be reprinted or reproduced or utilised in any form or by any electronic, mechanical, or other means, now known or hereafter invented, including photocopying and recording, or in any information storage or retrieval system, without permission in writing from the publishers.

Trademark notice: Product or corporate names may be trademarks or registered trademarks, and are used only for identification and explanation without intent to infringe.

British Library Cataloguing in Publication Data
A catalogue record for this book is available from the British Library

Library of Congress Cataloging in Publication Data
Names: Elliott, Cathy.
Title: Democracy promotion as foreign policy : temporal othering in
    international relations / by Cathy Elliott.
Description: Milton Park, Abingdon, Oxon ; New York, NY : Routledge,
    2017. | Includes bibliographical references and index.
Identifiers: LCCN 2016037848| ISBN 9781138669727 (hardback) | ISBN
    9781315618050 (ebook)
Subjects: LCSH: Democratization–International cooperation. | Democracy. |
    international relations.
Classification: LCC JC423 .E385 2017 | DDC 327.1/1–dc23
LC record available at https://lccn.loc.gov/2016037848

ISBN: 978-1-138-66972-7 (hbk)
ISBN: 978-1-31561-805-0 (ebk)

Typeset in Times New Roman
by Taylor & Francis Books

To my mum and dad, with love

Contents

List of figures	viii
Preface	ix
Introduction	1
1 What is democracy promotion?	22
2 Democratic representation	38
3 Disordering histories	55
4 Authoring the codes elsewhere: Colonial governmentality and teleological time	82
5 Blood in the codes: Liberal governmentality, democracy and Pakistan	106
6 Twelve months that shook the world: 1989 and the Salman Rushdie affair	126
7 The art of integration: Representing British Muslims	147
Conclusion: Democracy promotion, time and the "radical ordinary"	165
Bibliography	176
Index	196

Figure

2.1 Why politics will not fix Pakistan 38

Preface

On Friday 13 November 2015, we tragically saw yet another co-ordinated terrorist attack in a European capital city. Gunmen and suicide bombers in Paris attacked a rock concert, a sports stadium, and various bars and restaurants, killing 130 people and injuring many more (BBC, 2015a). A two-minute monologue by BBC TV political affairs presenter Andrew Neil condemning the attacks subsequently went viral on social media. It was later translated into French and made freely available on the BBC website in both languages (BBC, 2015b). This intervention summed up common discursive responses to such terrible events. The attackers, says Neil, are more in a long historical line of "fascists, Nazis and Stalinists" who have attacked Europe and "democracy" before. He proposes that France is a symbol of "civilisation" and cites as evidence a long list of distinguished French citizens. This is mainly a roll call of dead white men – including Sartre and Camus but not Simone de Beauvoir – though Juliette Binoche, Zinedine Zidane and the pop group Daft Punk do get a mention after coq au vin and before crème brûlée. He also refers to France's modern, up-to-date, progressive credentials: "cutting-edge science", modern medicine, "fearsome" security forces and nuclear power. The attackers, meanwhile, are associated with a "death cult barbarity" and "medieval squalor" that would "shame the Middle Ages". The future, he suggested, would be "won" by democracy and leave the terrorists as "dust". This temporal narrative, casting terrorists as "back in the past" and industrialised, postcoloniser, liberal democratic countries like Britain and France as on an inexorable and unbroken march towards an ever more civilised future is very familiar and we will encounter it many times in the forthcoming pages. It does not seem to be a discourse that is going away.

This book begins from the premise that identity is only possible as a function of difference. If someone is British, that is because they are *not* French or American or Pakistani and so on. This account of identity tells us very little, however, unless we flesh out the concrete empirical detail of the identities individual subjects have by virtue of what they are not: what matters is not the fact of these divisions but *how* they operate and with what consequences. I suggest that for contemporary practices of thought, the identification of "others" by means of *temporal* distinctions has become extremely important.

x *Preface*

I examine the temporal distinctions that constitute a British, democratic, national identity by positing an "other" that is barbaric, alien, despotic, violent and – most importantly – backward. This is what I refer to when I talk about "democracy promotion" as a form of "foreign policy", borrowing from David Campbell's influential terminology (Campbell, 1998).

The book has taken a long time to write. As I document in the Introduction, I can date its earliest beginnings to 7 July 2005. It really began in long conversations in my garden in Islamabad on hot evenings with British Council colleagues about the strange business of democracy promotion in which we were now engaged. I have been asking questions about democracy promotion for the last 11 years and counting. Figuring out what the important questions were, and even being able to hazard some answers, has amply filled my time in the intervening years.

First, I made the painful and gradual decision that I was in the wrong job and, frankly, the wrong way of life altogether. Then, having decided that the questions to which I needed answers were fundamentally *political*, I arrived at University College London (UCL) to study for a master's degree in the Politics Department. I later enrolled on the PhD programme thanks to the unwavering support of David Hudson and Sherrill Stroschein, who may not have completely shared my passion for Foucault, but seemed to agree that I might have some questions that needed answers. Bit by painful bit I started to notice just how curious the familiar day-to-day work I had been involved in really was, and I managed to research and write the PhD thesis that was the earliest version of this book. In contrast to the ever-accelerating life of the academy, then, this has been "slow scholarship" (Berg and Seeber, 2016), motivated – in the words of the great Edward Said – by "care and affection rather than by profit and [...] narrow specialisation" (Said, 1994: 82).

The puzzle that has been occupying me can be summed up as: why promote democracy in response to terrorist attacks in London and why in Pakistan? Yet, a lot has happened since those attacks in July 2005. In the UK, we have had three Prime Ministers since Tony Blair, as well as two general elections and two changes of government. Pakistan has returned to civilian, electoral democracy and is probably no longer thought of as the "most dangerous country in the world" as it was characterised in 2005. A "backlash against democracy promotion" has been increasingly apparent as political violence in Afghanistan and Iraq appeared to go from bad to worse (Carothers, 2006; Bridoux and Russell, 2012). The language, if not all the discourses, of the "war on terror" was consigned to history with the election of US President Barack Obama. My undergraduates scarcely remember 11 September 2001.

Nevertheless, the answers to my initial puzzle help us with other pressing questions that are still depressingly current: why (also) promote democracy – or advocate democratic regime change – in Afghanistan, Syria, Libya and elsewhere? Why is democracy support understood to be an appropriate answer to terrorist attacks in Tunisia (Zelin, 2015)? Why promote democracy as a response to "radicalisation" in Park View High School in Birmingham

Preface xi

(the school of the so-called "Trojan Horse" affair) (Hope, 2015), in the history curriculum (Evans, 2013; see Robinson, 2012: 100–109; Cannadine et al., 2011; Bowen et al., 2012), and in the public duty for schools and universities under the new Prevent agenda (HM Government, 2015)? We will see that there is a logic to all of these decisions which is intimately related to a widespread and taken-for-granted discourse about British history and the way it constitutes British identity and its "others".

The book focuses on a specific British context and history, attempting to put at risk a narrative that suggests that the story of democracy was authored here. However, I hope that the particular approach I take to democracy promotion, foreign policy and genealogy will enable myriad other research questions to be prised open and addressed. For example, other countries and international entities are constituted through a discursive commitment to the temporal and civilisational narrative of democracy, and conduct their foreign policy and Foreign Policy accordingly. The United States and the European Union are perhaps the most widely researched (Huber, 2015: 2), but the discursive appeal of democracy is very wide, with India one of a number of new prominent participants in both constitutive democracy promotion and conventional Democracy Promotion (Mohan, 2007; Huber, 2015). It is not within the scope of this book to look in detail at the precise ways in which democratic identities are produced and reproduced through the specific temporal and historical narratives used in diverse locations. Nevertheless, the book could certainly offer theoretical and methodological provocation for anyone interested in taking up the questions of how and in what ways democratic identities are promoted, and what and who is excluded in consequence.

Over many years, this book has been the product of an often intimate, patient and radically ordinary experience of collaboration, talk, mutual support and sometimes rather intense emotion. I have long been grateful to Mark Ferrigan for first introducing me to the ideas of Michel Foucault and other French "theory". I still use his explanations and examples with my students. I am also grateful to all my friends and colleagues in Pakistan, and to Tomáš Daňhel, for teaching me so much about this beautiful and fascinating country.

David and Sherrill were exceptionally kind and helpful to me as a bit of an unusual postgraduate student. I am especially grateful to David, my primary supervisor, for his patience, kindness, encouragement, time, tact and cups of tea, as well as his insight, ideas and intellect. I would not have been able to write this book without him.

My doctoral research was funded by the Economic and Social Research Council (ESRC). As a consequence, I was able to undertake an internship at the UK's National Archives, which considerably developed my research skills and was great fun, not least thanks to the support of Amanda Bevan and Liz Evans. Many thanks are also due to innumerable helpful librarians and archivists at the British Library and the House of Commons Library, as well as all the helpful staff at the Foreign and Commonwealth Office and Department for International Development who processed a huge number of Freedom of Information

xii *Preface*

requests with incredible efficiency. I am grateful to Peter and Hafsa Sanders for allowing me to use the image *The Tracks of My Tears* on the cover. Thanks also for the following permissions: Ingram Pinn and *The Financial Times* for the figure at the start of Chapter 2; Faber & Faber and Matt Charman for the epigraph to Chapter 1; *The New York Review of Books* and David Bromwich for the epigraph to Chapter 3; and Kenan Malik and Atlantic Books for the epigraph to Chapter 6.

I am deeply grateful to the School of Public Policy at UCL, especially Jennifer Hudson, Richard Bellamy, David Coen, Neil Mitchell and Nicky Henson, for awarding me the ESRC funding and for providing a stimulating environment in which to work, especially the great Monday night PhD seminars. Alex Hartman, Susan Gaines, and all the gang teaching Qualitative Methods at the School of Public Policy have been a great pleasure to work with, as have my students, who are always lively, interesting and thought-provoking. The same can be said of my former students at King's College London, and I particularly thank Adrian Blau for being a great boss, critical friend, and letting me loose on his undergraduates with all my French ideas.

I need to thank Louise Amoore, Victoria Browne, Graham Burchell, Niheer Dasandi, James Dawson, Matthew Dennis, Hannah Elias, Kathryn Fisher, Caroline Holmqvist, Viv Jabri, Patrick Jackson (and his brilliant Methods workshop at the International Studies Association – North-East), Laleh Khalili, Emily Linnemann, Aletta Norval (and her great summer school at Essex), Emily Robinson, Doerthe Rosenow, Christine Sylvester, Tony Taylor, an anonymous reviewer, and Jenny Edkins and Nick Vaughan-Williams as series editors of *Interventions*, for invaluable and insightful questions, suggestions and comments at various stages of the process. Lydia de Cruz and her colleagues at Routledge have also been brilliant.

Also to thank for warmth, love, friendship, music, wine and great conversation over the years have been Nick Evans, Marsha Healey, Richard Martini (also proof reader extraordinaire), Gill Sampson, Nichola Frances, Michal Polák, Lizzy Toon, Mike Grundmann, Andy Still, and especially Jenny, Nadeem and now little Noah and Esme. I would also like to thank all my friends at Republic for their support and understanding, especially Graham Smith. Particular thanks must go to Jill, Carlos, Luke and Sophie who have welcomed me into their life and home with unfailing love, support and occasional much-needed slave-driving. Luke in particular has been a worthy opponent at Scrabble and someone with whom I can always talk about ideas. I look forward to reading his PhD thesis one day. I scarcely know what I would have done without the wonderful Rachel Jones. Despite having troubles of her own, she has read more drafts than I can count, listened to my incessant chatting on, asked great questions, made brilliant jokes, cooked my tea, encouraged and looked after me. I thank her from the bottom of my heart.

Finally, and above all, my parents have made everything possible from the time they first taught me to read. They have put up with a lot, have given me a lot in all sorts of ways, and I love them.

Introduction

I had been living and working in Pakistan for nearly a year when I heard the terrible news that a co-ordinated bombing attack on the London transport system on 7 July 2005 had killed 56 people, including the bombers, and injured more than 700. The bombing had been perpetrated by British citizens on British soil, avowedly as a result of profound dissatisfaction with the policies of the British government. Nevertheless, the policy response to the attack that most affected me was that government servants in Pakistan were asked step up work on democracy promotion. This provokes two questions. First, why was *democracy* seen to be the answer to terrorism in London? Second, why should democracy be promoted not in Britain, but in *Pakistan*? This book provides a detailed answer to these questions, examining the logic and the modes of thinking that made such a response possible. It also shows why they matter for the way democracy is thought about, not only by democracy promoters in Pakistan, but also in Britain.

The book is about democracy promotion as a form of foreign policy. That is to say, it understands democracy promotion not only as a set of practices enacted by embassies and development agencies overseas, but also as a whole complex of practices of thought that enable distinctions to be made between who is "foreign" and who is not. It shows that a key element in contemporary understandings of otherness is the acceptance or rejection of a certain, narrowly specified form of liberal democracy.

This form of othering sets up democracy as emblematic of the modern, developed self: in British political, policy and popular discourse, democracy is understood as the outcome of a long progressive sweep of British history in which multiple threats to it have been struggled against and overcome. It is in encountering and constantly re-narrating these threats to democracy that the British come to have a sense of an imagined, democratic community that exists by virtue of what it is opposed to. Relatedly, democracy is understood as the endpoint of history, the ultimate best way of managing human affairs, which has been alighted upon through a long historical process in which worse alternatives have been discarded in favour of better. The precise form that democracy has to take, by this account, includes the familiar institutions of liberal democracy as well as a notional delineation between a public and

2   Introduction

private sphere implied by liberalism. Thus the borders between self and other, past and future, masculine and feminine, and public and private are all imbricated and mutually reinforcing.

This teleological version of history has been in circulation at least since ideas about progress first became common currency during the Industrial Revolution and a form of it was once known, after Whig politician Lord Thomas Macaulay, as "the Whig version of history" (Butterfield, 1965). Despite the pejorative implications of this name for evolutionary versions of history, however, I argue that from Macaulay to Francis Fukuyama it has been enormously influential in producing the practices of thought that inform and constitute British identities and democratic practices. The practices of thought that constitute teleological versions of history emerge and are constantly redeployed in order to manage an uncertain present. This is not only because if democracy is the end of history, then it is obvious that efforts must be focused on promoting it, but also that democracy itself offers useful tools for providing detailed knowledge about how to govern. If history can be taken for granted as a logical progression towards democracy, it concomitantly offers a reassuring programme for action: threats to democracy that emanate from other, threatening parts of the world can be contained and domesticated by bringing those places up to date and enabling them to progress through the same journey from a worse past to a better, more democratic, more governable future.

However, the second crucial argument I make is that it is possible – and politically preferable – to narrate alternative versions of history. In examining the emergence and pervasiveness of teleological versions of history, I show by my detailed research into the past that there is no necessarily progressive or improving logic to history. On the contrary, from a curtailment of political participation in the colonial era to the Partition of India and Pakistan to the daily racist violence suffered by British Pakistanis, democracy promotion has been fully implicated in messy, random and, above all, violent events. Rather, our contemporary modes of governance have emerged through the ways that various leaders, politicians, thinkers and policy makers have muddled through the confusion of history, creating teleological narratives to help them. Teleology is not the driving force of history, but rather emerges from the messiness of historical events. In making this argument, I show that the historical narrative that currently pervades practices of thought about British identity and democracy promotion is contestable, and that therefore it might be possible to think, act and live differently.

Teleological narratives, I suggest, are practices of thought: they are habits of thinking, unreflexive modes of interpreting the world. Michel Foucault, who has done so much to enable us to recognise the modes of thought we take for granted, made the following remark about the importance of thought:

> We must [...] stop regarding as superfluous something so essential in human life and in human relations as thought [...] It is something that is

Introduction 3

often hidden, but which always animates everyday behavior. There is always a little thought even in the most stupid institutions; there is always thought even in silent habits. Criticism is a matter of flushing out that thought and trying to change it: to show that things are not as self-evident as one believed.

(Foucault, 1988: 155)

This book is such a work of criticism.

To set the scene, I will next tell two stories about democracy, history and threatening others. The first concerns Democracy Promotion in Pakistan; the second is about a row provoked by the Archbishop of Canterbury. Both these stories show how identities are produced and reproduced through continuous narrations of a version of history that is haunted by a variety of undemocratic others. They both demonstrate how practices of thought produce a commitment to a democracy that is quite rigid in terms of the precise institutions that are considered democratic: the familiar institutions of liberal democracy. Finally, they both show how identity and democratic practice are grounded in everyday life including perfectly ordinary practices of thought: a citizen reading a newspaper or listening to a speech on the news; a civil servant doing her job; a clergyman giving a lecture or sermon; a teacher, a newspaper, a popular book or a television programme offering a version of history; a believer taking her claims to a religious court or scholar.

The first story brings us back to the puzzle at the start of the chapter. Why was *democracy* seen as a solution to "home-grown" terrorism? And why in *Pakistan*?

To begin with, it was not clear who had committed mass murder in London on 7 July 2005, but within the week the fact came out that the suicide bombers had been British citizens. This was shocking news, because the bombings had widely been reported as a war-like act that would have been easier to understand if they had come from a foreign enemy, rather than from young men who had "unmistakeably" Yorkshire accents (BBC, 2006b). In the weeks and months that followed, moreover, it transpired that almost everything about the attacks had been, in conventional terms, "domestic", including financing from a British bank loan, the technical know-how obtained from websites hosted in Britain and the apparent motivation which seems to have been directed against the actions of the British government (Bulley, 2008: 82; Townsend, 2006). It was therefore, on the face of it, strange that the *Foreign* Secretary was tasked with engaging with the media (Bulley, 2008: 83) and that people like me, working for the British government abroad, were involved in the policy dimension of the reaction.

One way of explaining intervention in Pakistan (amongst myriad other actions) as a logical concrete response to an attack by British-born bombers in the British capital city is to suggest that there must have been something foreign (Pakistani?) about the bombers, despite appearances. This would explain the enormous amount of attention that was paid to "links" they had in Pakistan (BBC, 2006b; Bulley, 2008: 82–83).

4   Introduction

In fact, various vague hints about possible trips to training camps or links to Al-Qaeda leaders have largely been discredited (ibid.; Townsend, 2006), and the Official Report of the London Bombings stated that "[t]heir indoctrination appears to have taken place away from places with known links to extremism" (Home Office, 2006: 25). Nevertheless, the same report devotes two pages to the question: "Were they directed from abroad?" These two pages make much of the two and a half-month visit Mohammed Sidique Khan and Shehzad Tanweer made to Pakistan in 2004–05, although again this is acknowledged to be hardly "unusual", given that 400,000 trips were made to Pakistan by UK residents in 2004 (ibid.: 21). Likewise, media reporting of the bombings was overwhelmingly framed by this supposed link with Pakistan, to the extent that the *Daily Telegraph* ran a story about the attack entitled "Pakistan wakes up to the hatred within", as if the bombers had indeed been Pakistani and not British (Rashid, 2005). This is emblematic of the perplexity engendered by the discovery that terrorism could be "home-grown": it seemed no longer clear who was British and who was not. This, then, appears to account for why Pakistan was the target of intervention: if the threat was foreign, then it could be contained by intervention overseas.

Tony Blair, the then-Prime Minister, explained the importance of intervention beyond the borders of the UK – as they are conventionally understood – in order to prevent terrorism by stating that the bomber, Mohammed Sidique Khan, "may have been born here. But his ideology wasn't. And that is why it has to be taken on, everywhere" (Blair, 2006). This is a move with two consequences. First, by pinpointing the ideology of the bombers as *foreign*, he was exteriorising the problem. The argument could then logically follow, as Blair (2007b) put it himself, that "what happens in Pakistan matters on the streets of Britain". This is how he attempted to legitimate the interventions in Pakistan that I experienced first hand. Second, though, Blair was suggesting that just because a person is "born here", that does not mean that he or she is necessarily wholly British. This disrupts the common-sense assumption that to be "born here" – traditional *jus soli* – is the first and, perhaps, fundamental criterion of belonging, of being British. The bombers, it is implied, were indeed in some way foreign because they did not share a British "ideology". The corollary of this is that it is not possible to *know* who is British and who is foreign, who belongs and who does not, from their appearance, or their accent, or their passport. Rather, the border between the domestic and the foreign can only be created and sustained by establishing what counts as an acceptably British "ideology" or set of values.

So, why was *democracy* to be the means of making the streets of Britain safer by intervening in Pakistan? To understand this, I need to begin by showing that an acceptable "British ideology" was understood to entail a commitment to democracy and to a narrative of national history that has involved facing down numerous undemocratic others. This will lead to a discussion of how the promotion of this ideology overseas was understood to be useful in containing the threat of terrorism, even as the distinction between home and overseas threatens to collapse.

The question of what was meant by British values (or the ideology informed by them) was the subject of a great deal of discussion in the media and by politicians at the time and, importantly, this was accompanied by a set of narratives about British history. For example, a leader in the *Sunday Express* on 10 July 2005 encouraged reflection on "what values Britain has to defend" against terrorism and suggested that an appropriate response would be to strengthen "Western [...] democratic values" against the threat that "sharia law [...] should take root in this country" by ensuring that all schoolchildren and anyone seeking British citizenship should "be taught about the evolution of democracy and the rule of law and the emergence of religious tolerance from the Magna Carta through the Civil War, the Glorious Revolution, the Great Reform Act and the fight to defend all those freedoms in the cauldron of the Second World War" (Shipman, 2005). By this account, one way of distinguishing the difference between someone who is, in some sense, authentically British and someone who is foreign comes from their understanding of an official historical narrative and a commitment to the democratic values that emerge from the history that British people share.

This idea of Britishness as embodied by a commitment to democracy, honed through a seamless process of evolution and fought for against multiple others was echoed widely in the press and by politicians. It is, perhaps, summed up by Donald Rumsfeld's words reproduced in large print across a double page in the *Daily Telegraph*: "For generations, tyrants, fascists and terrorists have sought to carry out their violent designs upon the British people, only to founder upon its unrelenting shores" (*Daily Telegraph*, 2005), which resonate with the more than 400 mentions in national newspapers of the London Blitz in connection with the attack in the three weeks following the bombings. Moments of British history that would be widely familiar were pressed into service in a narrative about Britishness as a history of struggle for democracy against threatening and foreign others.

The question of why democracy in Pakistan would help make Britain safe was also informed by understandings about the logic of history. If domestic identity had been established through a progressive, evolutionary history, this meant that other countries could likewise go through a similar version of history and thereby modernise, progress and come up to date, thus becoming domesticated and being made safe. This narrative of history as a necessary progression from worse to better times is implicit in notions about "civilisation" that date back to colonial rule (Bowden, 2009), and to more recent ideas about "development".

The relationship of a narrative of civilisation and development to the bombings is symbolised perhaps most vividly by a description on 10 July 2005, in the *Sunday Telegraph*. It paints a grizzly picture of St Pancras Church in London with both Make Poverty History ribbons tied round its pillars and blood splattered on its walls following the bombing of a crowded bus in nearby Tavistock Square (Porter, 2005: 2). The ribbons were there because the bombings were timed – seemingly deliberately – to coincide with

6 *Introduction*

the G8 summit in Gleneagles, which was focusing on issues of poverty and development. These juxtapositions of the Make Poverty History campaign and the G8 summit, on the one hand, with the destruction wrought by the bombers, on the other, offered a useful way of understanding and condemning the attacks. The "civilised" values of the G8, the UK government, the "British way of life" and the Make Poverty History campaign, were readily juxtaposed with the "barbarism" of the terrorist display of violence, as well as the barbarities of poverty, lack of development, bad governance and corruption (Douzinas, 2008: 195). The present, civilised, developed condition of Britain could be contrasted not only with the backward state the country would be in if the terrorists were able to prevail, but also with the current underdeveloped state of Pakistan, whence the danger of terrorism appeared to emanate.

Tony Blair, in his initial statement on the bombings, spoke in a language informed by these temporalities: "It is particularly barbaric that this has happened on a day when people are meeting to try to help the problems of poverty [...] our determination to defend our values is greater than their determination to cause death and destruction to innocent people [...] they will never succeed in destroying what we hold dear in this country and in other civilised nations throughout the world" (Blair, 2005a). In March 2006, Blair gave a speech that developed and extended the initial response to the bombings as the actions of "barbarians" against "civilised people": he furthermore suggested that "their [the terrorists'?] concept of governance is pre-feudal; their positions on women and other faiths, reactionary and regressive". The "battle" being waged, by this account, is "between progress and reaction, between those who embrace the modern world and those who reject its existence". Once again, an unspoken version of history as a directional force that moves countries and people forward in time from a worse past to a better future is here evident in a number of temporal and historical formulations, in which civilisation, modernity and progress are pitted against feudalism (a specific feature of European history), barbarism and poverty. This is a version of history that offers a useful potential solution in a crisis. Again, if terrorism is the opposite of development, progress and civilisation, then one answer to the problem is to domesticate foreign danger by enabling places like Pakistan to come up to date.

The answer to the question of why *democracy* and why in *Pakistan* is now much clearer. The values that emerge in his account as constitutive of "civilisation", "progress" and "modernity" are clearly spelled out by Blair as: "religious tolerance, openness to others, to democracy, liberty and human rights administered by secular courts" (Blair, 2006). These are recognisably the values commonly associated with liberal democracy, and it is no coincidence that "democracy" is invoked numerous times in this speech as the opposite of "extremism" or "terrorism". This then enables us to understand why *democracy* was understood to be what the British government in Pakistan should be concentrating on in order to domesticate, or make safe, the dangerous ideology that appeared to be threatening British citizens.

A teleological narrative of history, then, was understood both to shore up commitment to British values at home and to offer the means – through a development that had been achieved at home and was much needed overseas – by which threats to it could be challenged in Pakistan.

The second story is about a lecture given by the Archbishop of Canterbury in 2008 in which he suggested that different legal traditions, including *shari'ah* law, should be accommodated within the British legal system (Williams, 2008b). This was a measured and carefully argued speech, which drew upon the vast literature that suggests that it is desirable to incorporate a range of different voices into the democratic debate and conversation, and that this can only occur if different modes of identity and commitment, and different practical ways of making claims under the democratically constituted law, can be included.

The Archbishop was shouted down in fury as switchboards at Canterbury Cathedral, Lambeth Palace and the BBC were jammed by complaints (Gadher et al., 2008) and a torrent of around 500 newspaper articles appeared in the national press to dispute his views. Immediate condemnation came from the Prime Minister, the Head of Commission for Racial Equality, clergy from the Church of England and other churches, numerous MPs and even some Muslim leaders and politicians (Petre and Porter, 2008).

This story, like the first, is also puzzling. The puzzle it poses is why a lecture that carefully explored the possibility of making democratic law making and enforcement more plural and inclusive was attacked *in the very name of democracy*, and why it was widely interpreted as an existential threat to British values. Why were current configurations of democracy so passionately defended against innovations that might make them more democratic? Why were proposals for changes to the ways laws are democratically made and applied understood as threatening and *foreign*?

The fundamentally alien nature of *shari'ah* law was asserted by none other than the Prime Minister, Gordon Brown, whose spokesman distanced him from the Archbishop by suggesting that: "British laws would be based on British values" (Butt, 2008). Although a commitment to the principles of *shari'ah* law is part of the religious practice of millions of British citizens, its foreignness was taken for granted to the extent that it was widely repeated that anyone wishing to live under its provisions is welcome to "go and live in a Muslim country", establishing that British identity is premised on being those things that a Muslim country is *not* (Khan, 2008b; see also Baig, 2008; Diamond, 2008; Hartley-Brewer, 2008). The *Sunday Times* went so far as to suggest that the Archbishop has committed "treason" – the ultimate in existential threats to the nation – adding, in an echo of the Second World War narrative that regularly animated discussions of the London bombings, that his views are "appeasement to an alien set of values" (Marrin, 2008; see also *The Times*, 2008). Matthew d'Ancona (2008) put what is at stake here very clearly in the *Sunday Telegraph* when he stated that: "we are at war with fundamentalist Islam [...] They seek [...] the global imposition of sharia law." *Shari'ah* law is

8 Introduction

primarily understood to be foreign because it is connected to the foreign element of the London terrorists' ideology that is to be feared.

There are two elements to this perceived threat. The first is that there is some direct link between *shari'ah* law and terrorism itself. For example, the Director of the Crown Prosecution Service is quoted as saying that a map of "incidence of honour based violence", which is allegedly tolerated by *shari'ah* courts, and a map of "terrorist cells" would be "identical" (Seighart, 2008). This is despite the fact that the Archbishop made it clear, in a BBC interview prior to his lecture, that there could be no accommodation with "the most repressive and retrograde elements" that characterise stereotypes of Islamic law (Williams, 2008a). Meanwhile, the former Archbishop of Canterbury, Lord Carey, aired concerns that heeding Rowan Williams's suggestions "would be dangerous and would encourage some Muslims to try to turn Britain into an Islamic state" (Wynne-Jones, 2008). Thus the existential threat of terrorism appeared to be aided and abetted directly by these suggestions.

More widespread, however, is the second element of the threat: that any attempt to formalise systems of *shari'ah* law within the British system would in and of itself turn Britain into an unrecognisably foreign country – particularly insofar as it would impact negatively on women's rights – and would support the supposed aims of the terrorists by bringing about precisely what they wanted to achieve through violent means. The populist tabloid *Sun* newspaper was particularly keen to make this link. It condemned the speech on its front page next to a photograph of the burning bus in Tavistock Square (Pascoe-Watson, 2008), and claimed that the speech represented a "victory for terrorism" (Wilson and Pascoe-Watson, 2008). The implication is that the terrorists of 7 July 2005 showed what a violent place a Britain with *shari'ah* law might be like.

Given that ideas about *shari'ah* law were so bound up with the perceived threat to British identity from a foreign ideology, it is not difficult to see why the Archbishop's lecture was decried specifically in terms of *democracy*, even though his intention was precisely to expand and not foreclose British democratic practice. That is because of the already-constituted understanding of democracy as a quintessentially British achievement that is precisely what has to be defended against terrorism. If terrorists are opposed to Britain and to democracy and in favour of *shari'ah* law, then, it seems – despite the Archbishop's careful argument to the contrary – unthinkable that democracy and *shari'ah* law could be compatible. Thus, what is put forward as the set of values to be defended turns out to be the familiar status quo: the institutions and values of liberal democracy. *The Times* asserts, for instance, that "[i]t is fundamental to this democracy that there should be one law for everyone", adding that any accommodation with *shari'ah* law would "undermine the [...] strength of our parliamentary democracy" (*The Times*, 2008). Baroness Warsi, then shadow minister for community cohesion and social action, suggested that "[a]ll British citizens must be subject to British laws developed through Parliament and the courts" (quoted in Petre and Porter, 2008).

Introduction   9

Meanwhile a European court of human rights decision from 2003 is widely quoted as meaning that *shari'ah* law is "incompatible with European ideas of democracy" (Dyer, 2008). It is not so much democracy as a contested idea in political theory that is being defended, as a specific set of European institutions.

These institutions and their relation to Britishness is understood through a similar set of narratives about civilisation and British history that we saw in the first story about the London bombings above. Minette Marrin (2008) in the *Sunday Times* puts it like this:

> What is good and essential about this country is the [democratically made] law itself. It has evolved over centuries from medieval barbarities into something, for all its faults, that is civilised. Our law expresses and maintains the best virtues of our society. Anyone who does not accept it does not belong here.

Lord Carey (2008), writing in the popular tabloid the *News of the World*, invokes "the laws of our land which have been so painfully honed by the struggle for democracy and human rights". The seamless, teleological version of British history that is implied by these accounts of progression from a medieval barbaric past to a democratic, modern present is spelled out by the Daily Mail (2008a): "From Magna Carta to the Glorious Revolution, from the Great Reform Act to the Suffragettes, one golden thread runs through our nation's history." Yet again, then, we see a national identity and a commitment to a specific set of democratic institutions being shored up by a progressive narrative about British history.

Again, a specific narrative about British history intersects with a broader understanding of the logic of history, as civilised, modern values are contrasted with the barbarities of an uncivilised past, symbolised by *shari'ah* law (Wallis, 2008; Bunting, 2008; Seighart, 2008). Various breathless accounts of stonings, floggings, beheadings, limb amputations and so on are regularly provided to substantiate the out-dated modes of punishment the *shari'ah* allegedly sanctions (Murray and Giannangeli, 2008; *Daily Mail*, 2008b; Howse, 2008). A narrative about civilisation and the barbaric backwardness of *shari'ah* sits alongside a more specific story about British history and provides a broader understanding of history as offering a solution for parts of the world that are behind Britain in time: they simply need to make an entrance into history and come up to date.

Temporal othering

Lene Hansen suggests that there are three main forms of "othering" that take place in discourse and constitute a world of selves and others: spatial, temporal and ethical (Hansen, 2006: 12). There is now a considerable amount of work on the ways in which the discourses on terrorist attacks since 11 September 2001 have constituted spatial and ethical others. For example, Judith Butler (2004) has shown how discourses about what it is to be a human, and

10   Introduction

thereby legitimately entitled to benefit from the provisions of universal human rights, have produced classes of subjects who are ethically deemed less than human: lives that are unliveable and deaths that are ungrievable. Richard Jackson (2005) and Stuart Croft (2006) have both discussed the ways in which the "war on terror" discourse has produced a spatially polarised world in which particular states and individuals are constituted as "other" and thereby the legitimate objects of various kinds of violent force and disciplinary power.

There is furthermore quite a wide and growing literature on time in International Relations (Edkins, 2003; Hutchings, 2008; Puar, 2007; Jarvis, 2009; Lundborg, 2012; Closs Stephens, 2013), which has helped build a detailed understanding of how particular ways of thinking about time legitimate and reinforce contemporary forms of power: linear, teleological time is a key tool of sovereignty (Edkins 2003), for example, whilst understanding time as homogeneous and empty helps us account for the persistence of the nation-state (Closs Stephens, 2013). What is less common, however, is the analysis that this book performs: how do particular ways of thinking about time constitute the self and the other, the domestic and the foreign? With what effects?

One consequence of ignoring temporal dimensions of practices of othering is a tendency to understand the world in terms of sets of selves and others strung out in space. For example, Derek Gregory insists on understanding the "war on terror" discourse of civilisation and barbarians in terms of a colonial *present*. This then leads to an account of the work that discourse is doing in terms of its production of enemies and subjects of power *elsewhere in space*, in Iraq, or Afghanistan, or Pakistan:

> "Their" space is often seen as the inverse of "our" space: a sort of negative in the photographic sense that "they" might "develop" into something like "us" but also the site of an absence, because "they" are seen somehow to lack the positive tonalities that supposedly distinguish "us".
>
> (Gregory, 2004: 17)

However, both of the stories I narrated above enable us to see that there is a prominent discourse about barbarians and civilisation in which "being civilised" is a uniform endpoint to which *any part of the world* might aspire. The very idea of "development" in "other" *spaces* is reliant on the idea that *time and history* are forces that move forwards, towards the ultimate goal, or telos, of civilisation.

Acknowledging the temporal dimensions of othering, therefore, helps us to understand discursive moves and practices that otherwise would be incomprehensible. Whilst spatially constituted others can perhaps be more readily contained or subdued by conventional borders or by military force, temporally constituted others *might be anywhere*, might – frighteningly – be "born here" and look like "us", but might also bear within them the redemptive possibility of coming up to date. They might therefore require and be better served by more boring, more detailed, but no less important practices like democracy promotion to domesticate them and make them safe.

As Talal Asad (2003) has pointed out, ideas like "modernity" and "civilisation" are generally not descriptions of the present state of the world, but rather future-oriented projects that guide and condition present action. This is important particularly for the practices of thought that are concerned with encountering and managing the "other" of civilisation, because there opens up an historical trajectory into which others are understood to be able to enter. Foucault (2005b: 194–197) suggests that the "other" of civilisation need not be the barbarian – in our case, for instance, the unruly and ungovernable terrorist – who is, by definition, always the violent opponent of civilisation, contemporaneous in time and bent on its destruction. Rather, civilisation's other can equally well be understood as the "savage": that is, as a form of being that is further back in time but can be domesticated through the civilising course of history. In more contemporary language, the other of civilisation might be the *un(der)developed*, who can benefit from progress and be brought up to date.

This is a narrative that is *useful* in the wake of catastrophe, because it always leaves us with something to *do*. Hence a whole raft of practices that will bring civilisation wherever it is lacking by means of better governance can be instigated. Democracy promotion, then, regardless of its spatial location, can be understood as a kind of civilising mission, whose logic is both to control and contain the irredeemably foreign other – the barbarian, the terrorist – but also to domesticate the savage through the civilising rituals of liberal democracy.

Democracy Promotion as Foreign Policy

When Tony Blair stated that "[t]hey may have been born here but their ideology wasn't. And that is why it must be taken on everywhere", he performatively re/produces the idea that Britishness is constituted through a struggle against anti-democratic others. In doing this, he draws attention to the fact that the borders of the nation are not primarily spatially located on maps, in ports or airports or even immigration queues, but rather in the everyday practices that enable us to establish and affirm what is "foreign", in order that we might know who "we" are. "We", he suggests, are civilised, we belong, because we are democrats.

This helps us to understand the reaction to the Archbishop of Canterbury. If a commitment to liberal democracy is constitutive of the nation, then his attempt to broaden the scope of what can be considered democratic is a contestation of familiar bordering practices. In effect, he is attempting to *shift* perceptions of what counts as foreign and he is doing so by proposing novel forms of *democracy*. The condemnation he receives functions by means of a repetition of more familiar bordering practices, which reassert a commitment to liberal democracy as the primary mode through which we can distinguish self from other, domestic/ated from foreign.

Importantly, then, we can now distinguish two separate but deeply intertwined meanings of democracy promotion, mapping onto David Campbell's

12 *Introduction*

distinction between Foreign Policy and foreign policy, which is worth quoting at some length:

> The first is one in which foreign policy can be understood as referring to all [...] practices of differentiation, or modes of exclusion that constitute their objects as foreign when dealing with them. In this sense, foreign policy is divorced from the state as a particular resolution of the categories of identity and difference and applies to all confrontations between a self and an other located in different sites of ethnicity, race, class, gender or locale [... The] second understanding – Foreign Policy as state-based and conventionally understood – is thus not as equally implicated in the constitution of identity as the first understanding. Rather, Foreign Policy serves to reproduce the constitution of identity made possible by foreign policy and to contain challenges to that identity.
>
> (Campbell, 1990: 271)

Democracy Promotion is the conventional, state-based attempt to build and support the institutions of liberal democracy beyond conventional domestic borders. It is the work that the British Council, the Foreign and Commonwealth Office (FCO) and, above all, the Department for International Development (DFID) undertake in countries like Pakistan when they promote democracy and good governance. It can be understood to control and contain threats to democratic countries by building allegiances to the same values and institutions that ensure – according to Democratic Peace Theory – that democracies do not fight each other (Russett, 1993: 4).

As Campbell demonstrates, however, a conventional, state-based Foreign Policy that relies on spatial difference is merely one manifestation of, and depends on, the much broader range of everyday practices by which the border between the domestic and the foreign is established and reproduced. Likewise, democracy promotion can be understood as the practices – including but much exceeding Democracy Promotion – by which commitment to a liberal democratic identity is established and threats to it can be understood as foreign, suspicious and other. As we saw above, these practices are not primarily concerned with spatial differences, but instead rely on everyday practices including practices of thought that understand democracy *as* the endpoint of a long, teleological history, popularised through the media, political speech and history lessons.

How is an up-to-date democracy gendered?

This brings us to a question about what an appropriately "up-to-date" form of democratic life might look like in a plural society and what amendments to democratically decided laws might, or might not, be democratically proposed. In the stories above, we saw that contemporary practices of thought tend to require a commitment to the division between the public and private spheres which keeps religious practices private and maintains a public sphere that is understood as the rational, secular and legitimate sphere of democratic law making.

The particular modes of governance that are understood to be civilised have always been deeply bound up with the proper ordering of gender relations. As Gayatri Spivak has so influentially pointed out, the archetypal "civilising mission" has long been decipherable as the process of "white men saving brown women from brown men" (Spivak, 1987). The *Sun* newspaper's headline in response to the Archbishop of Canterbury – "What a burkha!" (Pascoe-Watson, 2008) – underlines the fact that civilisation is still thought about in profoundly gendered terms and much of the concern about *shari'ah* law both at the time of the London bombings and the Archbishop's speech was articulated around a perceived threat to the contemporary gendered status quo. Britain, it was suggested, cannot be understood as a civilised place if the specific rights of its women citizens are abrogated.

We therefore need to ask what *precise* gender relations are thought to be civilised and how far they limit the practices associated with conventional masculinities and femininities. The discourse of violent masculinities and "imperilled women" associated with Islam and the "war on terror" has been well documented (Razack, 2004; Abu-Lughod, 2002; Shepherd, 2006), and it functions to set up as the paragon of civilised behaviours the gendered relations of the liberal democracies. However, as feminist scholars have suggested, we need to ask what injustices are perpetuated and naturalised by the set of "women's rights" that are enshrined by liberal democracy. The *Sun* newspaper helpfully makes this completely visible. Turning the page from its outraged headline about the Archbishop of Canterbury, one is confronted – as every day – with a photograph of a half-naked young woman, paraded there purely for men's gratification. More on "Page Three" in Chapter 6, but for now we simply need to note that the position of women in the Western liberal democracies is not likely to be universally hailed as perfect. Yet externalising threats to women's rights and identifying them with foreign, uncivilised cultures that are still back in time, naturalises those hard-won rights that we do have and asks us to consider ourselves lucky, eliding the possibility that other ways of living might be thinkable.

However, the practices that constitute being a woman are not fixed and inevitable. As Judith Butler's (2006) influential work has made clear, just as the border between nations is created not through any natural or physical necessity, but rather through the constant practical assertion and reproduction of modes of belonging and exclusion, so the border between "male" and "female" is made up of innumerable, detailed performative practices. This is, of course, nowhere more evident than it is in the dress code. In Pakistan, as a woman, it was incumbent upon me, in all modesty, to wear trousers. In the UK, it was only in the last century that my grandmother's generation broke with norms of modesty and won me the right to do so. Indeed, almost none (if any at all) of the practices that constitute being a woman – the deeds that *constitute* the doer, as Butler puts it – are natural or inevitable.

14   *Introduction*

That being the case, it seems particularly curious that a given set of gendered relations – including implied practical restrictions on the dress code, especially the veil – is widely represented as *intrinsic* to a democratic way of life, rather than a matter of democratic contestation.

Democracy promotion as it currently functions implies a particular resolution of the world into public and private spheres characteristic of liberalism. This way of thinking about the world assumes that all people are autonomous, rational individuals who associate and cast their vote in the public sphere. Caring work, religion, emotion and the forms of socialisation that enable people to perform the culturally contingent roles of men and women are understood to take place in private and domestic spaces and are therefore not easily accommodated in the public sphere of democratic engagement, as the Archbishop of Canterbury found out. Thus women – their roles, practices and identities – are understood to be already constituted *prior* to democratic engagement, so that the main scope for gender in democratic debate is how the interests that emerge *out of* those practices can best be served and accommodated. For example, a debate about how childcare provision can be managed so that women can join the workforce is rather more common than a debate about why caring work is considered to be a peculiarly feminine role.

The division between what counts as public and what private is both incredibly important and pervasive and also extremely porous and fragile. Its location has shifted considerably through history and continues to be a focus of intense struggle (Gordon, 1991: 36). This observation, however, does not make the existence of that division any less important. The discursive reproduction of the distinction should not be understood as describing the world more or less accurately, but rather as enacting a separation that has concrete effects. Such effects are apparent in the story about the Archbishop, for example. The latter rightly claims that it is an "unsatisfactory account of political reality in modern societies" to suggest that "[beyond the uniform rule of law] all other relations, commitments or protocols of behaviour belong exclusively to the realm of the private and of individual choice" (Williams, 2008b). However, the accuracy or otherwise of thinking about a clear divide between the public and the private is less important than the way that this notional boundary can be *used* to silence the Archbishop's intervention. It is the notional boundary that enables Matthew Parris to argue in *The Times*, for instance, that "nowhere is our national discomfort with private laws more intense, or more justified, than when dealing with religious groupings" (Parris, 2008). The practices of thought that attempt to confine certain types of activity to the private sphere and deny their relevance for democratic contestation matter because of the way the line can be used to sideline and silence dissent. Thus matters of disagreement are relegated to a private sphere understood to be beyond the reach of government even as practices of governing are fully implicated in constructing and maintaining it.

The challenge throughout this book, then, is to show how the borders between domestic and foreign, feminine and masculine, private and public, intersect and interact in order to account for the particular form of democracy promotion that animates and limits political life.

Genealogy

This book is a genealogy. However, my approach to genealogical research is somewhat different from most others, and therefore modestly innovative. I provide an historical account not of an institution or a state of affairs, but rather of an historical narrative itself. I will discuss my methodological approach in some detail in Chapter 3, but for now it will be helpful to orientate the reader by providing an outline.

In his attempts to disrupt and criticise sedimented patterns of thought, Foucault was engaged throughout his life in the writing of history. Through looking at history in detail, he suggests, we can see the "accidents, the minute deviations – or conversely, the complete reversals – the errors, the false appraisals, and the faulty calculations that gave birth to those things that continue to exist and have value for us" (Foucault, 1991a: 81), thus enabling us to see the contingency in what had seemed inevitable, the accidental in what had seemed natural, the mutability of what had seemed eternal – and, above all, the hidden power relations in what had seemed neutral. This approach has been very influential in the study of politics and International Relations (for example, Der Derian, 1991; Bartelson, 1995; Jackson, 2006; Hansen, 2006; de Goede, 2005; and many others, as discussed in Miliken, 1999; and Vucetic, 2011), and has helped us understand a variety of practices and policies – from the Marshall Plan to sovereignty to international finance – in new ways.

When first working on writing the genealogy of Democracy Promotion, though, I was deeply struck by how much this set of practices is already talked about in historical terms. The taken-for-granted "official" history of Democracy Promotion is a narrative (as I show in more detail in Chapter 3) that assumes that Britain has been through an unbroken 1,000-year evolution described above towards the liberal democratic institutions that govern our lives. This evolutionary narrative implies that all countries should be able to grow to democratic maturity naturally, but, regrettably, that countries like Britain are understood to have been complicit in halting that natural evolution in parts of the world like present-day Pakistan. It was only – according to this version of history – with the postwar movements for national self-determination that Pakistan had any opportunity to enter into the normal course of history and to begin to develop, normal evolution having been stymied by the iniquities of colonialism. Moreover, the Cold War is thought to have complicated Pakistan's course through history by allowing short-term support of dictatorial, but anti-Communist, regimes to crowd out a principled commitment to allowing history to take its course. The story runs that it was only by 1989 that it began to be widely understood that liberal democratic capitalism was the one best way of running human affairs everywhere, at

16 *Introduction*

which point the moral imperative of allowing and enabling Pakistan to become thoroughly democratic became irresistible. Thus the civilising, evolutionary, inevitable story of the coming of democracy has come late and been much hindered in Pakistan, whilst in Britain it has long been part of our national story.

This much-repeated story of Democracy Promotion offers an intriguing methodological opportunity in terms of how to select what "moments" to study. To explain: a genealogy of an institution, a technology or a state of affairs – a genealogy of the prison, say, or of the practices involved in contemporary financial markets – would need to select such moments according to their importance in accounting for the emergence of the institution or practices in question. For example, moments of heightened debate about practices of punishment or financial speculation would be sought in order to show how certain alternatives came to be favoured over others. What is intriguing about a genealogy of a history, on the other hand, is that the stories we tell of ourselves already bear within them particular moments that are privileged and thought of as constitutive of who we are today. The habitual story about contemporary Britain as the endpoint of a struggle for democracy (along with the story of its struggling and backward other, Pakistan) contains various such privileged moments. These include the Age of Reform in the 1830s that seemed to inaugurate the importance and spread of electoral politics; the beginning of the age of "development" and decolonisation after the Second World War; the end of the Cold War with its narrative of a victory for "democracy"; and the so-called "war on terror" where democracy remains the value to be defended against an enemy who appears to represent the barbarous, primitive or medieval past. These are the four moments on which I have focused a chapter each, as these were the moments signalled by the discourse itself as constitutive of its own ancestry. I suggest, however, that we need to change the story. By selecting these moments as the focus of my study, I have been able to show that they already contain within them ways of narrating history differently and disrupting the teleological narrative we take for granted.

Teleological narratives have – as it turns out – for a long time been modes of making sense of and managing an uncertain world and providing a particular, taken-for-granted set of responses. Ideas about progress and civilisation first enabled British civil servants in India in the times of Lord Macaulay to make sense of an uncertain present and decide how to respond by means of setting up representative institutions. Teleological narratives continued to provide a frame of reference for understanding a seemingly complex and relativistic world in 1989, in which history seemed far from having ended, offering democracy promotion as a solution to the difficult problem of how to contain new enemies as old ones disappeared.

These narratives may seem to provide useful guides for future action in the face of present uncertainty, but they are not so helpful as a guide to what happened in the past. The "evolution" of British history is, as I shall show, easy to contest. The lack of inevitability or teleology in the detail of history is precisely the point, however. Historical research is a very useful mode of enquiry that shows us, as we will see, not only why we think in teleologies, but also what the (violent) consequences of teleologies are and how we might think differently.

Data

As my aim has been to make practices of thought about history and democracy decipherable, I have used a diverse range of sources that show the range of thought available in British society. This includes the standard resources of political history: secondary sources, government and parliamentary records, political speeches, and books written about political issues. These texts are included not because they *describe* government policy or political practices of thought, but because they are involved in producing and reproducing them, creating the options that are understood to be available. They also bear with them sets of historically constituted assumptions and beliefs that can be analysed; therefore broader practices of thought can be ascertained from them. This is not to say that the concrete practices, technologies and techniques of democracy promotion can be read off from them in an uncomplicated way: rather, they are crucial and privileged sites within an ongoing process of struggle. For example, the privileging of the election as a key technology for democracy in government policy documents does not tell us whether or not "free and fair" elections are taking place in targeted countries like Pakistan. It does, however, enable us to understand the particular rationality at work within democracy promotion policy, including what counts as democracy and what practices constitute "freeness" and "fairness". They are, then, policy in action: they can be said both to constitute and to be constituted by the discourses and practices of democracy promotion, and are therefore key pieces of evidence in an empirical study of such discourses and practices.

However, taking seriously the non-state-based nature of the practices of thought that constitute identity, I have also worked with a wide range of sources from what might be called popular culture. Important amongst these were the newspapers that are understood by democracy promoters to play such an important role in the list of institutions (a free press) that must be present for democracy to be meaningful. However, I also examined plays, cartoons, novels, television programming, films and photographs, discussing in the pages below those that appeared to me to be most important and exemplary of the practices of thought I have unearthed in my research.

These sorts of aesthetic representations are important for identity constitution because they not only exemplify, but also make available to a wide audience, prevalent practices of thought in concrete ways. They make visible and reproduce – but are also fully implicated in producing – the sets of choices and the possible forms of being and behaving that are understood to be available in contemporary life (Bleiker, 2001). Thus, I suggest, by reading a newspaper or watching a film, a subject (an ordinary citizen, for instance)

18 *Introduction*

does not so much see a picture of how others think and behave as understand what possible modes of thinking and behaviour are available (what practices of citizenship, how she might reflect on her vote and so forth). Again, then, these are pieces of important empirical evidence that provide ways of deciphering the concrete practices of everyday life in non-state-based locations.

Structure of the book

I begin in Chapter 1 by asking what it is that the UK – and by extension other countries and organisations – do when they attempt to promote democracy overseas. Starting from a description of the specific practices in which Democracy Promotion is engaged, I go on to discuss some critiques of these practices, which helpfully show that democracy promotion is – despite the best intentions of its practitioners – almost entirely engaged in promoting the institutions of liberal democracy. However, as the critical literature shows, given that democracy is one of the most contested concepts in the history of ideas, much is left out by this conceptualisation of democracy. The really important question, though, is why democracy promotion's practitioners are unable to think differently, or more broadly, about democracy. Using Campbell's work on foreign policy, I provide a distinctive answer to that question, showing that it is because commitments to the institutions of liberal democracy are intrinsic to distinctions between domestic and foreign identities.

Chapter 2 takes up the problem of why and how democracy promotion is needed. I argue that the difficulties of governing in an uncertain world mean that knowledge of populations is required in order to manage them: populations need to be both quantifiable and legible. I discuss the epistemological role of the familiar representative and deliberative institutions of liberal democracy to show that they are profoundly useful for the purposes of governing.

Chapter 3 looks in detail at how the narrative of democracy promotion functions through the logic of temporal othering. It looks in detail at the stories we tell of ourselves and shows what they are, how they work, why they matter and what can be done in response. Beginning from the narrative about an unbroken British history of progress towards democracy and its corollary, the story of an interrupted and broken path of history in Pakistan, I show that stories we tell of ourselves are ones about civilisation, development, modernisation and the benevolent spread of democracy. I examine in particular detail the "official" history of democracy promotion that I take from government and policy sources. This enables me to show precisely how it is that they make possible and legitimise the democracy promotion practices described in Chapters 1 and 2, by positing a "savage" other who must be brought up to date, developed or modernised. I next explain my approach to genealogy in detail. The official narrative consistently divides up the history of democracy promotion into three distinct periods: first, colonial times, when colonised countries were understood to have been blocked and denied in their aspirations to democracy; second, independence in the context of the Cold

Introduction 19

War, when "Western" countries like Britain were sporadic and instrumental in their support for fledgling democracy in decolonising countries because of broader geo-political imperatives; and third, the post-Cold War era, in which democracy is finally understood to be the one best form of governing. I show how this periodisation intersects with other teleological narratives.

The final and crucial move in this chapter is to discuss Foucault's *Society Must Be Defended* and show how these lectures make my particular and innovative approach to genealogy possible because of their emphasis on discerning and disrupting the historical narratives that provide guides to present action. What we need to do, I propose, is to change the story of how we got to where we are, and its accompanying assumptions about the nature of time, in order to help us see better what to do next. Thus, I explain my decision to engage in detailed historical investigation of precisely the moments that the democracy promotion discourse points to as its own ancestry: colonial reform, independence for Pakistan, and the end of the Cold War. It is these moments that provide the starting points for the subsequent chapters, in which I show that almost everything we take to be true about the history of democracy promotion is mistaken, and that other stories are not only possible and more plausible, but also politically preferable.

Chapter 4 then goes on to focus on the importance of the early colonial period for the emergence of teleological narratives and their relation to democracy promotion and identity constitution. It suggests that it was the encounter with India that profoundly changed, on a number of levels, modes of thinking about time and the forms of governing that were implied by them. Modes of governing in the eighteenth century had stressed the organic and accretive nature of time, in which wisdom was accumulated over the course of many decades and the main challenge was to preserve it. However, the uncertainty and epistemological confusion of governing in India made this mode of governing impractical. In response, James Mill in the early nineteenth century proposed a radical break with a past in India that he saw as barbarous. Macaulay and his contemporaries in India operated with a strange hybrid of these two ways of thinking, reversing the historical narrative of accumulated British wisdom in order to project a future for India that would resemble the British past written forwards. This represented the beginning of ideas about "progress" and it changed forever not only modes of governing in India but also democratic practices at home.

Chapter 5 provides a link between the colonial and postcolonial periods in what is now Pakistan. This chapter shows that the pivotal moment in the story we tell ourselves about the end of colonial rule can be narrated quite differently – as a story about continuity, rather than one of ruptural violence, in which the institutions of liberal democracy are fully implicated in constituting particular forms of national identity. I thus show that although liberal democracy is commonly thought of as a remedy for violence and unequal power relations, it is never innocent of them. I show that the notional division between the public and private spheres that first emerged as part of the

20 Introduction

teleological rationality of governing in the early colonial era remains important to this day in the creation and management of religious and gendered
identities, thus problematising the notion that decolonisation inaugurated a
new age of democracy and freedom that had been absent in colonial times.

Chapter 6 takes up the story of 1989, which is widely understood in the
democracy promotion literature as the inaugural period of democracy promotion as we know it. However, I tell the story from an unfamiliar angle that
casts doubt on the official narrative. The publication by British writer Salman
Rushdie of an allegedly blasphemous book, *The Satanic Verses*, led to widespread protests by Muslims around the world, including in Britain. This was a
time of confusion and uncertainty in which Muslims seemed to emerge for
the first time as an enemy, just as the threat of Communism seemed to be
receding. In the face of profound doubt about the future in a time of new and
bewildering threats, a teleological narrative about the end of history emerged
as a useful way of making sense of the contemporary world. I show that
stories about the end of history were less a description of the world in 1989,
than they were a continued means of managing the present and guiding
future action. Practices of temporal othering – through which anyone
opposed to the liberal democratic right to free speech was understood to be
foreign, primitive and despotic – emerged as fully complicit in violent practices that upheld a narrative of liberal democracy as the only possible future.

The preceding three chapters throw everything about the official history of
democracy promotion into doubt. Chapter 7 shows how the practices of
temporal othering, democracy promotion and teleology that emerge through
the challenge of colonial and postcolonial governance inform responses to the
London bombings, bringing the story back to where we began. I first show
the crude forms of temporal othering demonstrated in the tabloid press at the
time of the London bombings, and how the FCO attempted to disrupt them
with a photographic exhibition, *The Art of Integration*, which narrated an
alternative British history and a set of constitutive British practices in which
Muslims have long been fully and democratically involved. However, a critical close analysis of these photographs demonstrates that they are profoundly conservative and complicit in democracy promotion. In the last
section of this final chapter, I offer an alternative way of thinking about how
the contemporary narrative of democracy can be disrupted. I provide a close
reading of Chris Morris's 2010 film, *Four Lions*, which I argue provides a
more useful way into thinking about how we might live differently in our
concrete practices of thought.

I conclude by signposting some of the implications of this genealogy. If we
can no longer rely on the unspoken, taken-for-granted history of democracy
that constitutes our national identity, that provides a way of thinking about
our enemies and that offers a programme for the development of those benign
others thought to have been trapped in the past, we may feel that we are at a
loss for something to do. Should we still promote democracy, if democracy
promotion is a practice of inegalitarian power and, frequently, violence? I use

Romand Coles's work to suggest that we could make some room for man-oeuvre by renegotiating the divide between public and private spheres to craft an *intimate* and radically ordinary zone of democratic engagement (Hauerwas and Coles, 2012). This is the sort of work that will *take time*: precisely the sort of patient, slow time that is precluded by the teleological temporalities we have encountered in the official history of democracy promotion. I sketch out where these possibilities might be found in the multiple, radically ordinary counter-narratives about history and identity that we encounter in this book, and I propose that genealogy itself, with its slow, patient unearthing of counter-narratives, is a crucial tool for thinking about democracy differently and finding new democratic ways to live.

1 What is democracy promotion?

– We must all be transparent. That is what we are. We are impartial, transparent, bores.

– I can't stop thinking about ... voter registration.
– Oh my God, that is the saddest thing I've ever heard!

– And when we get bored of being able to vote, bored like Leeds, then we know we are truly democratic?

(Charman, 2009: 6,46)

These are lines from *The Observer*, a play by Matt Charman staged in 2009 at the National Theatre in London. Although fictionalised, it accurately encapsulates many of the technologies and techniques of Democracy Promotion that are likewise described by Thomas Carothers (2004: 83–89) in a more academic description of election observation. A far cry from the drama of "regime change" or military intervention, most of what we conventionally think about as Democracy Promotion takes place through the humdrum, boring and monotonous everyday practices and techniques of voter registration, election observation, polling, statistics and counting. This exists, of course, alongside a plethora of other technologies that enable and institutionalise particular forms of contestation, debate, participation, and the exercise of various rights and freedoms. What they have in common is that they all function not at the idealised level of a noble struggle for democracy, but rather through the detailed work of, for example, interpreting statistics or getting to grips with the detail of a participatory budget.

Democracy is presented in the play as a means for distributing power, for literally putting it into people's hands in the form of a voting slip (Charman, 2009: 62). This is a parcelling out of power that international democracy promoters, such as the ubiquitous election observers, merely oversee and in which they do not personally participate, in keeping with the importance of neutral and transparent procedures. However, the seemingly mundane and impartial business of election observation soon turns out, in this story, to be rather less objective than first thought. Interventions to encourage the registration of voters in one area and not another, the drawing of boundaries, the

What is democracy promotion? 23

positioning of polling stations, the hours during which voting is permitted and the declarations and (contested) opinions not only of the election observers, but also of international journalists, all seem to have the potential to render dramatic change possible.

As such, the seemingly neutral sets of rules and procedures turn out to have been produced by a kind of power that exceeds that vested in the voting slip, and which reproduces it in turn. During the play's violent denouement, the Western observation machine is shown to have been complicit in the unfolding of a particular result through the manipulation of rules that exist to offer neutrality and through the very maintenance of their impartial stance. Perhaps most tellingly, whereas immense change had seemed possible through the use of the election, by the end of the play the power relations between the West and the small developing country, between elites and the poor, between candidates and voters, seem to have been very little disrupted.

This dramatisation of the techniques of Democracy Promotion is useful because of the way it stages and problematises five particular ways of thinking about democracy and democracy promotion that are currently prevalent. First, that democracy is an uncontroversially good thing. Second, that we know what democracy *is* and what institutional form it should take. Third, that Democracy Promotion needs to take place through the mobilisation of the aspirations and desires of freely choosing people in target countries. Fourth, that through the mobilisation of Democracy Promotion overseas, the mundane and detailed practices of democracy in the Western countries of the democracy promoters will likewise be re-infused with aspiration and desire. Finally, that democracy promotion will render populations knowable and legible. In this chapter, I will look a bit more closely at each of these ideas as they relate to the existing policy and academic literature on democracy promotion.

The structure of this chapter is as follows. First, I provide a summary of the practices of Democracy Promotion in Pakistan and explain why they matter. In doing so, I show, in common with other critics of Democracy Promotion, that these practices are *not* neutral, but rather deeply implicated in international flows of power, in particular by narrowing conceptions of democracy down to the liberal democracy familiar in the West.[1] Second, I discuss Milja Kurki's suggestion that democracy should be promoted "as a contested concept". Third, I suggest that we need to think carefully about why such a suggestion is unlikely to be taken up. It is not, I argue, merely a question of policy makers deciding to think more imaginatively about their methods of Democracy Promotion, as if that were something they had somehow just forgotten to do. Rather, we need to question the ways in which Democracy Promotion is deeply bound up in relations of power that uphold the liberal democratic status quo at home and abroad.

Practices of Democracy Promotion: the power of the ballot paper

As Gayatri Spivak points out, democracy is one of those things that it is impossible not to want (Spivak, 1995: 158). Whilst it is therefore by no means

24 *What is democracy promotion?*

unusual to oppose wars purportedly conducted to install more "democratic" regimes, it might appear to be in rather bad taste to question the efforts of those development agencies, embassies and high commissions, non-governmental organisations (NGOs), local authorities and others who are working to strengthen electoral commissions, ensure that elections are conducted freely and fairly, combat corruption, support the protection of political and civil rights, and enable the political participation of women and minority groups.

However, detailed attention should be paid to these practices not least because of the way that power is mediated through them: a power that is not only capable, as in *The Observer*, of manipulating results in a cynical (or idealistic) way, but also a power that determines what we believe democracy and freedom are, who has what rights, what forms and practices democracy shall take and what the consequences will be for the kind of society we live in.

Since the publication of the World Bank's report on *Good Governance and Development* in 1992, the view that good governance is an intrinsic element of the good and developed life has become increasingly widespread in international development circles. In the intervening two decades, despite the uncertainties and disappointments of Democracy Promotion Efforts in Iraq, Afghanistan and elsewhere (Carothers, 2006; Bridoux and Russell, 2012), there has been increasing consensus that "good governance" includes, although it is not restricted to, "democracy" (UNDP, 2002; DFID, 2007b, 2008b). Democracies, the contemporary accepted wisdom suggests, are not only highly legitimate, but also richer, more competent, stronger, less likely to fight one another, and their populations are "better educated, more prosperous, healthier and happier" (Daalder and Lindsay, 2007; see also Hobson, 2008: 85–88). McFaul goes as far as to suggest that democracy is "an ideal system of government" (McFaul, 2004: 148). Democracy, we are compellingly told, is a "universal value" (Sen, 1999). In keeping with this tide of opinion, the United Nations Development Programme's (UNDP) *Human Development Report 2002: Deepening Democracy in a Fragmented World* concerned itself solely with making the case for more democratic governance in the developing world (UNDP, 2002). Democracy is promoted through donor conditionality, project support, diplomacy and, notoriously, although exceptionally, military force (McFaul, 2004: 156; UNDP, 2002; DFID, 2007b, 2012b), and a "right" to democratic governance is proposed in international law (Franck, 1992; Sen, 1999: 5; Hobson, 2008: 85).

Most important for the British context was a Department for International Development (DFID) White Paper, or policy document, published not long after the London bombings, which entirely framed its plans for British development spending in terms of commitments to "better governance" and discussed in detail the various practices through which this might be achieved (DFID, 2006e, 2007b). This appeared alongside a White Paper from the Foreign and Commonwealth Office (FCO), which included "[s]ustainable development and poverty reduction underpinned by human rights, democracy and good governance" as one of nine "strategic priorities" for the UK (FCO, 2006: Chapter 3).

What is democracy promotion? 25

In Pakistan, in the financial year 2008/09, DFID spent over £24 million, or just over 20 per cent of their total programme, on "the governance sector" (DFID, 2010). This included by their own account a £12 million tranche of "poverty reduction budget support", a direct payment into the Pakistani government's budget, which was part of a longer project worth up to £85 million over three years (DFID, 2006d). This was a very important investment for DFID in both political and financial terms, contributing significantly to the "doubling of aid" to Pakistan and signed off personally by the then Prime Minister, Tony Blair, in 2006 during a visit to Pakistan (BBC, 2006c; DFID, 2008a: 8). Under David Cameron's government, DFID has a budget of £220 million to spend on "government and civil society" (DFID, 2012b) in Pakistan, and the "top priority" for this money is: "peace, stability and democracy – for example, by helping another two million people (half of them women) to vote at the next general election" (ibid.).

DFID explicitly claims that "[g]overnance is all about the use of power and authority" (DFID, 2007b: 6). However, the way this claim is formulated betrays the particular conception of power that is held within democracy promotion policy: that power is something that people have and exercise (or do not), usually over others. DFID discusses, for example, "the way power is held, used and projected in different contexts" and targets particular concern toward "those without power and influence" (ibid.). Liberal democratic rationality relies on this way of thinking about power: it is what enables a ballot paper to be thought of as "power actually in their hands" (Charman, 2009: 62). As such, the task at hand is conceived to be the better, more equitable, distribution of power (DFID, 2007b: 20). It is furthermore important to note that the techniques of democracy promoters are conceptualised as entirely outside these power relations, seeking only to intervene in the distribution of power, not to exercise that power itself.

This conception of power has much in common with what Foucault influentially named the "repressive hypothesis", which is to say, the hypothesis that power mainly functions through exclusions, denials and prohibitions (Foucault, 1981: 10–12). Foucault does not deny that power can and does operate in this way: in the context of democracy promotion, a Foucauldian can acknowledge that people are indeed denied resources and freedoms, excluded from decision making, prohibited from joining political organisations and so on. The important point for Foucault, though, is that power is much more interesting, diffuse and productive than this, as we will see.

In the meantime, though, we need to note that DFID is, in the interests of neutrality, quite explicit that it is not its role to prescribe any one particular set of institutions or organisations that would constitute democratic governance:

> Like all aspects of governance, democratic politics cannot be transplanted to or imposed on a country from outside. Governance systems have many different forms, depending on local culture, society and history. It is for each country to design and implement its own democratic institutions.

> (DFID, 2007b: 20)

26   *What is democracy promotion?*

Furthermore, they suggest it is important to:

> ensure that "governance" initiatives at the country level are based on a much stronger, deeper and more nuanced understanding of context. This will mean [...] having no preconceptions about the "right sort of institutions" [...] Donors will need to recognise [...] different histories and build on them, and reject simplistic ideas of building institutions that "look like ours".
>
> (DFID, 2007b: 69)

The then British Foreign Secretary likewise argued, specifically in relation to Pakistan, that Muslim countries do not want "a floor-plan for democratic government" (Miliband, 2009) from the UK, and suggested that "democratization happens primarily because of local pressures and dynamics" (Miliband, 2008), whereas Sue Unsworth, academic and former Chief Governance Adviser at DFID, talks about the crucial importance of the "local political environment" and "home-grown ideas" (Unsworth, 2007: 27; and see also, amongst others UNDP, 2002: 4; Smillie, 2007: 65; Carothers, 2004: 5, 20).

Nevertheless, as other critical scholars have pointed out (Robinson, 1996; Abrahamsen, 2000; Ayers, 2006; Kurki, 2010, 2013), we regularly see surprisingly specific sets of prescriptions given the emphasis placed on local context. In the White Paper, DFID suggests that "democratic politics requires representative institutions to which there are free and fair elections, freedom of expression, a free media, freedom of association and inclusive citizenship" (DFID, 2007b: 19). They also emphasise "the rule of law, accountability, fair representation and effective participation and voice – and a set of values that recognise individual and collective human rights and freedoms" (ibid.). The FCO describes "democracy and good political governance" as "fair electoral processes, effective parliamentary institutions, public participation in decision making, independent judiciaries, and freedom of expression" (FCO, 2006: 56). These prescriptions look remarkably like the familiar institutions of liberal democracy.

Concomitantly, DFID spending on governance in Pakistan was likewise fully implicated in promoting what are clearly liberal democratic institutions. The rationale of the £12 million budget support credit (DFID, 2006d) was not only to put money into the country's public services contributing to health, education and the like, but also to ensure that it is the government itself that spends this money and that it is accountable for it, ideally to its own people. Thus, although the documentation for this sort of intervention may appear at first sight to be quite technical – rather than political – and more interested in the transparency of country accounting systems and the achievement of quantified Millennium Development Goals, it is an intervention that is deeply concerned with the promotion of particular institutions. Amongst the highest-level indicators for success for this project is "% of households satisfied with union councillor contact" (ibid.: 17), as well as other

What is democracy promotion? 27

public service provision, and one of the four broad areas (or "pillars") that legitimates the intervention is its preoccupation with "devolution" (DFID, 2006c: 2). Devolution is important not only because it "demonstrates a commitment to moving spending decisions closer to recipients" (DFID, 2006d: 5), which implies some form of democratic accountability, but also because at provincial level the assemblies were, even at that time, elected and provided some form of democratic legitimacy despite the military government still in power in Islamabad (DFID, 2006c: 5). It is therefore not surprising that around a further £5.5 million was spent on supporting provincial government in the same financial year.

Other projects also reflect that the thrust of DFID's governance work was to bolster specifically liberal democratic institutions, not least the £3.5 million programme to support "free, fair and credible elections in Pakistan" in 2007 (DFID, 2006b). Support for elections provided by DFID comprises mainly support for the Pakistani Electoral Commission and for international election observation, with some support for local civil society partially focused on building capacity for national election observation (DFID, 2006b). Furthermore, a four-year project worth £18 million was funded to strengthen civil society groups' ability to make demands to the devolved governments on the basis that "[c]itizens' engagement is key to a responsive and accountable state" (DFID, 2007c; see Kurki 2011, 2013 for more discussion of why civil society strengthening is a move that is particularly important for liberal democratic government). On a smaller scale, a two-year DFID-funded project run by US democracy promoters, the National Democratic Institute for International Affairs (NDI), worth £325,611 aimed at "strengthening the capacity of political parties to engage in local governance" (DFID, 2004). All of this expenditure takes place alongside smaller-scale FCO projects, which aim to support the right to freedom of speech and expression. In the detail of the projects supported, then, there is a thorough-going, although tacit, commitment to the institutions that together make up liberal democratic governance.

Despite the policy makers' injunctions to be sensitive to local contexts and histories, the academic literature, in fact, very widely acknowledges that what is to be promoted *is* liberal democracy: "Aid providers know what they would like to help countries achieve – the Western-style, rule-oriented systems they know from their own countries" (Carothers, 2004: 136). Samuel Huntington, in advocating a Schumpeterian, procedural version of democracy, indeed hails it as a desirable move that the question of what we mean by democracy appears to have been settled, because in order to promote democracy effectively it is necessary to know what it is: "fuzzy norms do not yield useful analysis" (Huntington, 1991: 9; Schumpeter, 2010).

The perceived advantage in using this particular conception of democracy again comes back to the notion that it can arbitrate neutrally between existing relations of power (Przeworski, 1999; Barro, 1999). Democracy is viewed as a set of "procedures" that are neutral and objective, that will distribute power evenly, and can be separated from the substantive decisions that are their

28 *What is democracy promotion?*

outcome: Larry Diamond exemplifies such a procedural conception when he sets out a lengthy set of rules that would constitute a "free and fair election" (Diamond, 2002). Concrete practices of democracy promotion are informed by this view, which is why donors invest in technologies such as election observation and the strengthening of neutral arbiters of process and procedures such as electoral commissions (Hyde, 2011; Carothers, 2004: 83–90). However, although the election here stands as a particularly powerful symbol of neutrality in the distribution of power, it is important to note that it is only one amongst a complex web of different institutions that make up liberal democracy. The position of the election as the cornerstone of a much broader set of democratic institutions is set out intriguingly by DFID thus:

> A holistic and large programme to support democratic institutions in Pakistan prior to the 2007 elections represents high risk without corresponding returns. Issues that merit careful and material consideration such as parliamentary capacity, transparency of political party funds and operations, and the media's role in promoting democracy, therefore, while crucial, cannot be dealt with in the absence of a clear and demonstrable commitment of sustained democracy from the Government of Pakistan. The 2007 election is a litmus test of this commitment.
>
> (DFID, 2006a: 7)

In other words, the election is not only the linchpin of the set of institutions that DFID intends to promote, but is also prior to them, both in the sense that it must happen first and in the sense that it takes priority. Paradoxically, then, the very desire for neutrality, based on the repressive hypothesis of power, which began by stressing the importance of local ideas, practices and traditions, also leads to a highly restricted vision of what democracy can be, in which the election both sets up the conditions for, and guarantees, the other institutions of liberal democracy.

Democratic theorising and power: is liberal democracy neutral?

The criticism of this approach to Democracy Promotion, as Milja Kurki has pointed out, is that one of the most contested ideas in political theory and popular imagination– democracy – is narrowed down to a particular set of concrete practices. Peter Burnell is one of the few mainstream commentators who does not merely pass over this point (Burnell, 2000: 4; others include Whitehead, 2002; and Schmitter and Karl, 1996; see also the more detailed discussion by Kurki, 2010: 369–370; Kurki, 2013; and Hobson and Kurki, 2012). However, despite his suggestion that "greater mass empowerment than has been commonplace in the West" (Burnell, 2000: 23) might emerge from taking democratic theorising seriously, he nevertheless ends up dismissing the possibility that a more radical or participatory conceptualisation of democracy could be entertained by Democracy Promotion.

What is democracy promotion? 29

This reticence in engaging with the possibilities of alternative theories of democracy is defended on the following grounds: "external actors can contribute very little to the development of truly popular or grass-roots democracy anyway" (Burnell, 2000: 4). The logic of this argument is somewhat curious because, unlike the many accounts of democratisation that fail sufficiently to acknowledge the importance of external actors (see Abrahamsen, 2000: 2–3), Burnell is very clear that "democracy assistance [...] could come close to being essential" (Burnell, 2000: 5) for democratisation under some circumstances and that "approaching two thirds of currently existing democracies owe their origins to deliberate acts of imposition or intervention from without" (ibid.: 7). In other words, he implicitly suggests that external actors *do* successfully intervene, but only when it is liberal democratic theory that animates them. It seems at least possible that in their suffocating elision of alternative modes of theorising democracy, they are likewise actively preventing the emergence of different, perhaps "truly popular or grass-roots", alternatives.

Burnell suggests furthermore that promoting "untried models" is too "risky" and that it lies beyond the ability of Democracy Promotion agencies (Burnell, 2000: 4). The logic here is to imply that the difference between promoting liberal democracy and other potentially democratic forms of governance is due to the distinction between practice and theory: it is safe, justifiable and ultimately possible to promote Western forms of democracy because they are known, tried and tested as practice, but beyond this we are in the untrodden and dangerous terrain of democratic theory. Burnell's privileging of practice over theory is problematic for two reasons. First, in countries where Democracy Promotion is advocated, the practices of liberal democracy are arguably often themselves "untried models" and the risks associated with their implementation during democratic transitions – even if judged worth taking – have been well documented and are often catastrophic (Huntington, 1968; Chua, 2004; Kaplan, 2001; Hawksley, 2009). Second, Burnell's implied dichotomy allows us to forget that liberal democracy is also entirely underwritten by theory. Sue Unsworth notes, just for example, that the "implicit model" is "the reproduction of Weberian norms and democratic political systems as found in OECD [Organisation for Economic Co-operation and Development] countries" (Unsworth, 2007: 21). Similarly, Swain et al. (2011) suggest that Democracy Promotion does, and should, rely on the notion – borrowed from Robert Dahl – of "polyarchy" (Dahl, 1977; see also Huber, 2015 and Robinson, 1996). Democracy as we know it in the West, then, is not an alternative to the dangers of democratic theorising, but rather a consequence of them. Not only this, but practices and theories are never separate from one another, but always in a process of interaction, acting on and constituting the world and each other as they do.

To understand this last claim in context, we need to return to the idea that liberal democracy functions using the "repressive hypothesis" of power. Foucault's essential contribution was to point out that repressive practices are localised tactics within a broader "general economy" of power that is also,

30 *What is democracy promotion?*

and primarily, productive. A Foucauldian approach is sceptical that procedures, "the rules of the game", and power can be separated out, rather viewing procedures as already implicated in the circulation of power. For our purposes, the procedures – however broadly defined – of, say, a democratic practice based on "free and fair elections" can be traced to a particular kind of individualisation which takes human beings as already constituted in their preferences and interests and amenable to counting and measurement prior to any democratic engagement. These procedures may, as in Diamond's account, institutionalise processes of contestation, but in so doing they also put in place a particular regime of political and civil rights that likewise stress individuality above, say, relations of care or the social or economic rights of the group (Burnell, 2000: 4). As such, then, discourses and forms of expertise (of individual rights, of counting, of combating electoral fraud) and the ways in which they intersect with non-discursive practices (the ballot box, recourse to individual legal redress), taken together, will constitute procedures that purport to be neutral but in fact produce and reproduce a whole way of looking at the world.

By broadening our conception of power, we can see that Democracy Promotion, far from being outside power relations in an adjudicative role, aiming only at the better distribution of power that is located in local hands, are rather fully implicated in the production and maintenance of power relations.

Promoting democracy "as a contested concept"?

As Kurki (2010, 2013) has shown in detail, both the precision of the conceptualisation of democracy at the heart of Democracy Promotion and the consensus that seems to surround it, are all the more striking considering that democracy is one of the most contested concepts in the history of political theory. If we were to take history and context as seriously as the authors cited in the previous section suggest we should, we must quickly recognise that there have been many forms and models of rule throughout history that have been considered "democratic", not all of which have featured any or all of the institutions of liberal democracy.

David Held counts at least eight models of democracy that have actually existed: the Greek city state, the republican tradition of active citizenship, social democracy, particularly in Scandinavian countries, and forms of "direct democracy", often advocated in socialist regimes, are the most immediately obvious (Held, 1996; see also Hobson, 2008). Kurki (2013) develops in some detail the argument that alternative models should inform contemporary democracy promotion policy and furthermore points to theoretical contributions to democratic theory as other sites of contestability (Kurki, 2010: 373; Kurki, 2013: Chapters 2–5). These include "participatory" democracy, which focuses on participation not only in public decision making but also in sites such as the workplace and civil society (Pateman, 1975); "deliberative" democracy, which advocates broader inclusion of citizens in democratic deliberation and the formulation of institutions and rules that would enable this to take place in ways that privilege fairness, equality and justice (Bohman, 2000; Dryzek, 2000); "agonistic" and other relational ideas about democracy which stress the importance of subject formation and the never-ending play of power in democratic encounters (Laclau and Mouffe, 2001; Mouffe, 1999, 2000, 2004; Norval, 2007; Laclau, 2005); and "cosmopolitan" democracy that takes engagement at a supranational or global level to be a precondition of democratic life (Held, 1996).

To this I would add the forms of decision making and dispute resolution that have their own specific and local histories, such as the "jirga" in northern Pakistan. The jirga is a:

> key mechanism of governance [...] representatives of affected parties meet and sit in a circle to "deliberate" and finally decide [...] Jirgas deal with disputes between people, but they also negotiate conflicts about lands and forests, and represent "the local" in dealings with state officials. Jirgas are still powerful.
>
> (Geiser, 2012: 713)

My intention in mentioning this form of local governance is not to idealise the jirga, as if it were some kind of unproblematic alternative, or to suggest that it is a form of governance that is somehow authentic or untrammelled by colonial or liberal histories. On the contrary, although the village jirga pre-dates the British, its history is complex and bound up with British rule (Beattie, 2011: 574; Tripodi, 2009; Sammon, 2008). However, the problem the British had with working with the jirga was that it was understood to be "extremely democratic" (Commissioner Derajat Division, quoted in Beattie, 2011: 579), and therefore unwieldy. It is more than a little strange, therefore, given that "democracy" is precisely what has come to be valued by British development practitioners, that the jirga is now entirely absent from official discussions about the region. These important institutions did not even merit a mention in DFID's 2011 "Pakistan Country Governance Analysis" (Coffey International Development, 2011): once considered profoundly democratic, grass-roots organisations, jirgas are no longer even discussed as part of Pakistan's existing postcolonial institutional landscape.

The point here is simply to note that concrete alternative models to the liberal tradition exist. Furthermore, the differences between them are far from trivial. Contrary to the idea that liberal democracy offers a set of neutral procedures that are in principle separable from outcomes, experiments with deliberative democracy, for example, have shown that changing the institutions and the "rules of the game" may shift the substantive outcome dramatically (Goodin and Niemeyer, 2003). Yet any alternative imagining of democracy or democratic institutions – perhaps rooted in local histories, perhaps imaginatively building on and exceeding them, perhaps borrowing from theoretical explorations or now-vanished models, probably always a

32   *What is democracy promotion?*

combination of these – is ruled out by the insistence of Democracy Promotion on a narrow range of institutions, values and techniques, despite explicit claims that this is precisely what they do not want to do. For example, when Sen suggests that the rich argumentative and deliberative traditions of northern India might pave the way for India's introduction of electoral democracy (Sen, 2006: 3–16), he assumes that the proper institutional form for continuing this tradition is liberal democratic, rather than considering other modes of institutionalising deliberation. Similarly, Gilmore and Mosazai describe modes of local governance in Afghanistan, they are at pain to mention that "[v]illages elect their representatives to shuras [local councils]", although electoral technologies were in fact introduced by donor organisations into these more traditional fora (Gilmore and Mosazai, 2007: 147). Even when other models or forms of democracy are mentioned, they are generally not considered with any seriousness as alternatives to liberal democracy, but rather as precursors or additions to it: liberal democracy has effectively colonised the ordinary modes of thinking about democracy.

Where I would depart from Kurki's account, however, is in a stronger emphasis on the relations of power that circulate within Democracy Promotion techniques. It is not merely an oversight that democracy is not promoted as a contested concept. When she puts forward concrete proposals about what might be done to promote democracy differently, she suggests that this might be "a lot to ask", but does not really say why this is, thus failing to uncover the sedimented relations of power that are involved in upholding liberal democracy as democracy (Kurki, 2010: 381). The clue, however, might be in her analysis that a more plural and contextual approach to Democracy Promotion would – by opening up debate on the criteria by which regimes can be judged as "democratic" – disrupt the "student-teacher relationship between the West and the rest" (ibid.: 380). In other words, promoting democracy as a contested concept would imply that we can no longer think of Western countries like the UK as perfect and uncontested models of how democracy should be done.

Democracy Promotion and democracy promotion

The Observer nicely depicts the way that desire – experienced as "massive popular demand for democracy" (DFID, 2007b: 20) – is incited by the drama and spectacle of people queuing to vote in the rain, hoping for dramatic change and televised by journalists who – along with election observers – are "stuck on this seemingly never-ending democracy-sort-of concert tour" (Charman, 2009: 39; see also Coleman, 2013: 2). Fiona Russell, the election observer of the play, puts it like this: "there's nothing like the excitement of an election night. A first election" (Charman, 2009: 14). As she explains, this compares favourably with a country in which these liberal democratic practices have become routine. Liberal democracy – along with the particular rights and freedoms that go with it – is revalorised and relegitimated on

What is democracy promotion? 33

television screens in Leeds (ibid.: 62) as well as in polling stations observed by Western missions. As such, Democracy Promotion can be seen to reinforce the notion that liberal democracy is the one best way of organising human affairs.

The link between Democracy Promotion overseas and the maintenance of liberal democracy at home (conventionally understood) can be understood through an analysis of Democracy Promotion as just one aspect of what David Campbell (1990, 1998) calls Foreign Policy. Campbell's *Writing Security* has been hugely important and is still one of the most influential texts poststructural International Relations. He argues that conventional Foreign Policy can only take place as a function of a whole range of practices he calls "foreign policy", which constitute and enable us to discern what counts as "foreign" in the first place. Any kind of identity can only be established by reference to what it is not. Therefore, it is only by a process of sorting out that which is "foreign", or "other", that identities, such as national identities, can be derived and maintained, and loyalty to them demanded.

Since the book came out two decades ago, there has been a great deal of interest in how the borders between domestic and foreign are produced and policed, which has created the agenda for a field of work called Critical Border Studies (Parker and Vaughan-Williams, 2009). Work in this field has stressed the non-territorial dimension of borders: in other words, the border between the UK and Pakistan is not located only in the immigration queues of Heathrow Airport, but in multiple technologies and forms of surveillance that track, police and assess the risk associated with the movements of bodies, establishing what, or who, is legitimate or illegitimate, foreign or domestic (for example Amoore, 2007; Bigo, 2000; Vaughan-Williams, 2008; Basham and Vaughan-Williams, 2012). Work in this area has provided a much more nuanced account of what a border is and the different sites in which it is performed. However, as R.B.J. Walker (2011: 6) has pointed out, the biopolitical focus of much of this work – extremely valuable though it is – has not yet yielded much critical attention towards how the border between the domestic and the foreign is produced and reproduced in ordinary techniques of governing "domestic" populations, in non-state-based locations and in the practices of everyday life and, also, towards the ways that the border between foreign and domestic intersects with and makes possible other boundaries, such as those that precariously delimit gender and "race".

Although Campbell does not use the language of "bordering", he offers pertinent examples of how the domestic and the foreign are produced at multiple sites and as a consequence of multiple exclusions, as well as giving us a language to think about how practices of Foreign Policy, such as Democracy Promotion, intersect with foreign policy and democracy promotion. As we saw in the Introduction, above, there is in the UK's recent history a clear "othering" process that takes place through the identification of a danger: in this case, the alien and the dangerous element is frequently the figure of the

34 *What is democracy promotion?*

Muslim (often implicitly Pakistani) terrorist: the barbarian. It is also crucial to note that this enemy is often mobilised through the often-repeated contention that "democracy" and "democratic values" are what is under attack and what is to be defended in the "war on terror" (Carothers, 2004: 1, 63–64, 73). Thus the enemy of "Britishness" is identical to the enemy of liberal democracy, which constitutes democracy itself as the intrinsic element of Britishness that must be defended and to which loyalty is required in order to demonstrate and qualify for belonging. Finally, the precise mode by which this othering takes place is a temporal one, which legitimates democracy as an intrinsic part of Britishness because threats against democracy, internal and external, have been struggled against *through history*, constituting the British people in opposition to them.

More on history in Chapter 3. First, though, let us see how the othering discourse relates to democracy promotion in practice. Tony Blair, for example, regularly spoke of "terrorism" as the opposite of "democracy", describing the wars in Iraq and Afghanistan as "a struggle between democracy and violence" and talking about "each revolting terrorist barbarity, each reverse for the forces of democracy". He furthermore reminded us that Mohammed Sidique Khan, one of the London bombers, was "free to speak out, free to vote" and dismissed the latter's professed anger at UK foreign policy by suggesting: "let Iraqi or Afghan Muslims decide whether to be angry or not by ballot" (Blair, 2006).

Tony Blair exteriorised the problem of home-grown terrorism and legitimated ongoing intervention in Pakistan by suggesting that the bombings have made it clear that, "[w]hat happens today in Pakistan matters on the streets of Britain" (Blair, 2007b). This feeds into the government's cross-departmental "Prevent" agenda, which casts one of the causes of "radicalisation" as "poor governance" (FCO, 2006: 29) overseas, to be tackled in part, as we have seen, by Democracy Promotion by DFID through its agenda on "good governance" (DFID, 2006e: particularly 38–40; DFID, 2007b), and the FCO's mandate – notably particularly for the "Muslim world" – to "[e]ncourage the spread of democracy and good political governance" (FCO, 2006: 56).

It should be emphasised, then, that democracy can here be understood to be promoted according to our two understandings of Foreign Policy/foreign policy. On the one hand, a construction of "democracy" as the opposite of "barbarism", legitimates the Democracy Promotion overseas in the, by now familiar, terms of liberal democracy. On the other hand, the construction of a British identity as the opposite of a threat to democracy, enables the articulation of a narrative with a strong positive content about what it means to be British, characterised as being "free to speak out, free to vote". The freely choosing subjects implied by a liberal democratic paradigm have the option to participate fully in the democratic practices of Britishness. This is an othering that is temporal, rather than spatial, and associated with the familiar teleologies of development, in which danger can be averted by developing, democratising, civilising, modernising, progressing and coming up to date.

I therefore argue that foreign policy in the contemporary UK is in practice concerned with upholding liberal democratic values through a process of othering that equates participation in liberal democracy with the self, or the acceptable practice of loyalty to a British identity, and lack of democracy with the external, the uncivilised and the foreign. In consequence, it should now be clear that it is possible to refer to Democracy Promotion as a sub-category of Foreign Policy – that is, as the state-based and externally focused process of reproducing a liberal democratic identity and containing challenges to it. As this discussion should now also have made clear, however, we also need to be mindful of the modes of democracy promotion that are not directly state based, and which may take place within conventional borders: the everyday practices of shoring up liberal democracy as a way of life and a mode of identification.

It is interesting to note that, even speaking from within the mainstream Democracy Promotion literature, Laurence Whitehead was able quite clearly to acknowledge this constitutive identity-based logic of Foreign Policy before 1989:

> The simplest and most fundamental motive for the promotion of democracy is to extend to foreigners the benefit of a system that is valued at home. Citizens of established liberal democracies readily believe in the superiority – both moral and practical – of their own form of government, and most would find it hard to doubt that the world would be a safer and happier place if it were generalised.
>
> (Whitehead, 1986: 10)

Whilst acknowledging that citizens of the Soviet Union or Iran might, at the time, feel much the same about their own systems, he suggests that Democracy Promotion "should be interpreted first and foremost as affirmation [...] of internal legitimacy" (Whitehead, 1986: 10).

However, what in Whitehead's 1986 account had been "established liberal democracies" are now characterised simply as "established democracies" (Carothers, 2004: 4). Likewise, Swain et al. (2011: 3) suggest that "the definition of democracy is often contested in transitory countries", implying that such questions in Western countries are now settled and closed. Maureen O'Neil, former Chair of the United Nations Research Institute for Social Development, suggests that there has been an "internationalization of the concepts underpinning developed countries' national experiences of redistribution, economic development and law-making" (O'Neil, 2007: viii). This generalises the particular "national experiences" of developed countries in a way mirrored by DFID, which suggests that "[t]he democratic institutions we have in the UK took centuries to evolve" (DFID, 2007b: 20). By positing the institutions of the West as an endpoint, they are established as the only, natural and inevitable consequence of a process of democratisation: whilst noting the temporality implicit in this, the point for now is that this appears to put them beyond question. As such, when Carothers suggests that "for elections

36 *What is democracy promotion?*

to gain international credibility, certain procedures must be followed", the logic of this is to legitimate, and make credible, the procedures followed in Leeds as much as in Islamabad (Carothers, 2004: 86).

As April Biccum has pointed out, DFID has explicitly attempted to promote a particular sort of British citizen in the UK citizenship programme in schools, with their *Developments* magazine and through their engagement with UK-based international NGOs. She demonstrates the thrust of this work is to promote quiescence in a liberal order of global governance, which has tended to co-opt even the most seemingly radical of social movements, as the organised spectacle surrounding the G8 summit in Gleneagles in 2005 "amounted to a stage-managed legitimizing of democratic representation, lobbying and debate" (Biccum, 2007: 1111–1126). If consent for the good governance agenda in development agreed at Gleneagles was the Democracy Promotion element of the event (DFID, 2006e: 12), democracy promotion occurs at the level of the individual British citizen and her commitment to the rituals of democracy and citizenship through her acts of lobbying, protesting and so on. Indeed, at the G8 protests in 2005 – just after the London bombings – the discourse of civilisation and the barbarian could not be more evident: Tony Blair condemned "[the] savagery [of the terrorists] designed to cover all conventional politics in darkness, to overwhelm the dignity of democracy and proper process" (BBC, 2005a). Once again, at home as overseas, democracy is promoted through glorification and othering, at the same time that it is reduced to a "process", a set of procedures that are held up as the one right way to do politics.

It is again Peter Burnell who demonstrates some subtlety in discerning the power relationship here: viewed from the "alternative standpoints" of those who would theorise about democracy rather than join the liberal democratic consensus, "fundamental reforms applied not least to the western liberal democracies themselves would follow as a principal recommendation" (Burnell, 2000: 23) of promoting democracy as a contested concept. Disrupting Democracy Promotion, then, by introducing alternative conceptualisations of democracy, would destabilise democracy promotion and the very edifice of liberal democratic identity that forms a crucial part of domestic, Western national identities. This is not a price that is likely to be paid easily and without considerable struggle.

Working at the frontiers

In this chapter I have sought to show that Democracy Promotion is a set of practices and procedures that is far from being neutral and free from the effects of power, as is claimed. Rather, it is deeply implicated in the productive power relations that enable the constitution of particular subjectivities, selves and others. I have also shown that Democracy Promotion is intimately linked to the practices of democracy promotion, which at various sites in society discursively constitute a domestic identity by reference to what is seen to be

What is democracy promotion? 37

threatening it: Pakistan is an important "other" in this process, by standing in as a site of identification for those "others", such as Mohammed Sidique Khan, who are understood to have rejected and to be violently opposed to democracy. As such, UK Democracy Promotion is mobilised in the service of eliminating and containing threats to the liberal democratic British identity that is promoted at home, not least through the spectacle of Democracy Promotion itself. In this way, dangers to democracy can be exteriorised: this process of exteriorisation is both the discursive means of promoting democracy at home, by offering democracy as a redemptive, temporal narrative and a set of rituals by which Britishness can be affirmed and demonstrated, and the legitimation for ongoing Democracy Promotion in Pakistan.

Identity, then, is not something we can take for granted: rather we see a constant, vigilant, detailed practice of building the distinction between who may belong and who may be excluded from a community, enabling us to understand what is expected of us in practical terms. The same, it seems, can be applied to democracy, which cannot be taken as a given, a simple good, a universal value, but rather as an edifice that is constantly under construction and never innocent of power. However, as Foucault puts it:

> We are not talking about a gesture of rejection. We have to move beyond the inside-outside alternative; we have to be at the frontiers. Criticism indeed consists of analyzing and reflecting on limits.
>
> (Foucault, 1991e: 45)

I have suggested here that in the contemporary UK, the frontiers of national identity and the limits of what counts as democracy are intimately linked and mutually constituted, and it is at this intersection that we therefore need to focus our reflections. That being the case, if we believe that democratic subjectivity might be differently constituted, we will need to think not only about what the limits of democratic identity currently are, but also why, for whom and for what purposes democracy is *useful*. These are the questions that will be taken up in the next chapter.

Note

1 Kurki (2013) rightly discusses the fact that "liberalism" and "liberal democracy" are not always and everywhere the same thing, but are much debated and contested ideas. Her patient teasing out of the range and variation in democracy promotion practice is heroic and much to be welcomed as it shows the possibilities for change within the status quo. There is no need to repeat that work here: I agree both with her analysis of the variation within liberal thought and with her contention that there is much that unites ideas about "liberal democracy" and that taken together liberal democratic ideas have been overwhelmingly influential for Democracy Promotion.

2 Democratic representation

The cartoon in Figure 2.1 appeared in the respected and serious daily newspaper *The Financial Times* on the eve of Pakistan's general elections in February 2008: elections that were to inaugurate democratic rule for the first time since the military coup led by General Musharraf in 1999. It sums up rather elegantly the ways in which Pakistan is quite often represented in the British media. The unseemly, highly masculine and incipiently violent struggle this cartoon suggests is a far cry from a benevolent picture of democracy as a universal value. Democracy in Pakistan is a problem.

Whilst the regularly anti-democratic military, with their haphazardly aimed nuclear weapons, is clearly pinpointed as significantly to blame, it is their disunited opposition, the squabbling politicians and disengaged, outward

Figure 2.1 Why politics will not fix Pakistan
Source: *The Financial Times*, 19 February 2008: 6. Ingram Pinn/Financial Times 2008. Used under licence from the Financial Times. All Rights Reserved.

(backward?) facing Mullah (the only representative of what liberal democratic discourse might call "civil society"), that are particularly relevant here. Power politics are standing in the way of progress and development: the imagined marginalisation of real developmental needs by politics is signalled by the small boys in school uniforms, being pushed out of the picture/off the edge of a splintering country. There are no women anywhere to be seen.

Above all, the basic requirement of liberal democracy – that there is a division of a particular and important kind between the public and private spheres – appears to be missing here. Thus the irrational passions of ambition and anger, the religious spokesman and allegiances to particularistic regional, kinship or sectarian identities should – for the proper functioning of liberal democracy – be firmly excluded from the rational public sphere. Meanwhile, the issues that should be represented in the public, such as the proper role of government in education or the needs and interests of women (as their identities are already constituted in the private domain of family life) are crowded out and remain unrepresented. Whole swaths of the population, made up of individual voters, are unable to speak for or represent themselves because they cannot shout loudly enough.

This cartoon is also part of a more generalised discourse that suggests that Pakistan is "the most dangerous country in the world". The front page of the internationalist and left-leaning *New Statesman* magazine in 2010 depicts the Pakistani flag in the shape of a bomb with the fuse lit (*New Statesman*, 2010), which is emblematic of the 282 articles in national British newspapers between 2005 and 2008 that refer to Pakistan precisely as "the most dangerous" country. (A broader search on "Pakistan" and "danger" yields nearly 2,000 articles during the same period.) In an editorial in the Pakistani *Friday Times*, Najam Sethi (2012b) named the top ten bestselling English-language books on Pakistan, which all had names like *Pakistan: Beyond the Crisis State* or *Pakistan: Playing with Fire* or *The Unravelling: Pakistan in the Age of Jihad*, to name but the first three. Every single book title participated in a whole system of representations which constructs Pakistan as "other", threatening, perilous, intersecting with the notion that Pakistan is the place where terrorist ideologies "are born" and which hosts and trains young British men who are intent on causing death and destruction in the UK.

Intimately intertwined with this discourse of Pakistan as a very dangerous place is the notion that Pakistan constitutes a profound epistemological problem. Pakistan is dangerous because it is chaotic: it cannot be properly known and is therefore intractable to being managed. It is this threatening unknowability that informs a later *New Statesman* cover (*New Statesman*, 2011), this time depicting a shadowy general looking through binoculars, one lens of which shows a US flag and the other Osama bin Laden. The trouble with Pakistan, it is implied, is that its inscrutable "double game" makes it impossible to understand. It is not the struggle between military and civilian governance, its Islamic and sometimes conservative cultural heritage, nor even its nuclear weapons that cause the most unease (other countries share such features); it is the uncertainty it provokes that causes most consternation.

40 *Democratic representation*

Indeed, the *New York Review of Books* even suggests that the key role of Pakistani novelists writing in English is to "assume the burden of representing their country to the world" and making it comprehensible to the Western reader (Mishra, 2011: 37).

In suggesting that politics can't "fix" Pakistan the cartoon is elaborating two related points that run through the discourse of Pakistan as a dangerous and unknowable place. First, democracy in Pakistan is not democracy as we know it. There is no sense, here, that power is evenly distributed amongst already constituted individuals. How could anyone be "free to speak out, free to vote" in this chaotic landscape, where the public and the private spheres are so woefully undelimited? How can interests be aggregated and voices be exercised when there is no possibility of free association, when half the population is nowhere to be seen, when the provision of public services is less of an election issue than the more properly private matters of allegiance to tribe, or region, or slogan? This might be politics, but it is not really democracy in the way understood by Amartya Sen when he describes democracy as a universal value.

Second, and of particular interest for this chapter, because of these deficiencies in the political landscape of Pakistan, democracy is inadequate to the task of knowing the country and its population. If they cannot be adequately counted and thereby represented in a separate public sphere, how can women's needs and rights be fulfilled and protected by the legislature? If power is not distributed equally, put directly into the hands of the people, how can development priorities be established and public services provided? If the population cannot be known through the usual democratic institutions of the free vote and the free press, unencumbered by the power relations of the private, domestic sphere, how will the elected government know what to do at all?

I want to suggest that this set of epistemological uncertainties are precisely what Democracy Promotion in Pakistan is attempting to manage and control. As the Department for International Development (DFID) put it, also shortly before the 2008 elections: "A free and fair election will provide Pakistan with [...] political stability and international credibility" (DFID, 2006a). I suggest that the attempt to stabilise Pakistan is envisaged to function through an attempt to make it knowable and thereby domesticate it, rendering it less dangerous and irredeemably foreign: in other words, Pakistan needs to be better represented. This is where Democracy Promotion becomes most *useful*: democratic institutions – both electoral and deliberative – function as a useful set of practices that offer to render the unknown quantifiable and legible.

To show how Democracy Promotion functions in this way, I focus on the institutions that liberal democracy provides and ask how they intersect with Foucault's account of the form of rule known as "liberal governmentality". I show how democracy functions as a useful set of practices that enable governmental rule. This will entail demonstrating how it enables populations to be known and individual subjects to be constituted and managed within its ambit. I will begin by discussing Foucault's ideas about governmentality as

How does liberal democracy produce knowledge?

I want to suggest that democracy produces freely choosing subjects who can vote and otherwise represent their interests so that those interests can be *known*. This is an argument that is heavily influenced by Michel Foucault's work on governmentality, although it makes a number of leaps about the role that the institutions of liberal democracy specifically play in contemporary governmental regimes. Although Foucault is explicit in *Discipline and Punish* about the role that parliamentary representative regimes play in the constitution and reproduction of power in industrial societies (Foucault, 1991f: 222), he wrote relatively little about the specific institutions of liberal democracy and he pays more attention in his later works to ancient democracy (Sawyer, 2016). Nevertheless, I suggest here that it is possible to use his work on power and governmentality to develop important insights about the epistemological role of liberal democratic institutions.

It is useful at the outset to make a distinction between the related concepts of "government", "governance" and "governmentality". For the sake of clarity, I shall follow the distinction made implicitly by DFID between "government" and "governance", although Foucault refers throughout to "government" to cover both meanings and denote the intimate interconnections between them.[1] However, as my concern is with the conditions of possibility of contemporary British democracy promotion, I will use and analyse the terminology employed by British state agencies, including the government, wherein the former is understood as the government of a country: the individuals and/or the political parties that people the ubiquitous executive and ministerial institutions of the modern state, including the offices of government ministers, Prime Minister and/or President.

Governance, by contrast, is much more broadly defined: "Governance is about power and authority and how a country manages its affairs" (DFID, 2007b). This takes in a much broader range of actors: "governance works at all levels in society: from the state down to household level [...] governance is about people and their relationship with the state [...] the formal and informal rules that determine the way things are done". As such, governance might be understood as the "conduct of conduct" within a given society (Foucault, 2007: 193). Importantly it is good governance that is the focus of DFID's interventions, and democratic politics is viewed as the "best framework" for achieving it (DFID, 2007b: 3).

Foucault describes the operation of "sovereignty" as a highly constrained form of power which is mainly "deductive" in its operations: that is to say, the sovereign had the right to collect taxes, demand time and services, and the ultimate "right to decide life and death" (Foucault, 1981: 135). By contrast, with the emergence of the Industrial Revolution, Foucault points to the growing

42 Democratic representation

importance of alternative forms of power, which work alongside sovereignty. These are no longer purely repressive or deductive, but rather they work to: "incite, reinforce, control, monitor, optimise and organise the forces under it: a power bent on generating forces, making them grow and ordering them" (ibid.: 136). The "disciplinary" modes of such power are explored in *Discipline and Punish*, which looks in detail at the ways in which the micro-techniques of measuring, examining and surveillance all allow for the production of "docile bodies" (Foucault, 1991f: 135–170). One crucial technique at the disposal of disciplinary power is the establishment, through individual measurement and examination and broader statistical techniques, of the "norm". This has a double purpose, not only rendering the differences between individuals useful, "by making it possible to measure gaps, to determine levels, to fix specialties" (ibid.: 184), but also by exhorting conformity to the norm (ibid.: 181–182).

"Governmentality" is a concept that appears particularly in Foucault's 1977–78 and 1978–79 lecture series (Foucault 2007, 2008). It refers to the systematic ways of thinking, or what Foucault calls "rationalities", that make the "conduct of conduct" possible in the contemporary world, as well as the technologies and techniques through which governance operates (Dean, 2010: 40–41). Governmentality shares with disciplinary power a concern for "fostering life" and putting it to use, as differentiated from the sovereign power to take life (Foucault, 1981: 138). However, governmentality can be understood as distinct from discipline in important respects. If disciplinary power works at the level of the individual, the "governmentality" lectures and the first volume of *The History of Sexuality* stress the ways in which discipline has been joined to a "bio-politics of the population" (ibid.: 139). The micro-practices that constituted and regulated the individual in the classroom, the drill ground or the prison, do not cease to proliferate, but for the purposes of governance, "the multiplicity of individuals is no longer pertinent, the population is" (Foucault, 2007: 42). Furthermore, and notably, along with the level of the population, what will be important is:

> a different level, that of the series, the multiplicity of individuals, who will not be pertinent, or rather who will only be pertinent to the extent that, properly managed, maintained, and encouraged, it will make possible what one wants to obtain at the level that is pertinent.
>
> (Foucault, 2007: 42)

For our purposes, two key consequences follow from this important insight. First, population is constituted as a level of intervention and concern. Whereas nothing escapes the panoptical attention of disciplinary power, governmentality is concerned rather with the broad consequences of individual practices: "the big picture."

To give an example, the election observers in Charman's play, *The Observer*, discussed in Chapter 1, are not required to take note of coercion at the micro-level:

Democratic representation 43

If thirty-two were coerced [...] Does it have an effect on the outcome? Palpably I mean [...] If we report things that don't affect the outcome of this election then we're not helping anyone get a clear picture.

(Charman, 2009: 33)

Second, whereas discipline concerned the management, control and optimisation of the body's capacities as a "machine" (Foucault, 1981: 139), governmentality operates rather as a function of individual freedom (Foucault, 2007: 48–49). The aggregate actions and choices of freely acting and choosing individuals are what must be "managed, maintained, and encouraged" for the optimum outcome for the population as a whole. Thus, provided that coercion is negligible, the voting subject acts freely and makes a choice. The question then is how the voter can be maintained in her identity *as* a voter and how she can be managed and encouraged to act responsibly in the exercise of her choice, through the incitement and mobilisation of her aspirations and desires.

Techniques regarding the "norm" remain important but they are also to be understood differently under regimes of discipline and governmentality, respectively. Discipline is constructivist in that it takes a desirable outcome as the "norm", asking what particular people, techniques or specialisms would be best for performing a particular task and then directed training and examination at a minute level of individuals in order finally to establish and separate those who are incapable from those who are normal (Foucault, 2007: 57). A disciplinary regime, therefore, might concern itself with the most efficient means of registering a democratic choice, with the best technologies of designing a voting system, a ballot paper, the processing of individuals through a polling station. It would also divide those entitled to vote from the abnormal categories who are deemed incapable or are otherwise disallowed.

On the other hand, a governmentality regime is more concerned with rendering calculable a reality that is understood to be external to itself and quasi-natural. It does not concern itself with establishing a norm, but rather with discovering it, rendering it visible and amenable to manipulation. This is achieved through "an interplay of differential normalities", in which certain distributions, once measured, can be considered more favourable than the others, which are then, in turn, to be brought into alignment with it (Foucault, 2007: 63). A governmentality regime, therefore, might assess voter registration figures in different areas and attempt to bring the norm in more disenfranchised areas into line with the general norm, whilst always assuming that the choices and interests of voters are already fully formed and with the right techniques can be made representable through the electoral process. In short, whilst sovereignty might be said to prohibit and discipline to prescribe, governmentality is rather a form of power that regulates, that is, maintains the proper arrangement and analysis of what is understood as a concrete, external, fully formed reality that is not tractable to decree, but rather can be known, managed, channelled and put to work.

44 *Democratic representation*

As the above examples might suggest, none of this is to suggest that the rationalities characterised by either sovereignty or discipline have been abolished by governmentality (Foucault, 2007: 107). Rather, they exist alongside it and are transformed and re-inscribed by it. The specific configurations of these forms of power in different times and places, the ways in which they operate and interact, the modes of ongoing transformation and re-inscription that they undergo, are all a matter of empirical investigation. I will therefore turn next to the specific configuration of liberal democracy to discuss how contemporary democratic practice is informed by governmentality.

Governmentality and liberal democracy

The history of governmentality is intimately linked with the history of both liberalism and liberal democracy, with its emphasis on electoralism. As Foucault (2008: 321) points out, there is nothing inevitable about the historical conjunction of liberalism, electoralism and democracy. It is also worth noting that there are myriad different forms that the connections between liberalism and democracy can take (Kurki, 2013: Chapter 2). We therefore need to explore the way in which a specific articulation of liberalism and democracy is enabled in contemporary governmental regimes and the important consequences this has had for the way democratic institutions can be imagined by democracy promoters.

According to Foucault, the emergence of liberalism as a rationality accompanies the discovery of a way of thinking about the economy, which is for the first time understood as a quasi-natural realm that aggregates individual decisions within the realm of the market and which it is the primary job of the state to manage and control. This discovery emerges alongside the invention of statistics as a technology of the state that can measure and make visible the population, providing information about how decisions at the individual level are aggregated that can then be put to further use to optimise outcomes (Foucault, 2007: 87–110).

With the development of the population as a level of analysis and the means to make it knowable (legible, calculable and analysable), the correlative objective of governance is: "to improve the condition of the population, to increase its wealth, its longevity and its health" (ibid.: 105). Liberal democracy is a rational means of organising government within liberalism, analysed as a way of thinking, with its emphasis on the individual: "the rationality of the governed must serve as the regulating principle for the rationality of government" (Foucault, 2008: 312). Although Foucault does not focus on the technologies of democratic rule, it is nevertheless against this backdrop that the calculative technologies of electoral democracy are developed. The individual – conceptualised as independent and autonomous, with interests and needs that are fully transparent, knowable and representable by a simple cross on the ballot paper – is enshrined as the basic principle, and unit, of legitimate government (Dean, 2010: 143; Coleman, 2013: 28–33).

Above all, the election – this simple, quantitative means of obtaining information about the interests and preferences of individuals in a way that can be aggregated at the level of the population – is useful. Foucault suggests that, "participation of the governed in the drawing up of the law in a parliamentary system is the most effective system of government economy" (Foucault, 2008: 321). It provides the means, along with other statistical techniques, particularly opinion polling, and the burgeoning concomitant expertise that goes with it, of determining the various distributions of norms, the various needs, desires and interests of the electorate, the better to manage them. It also constitutes identities: constructing the electorate as a population amenable to measurement and enjoining the individuals within it to consider themselves as voters and citizens, to reflect upon their vote and exercise it freely and responsibly. If it is the role of governance to manage the affairs of a country in order to ensure citizens' flourishing and prosperity, the election provides both the information and legitimacy to pursue this end.

It may be tempting to join Fiona Russell in *The Observer* and remark the never-ending failure of the election – "[n]othing changes" (Charman, 2009: 61) – rather as Foucault points out the "perpetual failure" of the prison (Foucault, 1991f: 264). Those hoping for really radical change are indeed, it seems, destined to be disappointed by the technology of the election, because of the limitation and regulation of participation that is written into its very design. Nevertheless, the democratisation of state sovereignty has had concrete consequences, many of which are part of the explicit programme of those who recommend liberal (or social) democracy (Sen, 1999, just for example), in terms of the opening up of space to make and meet "social" demands to foster life, for health care and education, poverty reduction and generation of economic growth, environmental projects and the protection of natural and cultural heritages, to name but a few.

It is important to understand, for my purposes, however, that this space is opened up as the result of a specific history and in the service of particular rationalities and power relations. This concerns not least the creation and always vigilant maintenance of – and constant struggle over – the separation between what counts as "public" and contestable, and what is considered "private" and (in theory) beyond the sphere of governmental intervention. If the basic problem of liberalism is to draw the balance between "governing too much and governing too little" (Dean, 2010: 144), then the participation of individuals in the exercise of sovereignty provides an elegant solution to this problem by displacing the problem back onto the individuals from whose autonomy and rights it originates. A particular institutional design is implied by liberalism, for if government is understood as something to be limited, then participation must also be regulated and limited. This is achieved through institutions, which include representative, rather than more broadly participatory, mechanisms, a separation of powers, the independence of the police and judiciary, freedom of speech, and the broader principle of the "rule of law", understood to apply to all equally and in theory neutrally. This is

46 *Democratic representation*

why liberal democracy is understood as more than merely electoral democracy, despite the undeniable importance of elections: a whole range of technologies is inextricably united in producing and reproducing the citizen, the electorate, the law and the government.

Democracy promotion, governmentality, power

In Chapter 1, I discussed how the conception of power frequently used in Democracy Promotion has much in common with what Foucault influentially named the "repressive hypothesis", which is to say, the hypothesis that power mainly functions through exclusions, denials and prohibitions (Foucault, 1981: 10–12). Democracy Promotion relies on being considered neutral: the premise is that democracy will distribute power evenly, but democracy promoters are not understood to exercise power *over* anyone. The assumption of neutrality means that the productive flows of power that are intrinsic to Democracy Promotion are not seen and not questioned. However, governmentality is a web of productive power.

Let us begin with the election. The importance and centrality of elections as a democratic practice is not, as we have seen, much questioned in the literature. Its function as a governmental technology is signalled by Carothers, who suggests that the main reason for putting significant emphasis on the election, rather than other democratic practices, is not only its symbolic value, but also because it is "the best way of concentrating the energies and attention of a society in transition [...] toward a broad, participatory act of political self-determination" (Carothers, 2004: 15). In other words, an election is what enables, and requires, individuals to reflect upon their vote and make a free choice: they are moulded as subjects through this technology.

DFID justify their financial support to the elections in Pakistan in exactly the following terms:

> Research and monitoring on electoral behaviour will promote an improved understanding of social and poverty issues that influence voting behaviour thus enriching the policy dialogue.
>
> (DFID, 2006a: 9)

Thus the voting population is understood to be calculable and knowable through its electoral behaviour, in ways that are useful for government in its crucial role of fostering life. Furthermore, "special initiatives [will] address knowledge/information gaps that lead to lack of electoral participation among marginalised groups" (DFID, 2006a: 9). In other words, those voters who are unable to reflect freely and responsibly on their vote – probably because they are illiterate, or isolated because of social status (ibid.: 9) – need to be enabled to do so. This is viewed as a straightforward matter of providing "knowledge/information", which in principle is objective and can freely be reflected on by voters themselves.

Furthermore, the election (along with rights to free expression and association, which I will discuss below) constitutes a public sphere in which these choices can all be made visible and representable. The aggregate counting of ballots then enables the overall sum total of individuals reflecting on their vote to be understood more broadly, so that a government can not only be inaugurated but also that it might, because of the participation of the electors, know what it legitimately ought to do.

This process of rendering a population visible and knowable occurs not only at the level of the country holding the election, but is also implicated in larger, international flows of power. Susan Hyde notes that the ubiquity of the international election observer has developed into a mode of "signalling" (Hyde, 2011). Whether or not a given election is "free and fair", there is a general expectation that the election will be held and that it will be internationally observed. In a world in which there are significant rewards for holding democratic elections in terms of aid, investment, trade and membership of international organisations, there is a strong incentive to "signal" this in credible ways, particularly through the practice of election observation (ibid.: 9). Without this form of international visibility, there is an assumption that the election was not valid, which means that even elections which are less than "free and fair" are more likely to be observed, so as to maximise the potential benefits from holding them in the first place. Hyde argues that although the "signals may not be perfectly informative", refusing to send the signal itself becomes a source of relevant information, whereas the practice of observation itself generates reports which bring yet more information (ibid.: 12). The important thing to note here is that the election becomes part of a broader system of inscription and power, in which the competitive logic of international governance requires states to compete against one another for aid and other benefits by making their own performance – against externally defined targets – visible and calculable (Gould, 2005: 10).

This signalling functions alongside a whole industry of "country governance analyses" which aim to know in minute detail a whole range of information about how political and economic affairs are managed in countries, well beyond merely analysis of electoral practices (Unsworth, 2007: 32; DFID, 2007a; for Pakistan's own country governance analysis, see Coffey International Development, 2011). In all these ways, whole swaths of populations become representable, knowable and visible both as individuals with particular preferences and interests, and as citizens of states that have (or not) particular valued characteristics.

Equally tellingly, such anxiety as exists surrounding elections is generally related to concerns that elections do not always provide the most accurate way of representing populations, as the cartoon discussed at the start of this chapter implied. Thus Carothers warns that although the "mechanical process of voting" may be perfectly accurate and fair, it is always necessary to guard against the possibilities of "a biased election commission, a lack of any civic-education efforts, grossly unfair campaign coverage on television, or blatantly

48 *Democratic representation*

unequal resources" (Carothers, 2004: 88–89). Any such irregularities in the broader "neutrality" of democratic practices, it is implied, will skew the information derived from the election such as to make it impossible to read.

This anxiety likewise informs concerns over the possibility that donors might, unwittingly, interfere with democratic mechanisms of demand and bargaining that occur between the public and politicians (Unsworth, 2007: 28). Similarly the ever-present worry about "patronage" in Pakistan also centres on the way that practices of patronage will interfere with the accurate representation of the population (Coffey International Development, 2011: 11). The concern over the possible inadequacies of the election then entails an interest in other democratic practices that can supplement it: these include the institutions of a free press, freedom of association and public debate.

Freedom of speech and association

Liberal democracy relies upon the right to freedom of speech and freedom of association alongside elections, so that freely choosing individuals can test out their opinions in the public sphere, and worse options, ideas and beliefs can be discarded in favour of better ones. This is the precondition of being able to make a rational decision at the ballot box in possession of all relevant information and provides the opportunity for individuals to discover what their interests are in debate and conversation with others. Through processes of debate and contestation, a population will be able to represent its needs and interests, such that politicians will be able and obliged to understand and respond to them.

If one of the crucial logics of liberal governmentality is to produce and maintain separate public and private spheres, the state is understood to play a crucial role in constructing a broader public sphere in which representation can take place. This includes not only state institutions, but also a public sphere that is free from censorship and the construction of a "civil society" in which "citizens associate according to their own interests and wishes", which is understood to exist only insofar as a strong and capable state is able to guarantee and facilitate it (Diamond, 2008: 13; see also Kurki, 2011). Thus the state is fully implicated in modes of everyday democracy promotion, even when they are formally divorced from state institutions.

Free speech and association is the lifeblood of liberal democratic life in that it enables a range of policy options to be represented and developed in the public sphere and provides ongoing government action with legitimacy through the process of public debate. If the election renders the interests of the population *visible* and *quantifiable*, it is freedom of speech and association in civil society that makes populations truly *legible*. This focus on legibility explains the emphasis on visible "demand" that is found in the Democracy Promotion academic and policy literature (Unsworth, 2007: 28; DFID, 2007b: 16, 23, 32, 34). This is often articulated around practices of "bargaining", not least the ways in which citizens mobilise around how money raised through taxation should be spent, which particularly informs the logic

Democratic representation 49

behind putting budget support into government coffers as a mechanism for delivering aid (ibid.: 62; Smillie, 2007: 60; Moore and Unsworth, 2006: 710).

What is crucially important here is that citizens are more often than not conceptualised as engaging in speech in the public sphere with their interests, values and identities *already* fixed and decided: as in the classic liberalism described by Graham Burchell, "[i]nterest, then, functions as the principle of a personal choice which is unconditionally subjective or private" and therefore "irreducible" (Burchell, 1991: 130). As should by now be very clear, this liberal formulation of the rights of free speech relies on the repressive hypothesis of power, masking the ways in which power also enables what it is possible to say, the ways in which it is possible to say them and even the subjectivities of the individuals who get to speak. Just as electoral democracy is understood as a neutral forum which puts power directly into the hands of the people in the form of the ballot paper, likewise individuals are understood to hold and exercise power by dint of the right to hold and share their own opinions in a free, democratic country.

Thus Quadir, for example, suggests that the importance of "participatory governance" is in "representing the concerns of gender, age, caste, ethnicity, wealth and class [...] based on the voices of ordinary citizens in decision-making" (Quadir, 2007: 116). The logic of participation here is not to transform subjectivities, which are taken as given, but rather to ensure that they are fully representable, and therefore governable. Unsworth (2007: 33) finds this kind of representation more troubling, however, suggesting that "political mobilisation is often along ethnic lines rather than around economic or other interests that would facilitate compromise over time." This makes a particular set of assumptions about what ought to be represented in the public sphere – with loyalties related to ethnicity perhaps understood as unfit for the public sphere because they are understood to be mainly appropriate to the private, domestic relations of family and kinship – but still assumes that identities and interests precede democratic engagement.

The freedom of the *press* is clearly a crucially important element of the right to free expression. As Benedict Anderson (2006) has so famously shown, it is the daily practice of reading the same newspapers that enables a large population of individuals who will never meet to *imagine* themselves as a homogeneous community, governed by the same laws and norms, preoccupied by the same concerns, united by certain recurring narratives. The freedom to publish entails the ability to be represented at this crucial national level, where much governing still takes place, and to ensure that the opinions and beliefs that are formed in the private sphere can be represented to the institutions of government.

The role of the press is characterised in the Democracy Promotion literature as representing sets of identities and interests that exist prior to and can therefore be reflected transparently by the media. For example, in Larry Diamond's book on Democracy Promotion there are 36 references to "media and press" in the index, each of which either praises a press that is "free" or expresses concern about media that have been "censored" or "co-opted" by the government or incumbent in power (Diamond, 2008). One entry seems

50   *Democratic representation*

more nuanced than this, showing a politician (Alejandro Toledo in Peru) effectively hounded out of office by an elite-dominated and hostile press. Even here, however, Diamond's conclusion is that "a president must battle for public opinion" (ibid.: 175), thus failing to dissociate press and public or give a meaningful account of how they are co-constituted.

Freedom of speech and association is understood to exist in the *absence* of censorship or coercion. The power that produces gendered, racialised, ethnic or class identities, that enables subjects to understand themselves as belonging to a particular religious or tribal group rather than to a particular class, for the purposes of voting, is ignored here as attention is focused on the power that says "no", that censors, that forces a constituent to vote in favour of a more powerful landlord instead of in her own, already constituted interest. The press is not understood to have a role in actively constructing what might count as the truth. This is an important omission.

Democratic talk

Unsurprisingly, in light of the previous discussion, when the DFID "Pakistan Country Governance Analysis" assesses the role of the media, it predictably focuses on "transparency", the problem of "intimidation", and the role of media in enabling audiences to understand government policy and "hold government to account" (Coffey International Development, 2011: 10). What is therefore more interesting is the statement that the media must be supported to "contest militant viewpoints" (ibid.: 10). This is very different from an assumption that all that needs to be done is to ensure there is no censorship. Thus at the limits of Democracy Promotion, where the attempt to know, manage and civilise the unruly other comes up against the irredeemably unmanageable barbarian – the terrorist, the militant – the power of representation to create, not just reflect, identities is unusually acknowledged. Whilst there is no scope here to review the vast literature on democratic talk, including deliberation and reason giving in democracies,[2] it is worth drawing out some of the important productive dimensions of power that play a role in democratic contestation and speech.

At this point it is useful to consider the two interlocking meanings of "representation" identified by Spivak (1987: 275):

> Two senses of representation are being run together: representation as "speaking for", as in politics, and representation as "re-presentation", as in art or philosophy. These two senses of representation – within state formation and the law, on the one hand, and in subject predication, on the other – are related but irreducibly discontinuous.

The literature on democratic representation is particularly concerned with representation as a process of proxies "speaking for" others. Hanna Pitkin's (1967) classic and still influential study of traditional electoral representation identifies four different ways of thinking about representation, all of which in some way rely on the broad notion of a representative as a person who stands in for some (group of) other(s): this conception is still very prevalent in ways of thinking about electoral representative politics (Dovi, 2011).

Meanwhile, work on non-electoral forms of democracy, whether that be in citizens' juries, mini-publics or broader forms of public deliberation and debate (Bohman, 2000), likewise regularly involves some kind of speaking *for*. This may be through a variety of mechanisms, including the scientifically representative sampling of smaller groups that deliberate on behalf of some larger population and may then be able to make recommendations to an elected body (Goodin and Niemeyer, 2003; Goodin and Dryzek, 2006). Alternatively, public debate may be conceived as a key institution in its own right which enables not only better-informed preferences but also itself functions as a mechanism for their transmission to proxies within decision-making bodies (Dryzek, 2000; Bohman, 2000).

If we consider representative politics to be constitutively concerned with speaking *for*, then Spivak's second sense of representation modes of speaking that are possible – which statements can be uttered and which are ruled out by contemporary ways of knowing and thinking – are of the utmost importance. In her classic essay, "Can the Subaltern Speak?" (Spivak, 1987), she is concerned with the ways in which Indian women were rendered absent and invisible not only by the systematic exclusion of their voices, but also by the way that feminine practices and identities were struggled over by men, in the attempt to define what ways of speaking by and about women would be possible.

The importance of discursive representation is obviously not restricted to the practice of speaking for, or representing, someone else. The practice of speaking for oneself, including in organised deliberative settings, also requires participation in available discourses: indeed without this participation, there is no subject. Even Spivak's silenced subaltern woman has a subjectivity that is defined, although not determined, by prevailing discursive practices.

An example from her essay can help us understand this point: she describes a suicide of an unmarried Indian woman who waits until menstruation before killing herself, in order to provide evidence that she was not pregnant, or in "imprisonment within legitimate passion with a single male" (Spivak, 1987: 308). She reads this act as "an unemphatic, ad hoc, subaltern rewriting of the social text of sati-suicide", not least because sati is forbidden during menstruation. Spivak is interested in the (always indeterminate) meaning of the suicide, as if it were – in Foucault's words – a "document", which can be enquired into hermeneutically. However, I want to suggest, rather against the grain of Spivak's own emphasis, that we can more fruitfully treat it as something more material and concrete – a "monument" – and enquire into its conditions of possibility and its function (Foucault, 2002: 148, 156).

The subaltern's subversive agency, and Spivak's reading of it, are only made possible by the existence of the prevailing discourses and practices of sati, and its intersection with women's sexuality, in the first place. We can discern from

52 *Democratic representation*

an understanding of the history of struggles over sati how such an act of suicide and its timing becomes possible, what forms of subjectivity it implies and how they interact with the subjection to power relations of the subaltern-subject: what ways of being a woman, what practices of femininity, are possible in this given society? We can demonstrate that sati reproduces and re-inscribes existing power relations, but also that these power relations enable creative (if ultimately destructive) resistances. For all the inequalities and oppressiveness associated with such historically constituted practices, they are also the very ways in which subjectivity, and concrete action, is rendered possible. As such, the subaltern, though she may not speak, (re)presents a "body totally imprinted by history" (Foucault, 1991a: 83), which cannot just be read and understood only according to the relations of power circulating in Indian society at the time and the concrete practices that they produce, but furthermore *can only act* by means of them and the slender room for manoeuvre that they offer. What I want to say here is that Spivak is in danger of assuming that the subaltern woman possesses an essence or agency that precedes her insertion into discourse. This is precisely what I want to deny, drawing rather on Judith Butler in affirming that "gender is always a doing, though not a doing by a subject who might be said to preexist the deed" (Butler, 2006: 34), and that the subaltern woman's subjectivity and agency is only possible as a function of discourse. This has important consequences for understanding democratic practice.

Discourses are clearly not reducible to signifiers that represent an objective reality, but rather they are "practices that systematically form the objects of which they speak" (Foucault, 2002: 49), *including* the possibility of particular speaking positions. Or, to put it another way, a "system of relations establishes a discursive practice that sets the rules of the game: who can speak, from what points of view, with what authority, and according to what criteria of expertise" (Escobar, 1994: 41). Thus when, as freely choosing subjects, voters are asked to reflect on their choices and represent themselves at the ballot box or in deliberative institutions, the processes of thought in which they are engaged are already closely interwoven with power relations.

Representation, then, is always an active process of producing, and also struggling intersubjectively over, the world from within an inegalitarian web of power relations. Within democratic deliberation, the ways we have of knowing and of judging what sorts of statements may count as true, and what sorts of reasons are acceptable, are always conditioned by the workings of power (Foucault, 1981: 92–93). Discursive struggles take place precisely over the field of what may be recognised, or taken seriously, as truth, or as good reasons. For example, is it appropriate to take seriously a Pakistani villager who said that he had a thing or two to teach me about democracy, given the highly consensual and inclusive decision-making forum that existed in his village? Or is this proposition absurd, given the hierarchical structure of the forum and its exclusion of women and non-Muslims? Do we want to take seriously his discursive attempt to take control of the word "democracy" and claim it for a different discourse from the conventional ("Western") one of liberal democracy? When I put this question to a British political activist, who had just expressed his distaste for the habit of British Pakistani populations in his local area voting as a block, he suggested that, "it all depends on whether that is 'true' democracy, but I suspect that it isn't". This example is given as a way of illustrating how truth is struggled over: the ability to be taken seriously as a speaker of truth is a form of power, and conversely power is exercised over us as we attempt to, and are socially obliged to, voice what will be taken to be good reasons in our kind of society.

The intersection of power with truth, and therefore knowledge, is crucial to a Foucauldian understanding of the world. In the original French, this is always expressed as *"pouvoir-savoir"*, which – like *savoir-faire*, perhaps – has an everyday, concrete feel and connotes the local and specific practices through which we come to have the ability to know (Spivak, 1995): the ability to recognise democracy when we see it, for example, as well as the ability freely to represent ourselves by means of it, whether that be through practices of contestation, reason giving, voting, or all three.

Conclusion: the politics of representation

In this chapter I have shown the contingent ways in which democracy and representation are bound up in one another and in relations of power/knowledge. Liberal democratic governmentality enables the emergence of a particular kind of democratic subjectivity, which in turn enables and requires us to be represented, and to represent ourselves, in particular ways. Above all, the democratic practices of representation – whether through counting votes or through more deliberative means of giving reasons and persuading – are *epistemologically useful* in that they enable populations to be understood, known, governed and managed in particular ways.

Representation produces and reproduces truths, knowledges, discourses, identities and populations: representative practices need, therefore, not to be interpreted, but rather to be understood and traced in their logic and effects as they intersect with democracy promotion. I therefore do not treat practices of representation as forms of meaning, whose deeper intentions can be discerned hermeneutically. Rather, representation functions as a set of concrete practices: I am interested in what representation – in both senses – *does*, what functions it performs, what possibilities it may rule in or out, what subjects it produces and what action it makes thinkable.

In the next chapter I will return to the temporal narrative of democracy promotion, and the story of the barbarian and the savage, to show exactly why, how and in what specific ways such knowledge comes to matter.

Notes

1 Bevir and Rhodes (2004) suggest that "governance" is a relatively recent construct in Western democracies, denoting a move away from centralised institutions to

54 *Democratic representation*

diffuse networks and multiple organisations. However, as Foucault's work suggests, this tendency towards the diffusion – rather than centralisation – of power is a key feature of any kind of governmental rule.
2 James Bohman (1998) provides a good, although now somewhat out-of-date, review. For an excellent and full discussion of deliberative democracy from a poststructural perspective, see Norval, 2007.

3 Disordering histories

[O]f-course developments and in-the-end inevitabilities suggest the grip of tele-ology: the turn of mind that tells us things had to come out the way they did because they were always leading to us, and how can we imagine "progress" toward something different from ourselves?

(From *The New York Review of Books*. © 2011 by David Bromwich)

There is a character – Jim – in Mohsin Hamid's bestselling novel *The Reluctant Fundamentalist* whose fundamentalism is not so reluctant. The joke of the novel's title is that its depiction of "fundamentalism" concerns not educated and disillusioned Pakistani narrator Changez – despite the increasing radicalism of his opinions – but the American asset-stripping firm for which Jim works. Here the motto is: "Focus on the fundamentals [...] It mandated a single-minded attention to financial detail" (Hamid, 2007: 112). It is Jim, this fundamentalist, who suggests (all the while playing with a technologically advanced and highly engineered watch) that, "[t]ime only moves in one direction. Remember that" (ibid.: 109). He goes on to add to Changez:

The economy's an animal [...] It evolves. First it needed muscle. Now all the blood it could spare was rushing to its brain. That's where I wanted to be. In finance [...] And that's where you are. You're blood brought from some part of the body that the species doesn't need any more. The tailbone. Like me. We came from places that were wasting away.

(Hamid, 2007: 110)

Jim's account implies a certain version of history which – as we will see – is rather common. It suggests that history is an evolutionary,[1] or teleological, process in which time moves ever forwards and in doing so leads to improvement and progress. Progress is generally understood in technological terms as well as privileging rationality, or "the brain". This might remind us of the familiar and seamless teleologies of development and modernisation, as well as the narrative of civilisation as an ongoing movement through time towards higher and better modes of life. We might equally bring to mind Francis Fukuyama's (1993) famous contention that the march of history

56 *Disordering histories*

came to an end in 1989 as the battle of ideas was allegedly settled. Fukuyama here seems to join with Jim in suggesting that the history of ideas works according to an evolutionary logic, in which worse ideas are tested out and discarded in favour of better alternatives until humankind alights upon an endpoint on which all might agree.

Changez, however, emerges from a different, postcolonial history and can therefore provide an obvious foil to this type of thinking. Within a few pages he reminds the reader that:

> we were not always burdened by debt, dependent on foreign aid and handouts; *in the stories we tell of ourselves* we were not the crazed and destitute radicals you see on your television channels but rather saints, poets and – yes – conquering kings. We built the Royal Mosque and the Shalimar Gardens in this city, and we built the Lahore Fort with its mighty walls and wide ramp for its battle-elephants. And we did these things when [the United States] was still a collection of thirteen small colonies, gnawing away on the edge of a continent.
>
> (Hamid, 2007: 115–116, my emphasis)

This chapter is about the stories we tell of ourselves and why they matter.

I suggest that versions of history underpin in crucial ways our experiences of our own subjectivity, our sense of belonging to a community, our democratic identities and our understanding of what our relation to the future ought to be, what options are open for further action. A question then opens up about whether or not history might be thought about differently. What difference might it make for our experience of the present and hopes for the future, if we were able to think about history in different ways?

This is not a question of inventing fictions, but rather – like Changez speaking of Pakistan – questioning whether there might not be other, more defensible, ways of narrating our identity as subjects of history. At stake, as a matter of political strategy, would be different orientations towards the future and different forms of relation with oneself and with others.

In the first main section of this chapter, I investigate the narratives about history that currently circulate in discourses of democracy promotion, focusing on three interlocking ways of thinking about history: civilisation, development and the slow but inexorable spread of democracy. I look in detail at how these three narratives *function*, in all their diversity. The second section builds on this to show precisely *how* the narratives constitute othering practices in temporal teleological terms: the other is the savage or the barbarian, outside of civilisation but also *before* it. The next section explains why this matters. It explores in detail the political programmes that emerge from attempts to contain or domesticate the barbarian and the savage, respectively, looking at the ways in which they open up and foreclose different ways of acting. To conclude, I return to Foucault in order to ask how history might be re-fictioned to provide an alternative politics. This final section will elaborate on the precise opportunity offered by the histories that animate our contemporary practices of thought for exploring a somewhat novel form of genealogy. This discussion provides the framework for the alternative history that constitutes the final four chapters of this book.

The stories we tell of ourselves

I suggest that we need to be concerned with three distinct, but deeply interrelated, stories that we tell about ourselves. They are all teleological. The first is a story about civilisation, the second is about development and the third is about democracy promotion. Let us take each in turn.

Civilising histories

As we saw in the opening pages of this book, the language of "civilisation" is a commonplace way of securing identity and identifying and condemning threatening others in temporal terms. After the London bombings, as we have seen, Tony Blair (2005a) stated that: "they will never succeed in destroying what we hold dear in this country and in other civilised nations throughout the world." This was echoed by a joint statement of the G8 leaders (ibid.), who declared that "this terrorism" is an "attack [...] on all nations and on civilised people everywhere". Lest there be any doubt about what a "civilised" identity might comprise, Tony Blair (2006) spells out that it is "religious tolerance, openness to others, to democracy, liberty and human rights administered by secular courts". These are institutions all clearly recognisable as emblematic of liberal democratic governance and explicitly inimical to the kind of democratic innovation proposed by the Archbishop of Canterbury in 2008.

It is this widespread political discourse that posits "civilisation" as the opposite of barbaric terrorism that animates at least some of the resistance to the Archbishop of Canterbury's proposal for an accommodation with *shari'ah* law in the UK. Take, for instance, remarks in the *Daily Mail* by Mark Dooley (2008), who suggests that "when the future of Western civilisation is under threat, such posturing [by the Archbishop] is suicidal", or Melanie Phillips, who argues that sacking the Archbishop would be a "powerful statement" that "Britain really wants to defend itself and Western civilisation" (Phillips, 2008). Without reference to a civilisational discourse that refers to *shari'ah* law (understood to be an aim of terrorism) as a barbaric and existential threat, these statements would be simply unintelligible. They resonate with the scores of other references to barbarity, primitivism and the apparently medieval values of *shari'ah* law that appeared in the newspapers that week, and press into service an established and readily available narrative that functions to condemn threats to an established identity.

The immediate conditions through which this civilisational discourse is so readily intelligible are, of course, the historical context of the "war on terror" and a similar, at this point established and hegemonic, response to attacks on

58   *Disordering histories*

New York and Washington, DC, four years earlier on 11 September 2001 (Bowden, 2009: 177–178; Croft, 2006: 70). It was in terms of this discursive splitting of the world into "civilised" and "uncivilised" – the familiar discourse of "you are either with us or against us" espoused by US President George W. Bush – that Pakistan was exhorted to join the side of "civilisation" in the war, and subsequent attempts to establish liberal democratic government, in Afghanistan (ibid.: 156). Thus this narrative is already deeply involved in the domestication of a foreign enemy.

It would be wrong, however, to focus too closely on this immediate context if that were to occlude a much longer history of uses of the notion of civilisation. The history of this word, and the practices associated with it, has been painstakingly traced by Brett Bowden. He shows in detail the way that civilisational discourses have been used since colonial times to demand conformity to the practices characterising those countries that think of themselves as the "West" and to rule out competing practices as "barbaric" (Bowden, 2009). Bowden has shown that "civilisation" has, since the word's emergence, been defined as particular (changing) ways of *governing* familiar in the West (ibid.). It is against this historical involvement in practices of governing that any analysis of the civilisational narrative must be understood, as it alerts us to the deep entrenchment of thinking about "civilisation" *as* liberal democracy (see Hobson, 2008).

To talk of civilisation is to engage in a set of assumptions, a practice of thought, about the history of the world. To examine this idea, we must first of all distinguish between two ways in which "civilisation" is mobilised. On the one hand, Samuel Huntington's (2002) influential language of a "clash of civilisations" draws on ideas about multiple civilisations co-existing in time but separated by space and distinguished by different cultural values: "civilisation in the plural" (Jackson, 2006: 82–87; O'Hagan, 2007; Hobson, 2008). Competing with this, importantly, is a notion of "civilisation in the singular", which sees civilisation as "both a process and a goal [...] a term for expressing the distinguishing characteristics of a good society and also the process by which people are made fit for this society" (Jackson, 2006: 83). This latter conception of civilisation operates using a different conception of time: it is a teleological narrative in which some people or parts of the world are situated further back in time, along the trajectory towards civilisation, in a past that the "civilised" peoples have already gone beyond (ibid.).

It is no coincidence that the particular point in history when the term "civilisation" first comes into widespread English usage (between 1772 and 1836; Bowden, 2009: 31), also happens to be the time of the beginnings of the British Empire, when a vexed political debate was taking place regarding the best way to govern, amongst others, that part of the world which later became Pakistan. Here, then, we have the premise of the colonial "civilising mission", an endeavour which consistently represented non-Western countries as temporally backward, but not without the possibility of catching up, often understood through the metaphor of im/maturity. Thus, indigenous people are understood to be "wards" of the civilised nations (ibid.: 148–149) who – with time and proper tutelage – may grow into the "mature adults" of the Enlightenment (Foucault, 1991e: 49). Thus the history of the civilisational discourse is inextricably intertwined with a sense that places like Pakistan – understood to be the point of origin for the "foreign" and "barbaric" ideology of the terrorists – are behind places like Britain *in time*.

The two conceptions of civilisation – plural and singular – are never used completely in isolation from one another, but always interact, and usually in ways that reproduce the notion that "civilised nations" are also those belonging to a specifically Western "civilisation" which is both distinct from other "civilisations" or cultures and also better, less barbarous, more developed and modern (Gregory, 2004: 57–58). However, as we have seen, the notion of "civilisation" that is mobilised in response to the London bombings and the Archbishop is dominated by the latter conception – "civilisation in the singular" – as evidenced not least by the constant references to the "medieval" or "primitive" aims of the bombers, or practices of *shari'ah* law.

The temporal narrative of civilisation is underlined by the title of the speech, given by Tony Blair in March 2006 (the year of the good governance White Papers), in which he reflects both on terrorism and on UK foreign policy: "Not a clash between civilisations, but a clash about civilisation", a title which brings into play both these notions of civilisation before settling on the singular (Blair, 2006). This speech depends on a whole set of binary formulations which develop and extend the initial response to the bombings as the actions of "barbarians" against "civilised people" and they are reliant on the teleological temporalities of the "civilisation in the singular" narrative, suggesting, for example, that the "battle" being waged is "between progress and reaction, between those who embrace the modern world and those who reject its existence". This kind of language explicitly rejects the idea that multiple civilisations could co-exist in the world and therefore implies that those who are not (yet) civilised must be taken on, become civilised or be destroyed, in the "battle of values and progress" (Blair, 2006).

We will return to examine the political consequences of the story of civilisation, but first there is another temporal word often used in tandem with "progress" in Pakistan, and this brings us to our second story: development.

Development

The attacks in London appeared to have been deliberately timed to coincide with the G8 summit in Gleneagles. This was a summit about development. "It is particularly barbaric", said Tony Blair (2005b), "that this has happened on a day when people are meeting to try to help the problems of poverty in Africa." This quite obviously enacts a linking of the two temporal narratives of civilisation and development: the supposed "civilised" values of the G8, the UK government and the Make Poverty History campaign, as opposed not just to the "barbarism" of the terrorist display of violence, but also to the

60 *Disordering histories*

barbarities of poverty, lack of development, bad governance and corruption (Douzinas, 2008: 195).

The idea of "development" pre-dates, but is intimately linked to, the emergence of modernisation theory, which was inaugurated in Rostow's famous article, "The Stages of Economic Growth" (1959). This is the theory that assumes that economic development as it occurred in Western Europe and North America was not dependent on an historically specific set of circumstances, but is rather a progressive and benign process that every region in the world would, or should, go through as part of the inevitable process of history leading to a modern and prosperous future. This assumption that "developing countries" are not essentially different from those that are "developed" but rather situated, or even stuck, further back in time at earlier "stages" of development is evident in the very vocabulary of "developed", "developing" and even "under-developed". It is a mode of thinking that underpins the enormous industry of "development", in which "experts" from developed countries attempt to guide the developing world through these stages and towards the goal of "development", by which is generally meant a similarity to the West (Escobar, 1994).

This temporal logic remains prevalent despite the range and subtlety of development practitioners and scholars, many of whom are highly thoughtful and critical (see Kothari, 2005, for example, for a range of critical ways of thinking about development). The specifically temporal and teleological notion of what development is, and its relation to the idea that history has a directional and progressive force, is rather neatly summed up by Phil Vernon (2012), a development worker and director of programmes at International Alert: "One clue how to frame our aspirations is to imagine how historians in a hundred years might frame the history of human progress [...] Put simply, development planning is history looking forwards." The very title of the "Make Poverty History" campaign – so prominent at the time of the London bombings – is reliant on this understanding of time as a civilising force moving forwards in the service of progress and development.

It was this same G8 summit on development that provided the context for the Foreign and Commonwealth Office (FCO) and Department for International Development (DFID) White Papers of 2006, the documents that so clearly spell out the UK government's commitment to the agendas and technologies of Democracy Promotion and good governance as an intrinsic element of development. It had not always been the case that democracy and development were considered to be so deeply intertwined. Indeed, the protracted debate about whether democratisation inhibits or promotes economic development (Lipset, 1960; Hadenius, 1997; Przeworski et al., 1996; Przeworski and Limongi, 1993; Helliwell, 1994; Gillies, 1993) has only died away in the last 15 years. Yet, as the White Papers attest, there is now a powerful articulation of liberal democracy and development in policy thinking, such that development is by *definition* characterised by the presence of democratic institutions (see Chapter 1 above and also Quadir, 2007: 99; Smillie, 2007: 57;

Burnell, 2000: 4, 5, 15, 20, 28). To understand this, we need to look more closely at the third story we tell of ourselves: the story about the spread of democracy.

The official history of Democracy Promotion

The democratisation/development debate was less about whether practitioners should promote development *or* democracy, than about which should come *first*. This is because, just like the story of development, the story of the spread of democracy is animated by constant analogies between European history and the history of other parts of the world. By viewing contemporary Europe as a developed and democratic ideal endpoint, this narrative both idealises the institutions we now have and assumes that history elsewhere will follow a similar path.

We have seen that a common and idealised historical narrative told about Britain is one that stresses a slow but continual process of struggle and development that has brought us democracy (see Colley, 2009). As part of this narrative, certain key events – the Magna Carta, the Glorious Revolution, the Great Reform Act, votes for women, the Second World War – are totemic moments that can be appealed to in order to remind democratic citizens of the hard-won nature of their rights and secure commitment to a liberal democratic identity. Compare this with DFID's assertion that, "[b]uilding democratic values and institutions takes time. The democratic institutions we have in the UK took centuries to evolve" (DFID, 2007b: 20). These stories we tell of ourselves are deeply influential for the manner in which Britain engages with its undemocratic others.

Thus, despite the concern with local histories and contexts that we saw in Chapter 1, other countries – like Pakistan – can appear as ciphers of an idealised Western history. Democracy is very often assumed to be an inevitable outcome of the history the West has been through. Furthermore, events from a specific Western history populate accounts of Democracy Promotion, as though other parts of the world were just empty vessels waiting to be filled via the same trajectory. For example, Sue Unsworth suggests that: "An example from the history of Western Europe is the long process of (often violent) bargaining between rulers and citizens that resulted in the creation of civil, political and economic rights in return for recognition of obligation to pay tax" (Unsworth, 2007: 33). Similarly, Sheri Berman defends a social democratic approach to Democracy Promotion in these terms: "During the nineteenth and the first half of the twentieth century, Europe was the most turbulent region on earth [...] Yet during the second half of the twentieth century it was one of the most stable, a study in democracy, social harmony and prosperity" (Berman, 2012: 68); going on to conclude that "democracy promoters have lessons to learn from Europe's experience" (Berman, 2012: 83). Western history is understood and narrated as a difficult yet inexorable progress towards a set of institutions that have offered democratic rights to

62 *Disordering histories*

the poor and the powerless. Thus, it seems perfectly logical to prescribe a similar path for the poor and powerless elsewhere. Jeremy Gould (2005: 11) – who otherwise provides a nuanced account of postcolonial flows of power – also offers an idealised version of Western history by suggesting that in Western countries "demands for public consultation and participation" were decisive in the development of liberal, democratic institutions in ways that are denied to contemporary developing countries.

In light of the pervasiveness of references to Western history as a model, it is unsurprising that an underlying teleology, underwritten by references both to civilisation and to development, is easy to trace in the mainstream democracy promotion literature: DFID, for example, makes reference to poverty and poor governance as a state of "lagging behind" (DFID, 2006e: 44), as well as suggesting that "[b]uilding democratic values and institutions takes time" (DFID, 2007b: 20). Thomas Carothers proposes that "[b]y sending out more and more delegations to monitor elections [...] the established Western democracies have reinforced the basic idea that holding elections is something that civilized countries do" (Carothers, 2004: 87). Meanwhile, Larry Diamond speaks about "progress" towards the notion of democracy as a "universal value" (Diamond, 2008: 13). Sue Unsworth, on the other hand, narrates a cautionary history of Democracy Promotion itself as a series of failures, a long series of "fixes", unsuccessful practices that have moved into, then quickly out of, fashion (Unsworth, 2007: 23–27), but nevertheless suggests that certain more recent practices are an "advance" (ibid.: 31). All these examples imply that history itself has an evolutionary logic.

This is the case even for some writers who are critical of the liberal democratic order. Consider, for example, William Robinson's suggestion, within his Gramscian analysis of contemporary democracy promotion, that "[w]hat was 'discovered' [in 1492] was not the Americas, but universal human history and the world as one totality" (Robinson, 1996: 4). This sentence draws upon the discovery of the "savage" and the Enlightenment understanding of him as a figure who represents the past – a representation of what Europe once was like – which concomitantly offers our own society as his future and his destiny.

More on the savage below, but first it is important to say that not all accounts of Democracy Promotion are complacent about offering the benefits of history to the undeveloped. This is often because of the confrontation between the broad teleologies offered by this version of history with the actual historicity of events. Sue Unsworth, for example, offers a rather different take on what might be learned from history: "This process of institution building is inherently messy, conflict ridden, incremental, uncertain, and long term" (Unsworth, 2007: 33). Despite the open-endedness she claims to find in history, she nevertheless takes it as a basis for her claim that "[h]istorically poor people have almost always made progress in alliance with more powerful groups" (ibid.: 38). She has an endpoint ("progress") – and a set of universal processes ("institution-building", "alliances") as ways of getting there – in mind, even if chaotic events might get in the way.

This identification of historicity as an obstacle is reminiscent of Larry Diamond's view that "we have to identify the historical and structural obstacles to democracy around the world" (Diamond, 2008: 6). History is what appears to be getting in the way of progress: "History has seen no shortage of [human failings], which have played a large role in the breakdown of democracy. But human progress follows from the capacity to learn from and transcend our failings" (ibid.: 13). An acknowledgement of the contingency and open-endedness of history, then, does little to disrupt the underlying teleology. Various ways of describing the disappointments of Democracy Promotion underline this point: there has been "backsliding" (Carothers, 2004: 2), "democratic recession", "setbacks", "deterioration" (Diamond, 2008: 12) and "reversals" (Swain et al., 2011: 1). All these words connote an endpoint towards which there is the possibility of linear progress or regress: but no real notion of the multiple possibilities that a truly open-ended version of history might proliferate.

Now that the profoundly teleological logic of the story Democracy Promotion tells of itself has been unearthed, it is easy to understand the deep intertwining of developmental and Democracy Promotion narratives. On the face of it, the democratisation/development debate had appeared to take issue with the assumption (much coloured by modernisation theory) that all good things go together. However, it is important to note that at root the debate never really contested the idea of democracy as an endpoint. Rather it took as its target the concrete ways in which democratisation and economic development should be *sequenced* within an overall narrative that took the Western developed countries as their model. As such, it offers no genuine critique of liberal democratic capitalism as the ultimate endpoint – merely doubts about how to get there.

The stories that practitioners of Democracy Promotion tell about the Cold War, and its end, appear to quell those doubts.

Key moments in the history of Democracy Promotion

Democracy Promotion is readily understood as having emerged as a Cold War project. It is widely considered to have its origins after the Second World War with the beginnings of struggles for national self-determination and the end of the colonial rule that had blocked the normal teleological progress of history, coinciding with the emergence of a country called Pakistan. Whilst Kurki (2013: 122) and Huber (2015: 11–12) note that American Democracy Promotion began after the First World War, they also note that it is during the Cold War that it really takes off. Both Sue Unsworth and Ian Smillie offer potted histories of democracy promotion that begin in the late 1940s and acknowledge the role of democracy promotion as a Cold War strategy (Unsworth, 2007: 23–27; Smillie, 2007; see also the discussion of Laurence Whitehead's work above in Chapter 1). This reading of history suggests that the initial articulation of democracy and development was a specific response

64 *Disordering histories*

both to a shameful past of imperialism and, importantly, to alternative models of development offered by the Soviet Union. Take, for example, President Truman's inaugural address in 1949, at which he said:

> The old imperialism – exploitation for foreign profit – has no place in our plans. What we envisage is a program of development based on the concepts of democratic fair dealing.
>
> (quoted in Esteva, 1992: 6)

It seems that from its very beginnings, Democracy Promotion is understood as a ruptural break in the 1940s from an oppressive history of civilising missions.

Somewhat similarly, Brigg points out that a metaphor of "colonisation" is regularly employed by writers in the "post-development" school who critique the teleologies of development. He compares the colonial period to Foucault's conceptualisation of "sovereign power", which relates above all to violence, the ability of the sovereign to take away the life of subjects (Foucault, 1981: 135–136), and argues therefore that metaphors of colonisation are wrongly applied to the modern "development" era since 1945, because "development operates through the mobilisation of interests and aspirations of Third World subjects" (Brigg, 2002: 424). The meaning of 1945 is readily understood, then, as a ruptural moment when power was redistributed from imperial rulers to a multiplicity of local individuals, ideally via a ballot paper.

However, the story runs, the experience of the Cold War means that this process was initially deeply imperfect, with the principles of democracy frequently being "betrayed" (Diamond, 2008: 1–2) by cynical Western leaders, keen on short-term gain in the struggle with the Soviet Union, even at the price of the very principles of democracy they were ultimately attempting to defend. This is, of course, a common element in the story we tell of our relationship with Pakistan. Particularly widespread is the story of anti-democratic military dictator General Zia ul-Haq, whose rule was propped up by funding and support from America in return for his support for the Mujaheddin's struggle against the Soviet Union in Afghanistan (Mohan, 2007; Rashid, 2008: 184; Cohen, 2004: 302–303). This is a narrative about Pakistan that is still regularly told: for instance, a box office hit, the film *Charlie Wilson's War* (Nichols, 2010), narrated in detail – in cinema multiplexes and living rooms – the story of the compromises with anti-democratic power that took place in the name of the fight for democracy itself in Pakistan in the 1980s. The film ends with the worrying spectre of a resurgence of anti-democratic power as the Taliban take over Afghanistan.

Meanwhile, J.T. Rogers's play, *Blood and Gifts*, which takes as one of its concerns British acquiescence in these events, was staged at the National Theatre in London in 2010. This play demonstrates the ongoing perception that the story of the Cold War struggle in Pakistan is relevant to the growth of "barbaric" and anti-democratic forces. Western funding is portrayed as causing the desire of the Afghan Taliban to "cross oceans" in order to "spread" Islam (Rogers, 2010: 124). Whilst it might be objected that the Afghan Taliban are not known for crossing oceans to proselytise or commit terrorist crime (Gardner, 2010), the point to note is that the ultimately self-defeating nature of supporting undemocratic dictators in the name of democracy is now quite widely taken as read. These sorts of stories continue to function as a cautionary tale about the dangers of blocking the progressive path of history with short-term political machinations.

Despite this critique of Cold War practices, however, the period is still viewed as the last stage in a teleological history that was leading inexorably to the triumph of democracy as a universally acknowledged set of values. Larry Diamond thus provides an account of the Cold War as a narrative of two possible alternatives – democracy or Soviet-style communism – rather than any sense of multiple or open-ended trajectories (Diamond, 2008: 4).

If the Cold War can be understood as an era of contestation between two possible ways of governing, then its conclusion lays down the conditions of possibility for seeing liberal democracy as the only contender after the fall of Soviet communism. This seems like an obvious point. The importance of 1989 as a decisive and ruptural moment is almost undisputed: 1989 is understood as the "twelve months that shook the world" (Smillie, 2007: 48; see also Unsworth, 2007: 24; Carothers, 2004: 19). This was the era that was dubbed "the end of history": the (dialectical) battle of ideas was understood – and not only by Francis Fukuyama – to have been decisively won by one side, such that the one best way to govern was no longer an open question (Fukuyama, 1989, 1993; McFaul, 2004).

The ruptural end of the Cold War leaves us in no doubt as to where the logic of history has brought us. The important and influential four-volume study of democracy in developing countries published in 1988 states in its introduction that "democracy is the only model of government with any broad ideological legitimacy and appeal in the world today" (Diamond et al., 1988: x). Viewed after an intervening period of 20 years, for one of the authors, the "third wave" of democratisation that 1989 inaugurates is celebrated as "the greatest transformation of the way states are governed in the history of the world" (Diamond, 2008: 6). The FCO introduces its 2006 White Paper with the words: "With the collapse of the Soviet Union, the order that had set the framework for international relations for nearly 50 years came to an end. Markets and democracy spread across much of the world" (FCO, 2006: 6). In the words of Slavoj Žižek, "[i]t is easy to make fun of Fukuyama's notion of the End of History, but the dominant ethos today is 'Fukuyamaian': liberal democratic capitalism is accepted as the finally found formula of the best possible society" (Žižek, 2008: 421).

Even in more critical accounts, there is nevertheless a sense of a pivotal moment: William Robinson denies that we have reached "the end of history" but writes that "we are living in a time of transition from one great epoch to another; we stand at a great historic crossroad, the fourth in modern world

66 *Disordering histories*

history" (Robinson, 1996: 4). Meanwhile, Christopher Hobson detects a "new standard of civilization" emerging after 1989 which asserts that "truth and 'rightness'" of liberal democratic governance in ways that exclude alternatives (Hobson, 2008: 83–85).

These various readings of history all function on the basis that the world of democracy promotion now is understood to be, in important respects, different from the era of the Cold War. Particularly in the more mainstream accounts: if at that time, democracy was promoted strategically and sporadically, with an ideological enemy in view, now it is promoted ethically, as the one proper path through history. The final obstacle to the correct passage through history – alternative models offered by the Soviet Union – has now been lifted. As such, it is no surprise that democracy promoters distance themselves not only from modernisation theory but from the tactics (Carothers, 2004: 19) and institutions of the Cold War (DFID, 2006e: 8).

A moral tone and sense of dramatic promise pervades the discourse of Democracy Promotion at the time and in subsequent years, which – as both Rita Abrahamsen (2000: 36) and April Biccum (2005) have separately pointed out – in fact suggests a profound continuity with earlier colonial, civilising practices. Thus, Douglas Hurd in 1990 is able to talk about a "moral duty" (both towards the citizens of other countries and British taxpayers) to promote democracy (Hurd, 1990: 4), whilst the subsequent Labour government, at least in its early years, made much of its "ethical foreign policy" (Cook, 1997a, b) and the moral dimension of its aid programme (Marriage, 2006).

Given the continuity of a teleological Democracy Promotion narrative with older practices of civilisation and development, it is all the more remarkable that 1989 has come to be understood as a moment of rupture and change. This mode of talking about history, however, serves an important purpose, enabling democracy promoters to dissociate themselves from a shameful past, whether that be colonial oppression or Cold War manipulation. The End of History, and the way that it appears both to demonstrate the progressive nature of history and unblock the last impediment to its realisation, provides a justification for present and future-oriented Democracy Promotion.

Civilisation, development and the spread of democracy are pervasive stories that we tell of ourselves: stories that orient us towards the rest of the world and secure a developed identity by showing us an other who is poor, backward, badly governed and in need. It is worth pausing here to note that the success of a discourse or set of practices need have little to do with whether or not it achieves its stated aims. On the contrary, Foucault (1991f) shows us that the prison's self-perpetuation and apparent inevitability are extraordinary precisely because of its utter failure to reform criminals or deter crime. Its success resides in the way that it now seems indispensable. Its techniques and technologies have extended beyond itself, crafting ways of living and being (discipline, panopticism, individualisation) that reach beyond its heavy walls.

The success of the project of development since the end of the Second World War, with the incorporation of Democracy Promotion as an integral element of it particularly after 1989, can be described in similar terms. Despite the failure of development and good governance projects and programmes to reduce the prevalence of poverty and inequality in the global South, our understanding of the world is powerfully influenced by this division into "developed" and "developing" countries (Roy and Shaw Crane, 2015), and it is hard to imagine contemporary international relations without the ongoing technologies, practices and identities that are linked to developmental thinking. Before looking in more detail at these technologies and practices, let us consider the identities that these teleological stories produce.

Who are the others?

The three teleological stories we have examined inform and map onto each other in complex ways, but what they share is a mode of thinking that constitutes the self by reference to an other who is backward, trapped in the past and in need of moving forwards through the trajectory of a history that is given in advance. Let us now examine *exactly how* the distinction operates.

Uncivilised others: the savage and the barbarian

What is logically implied by the narrative of civilisation-in-the-singular is that not all the others of civilisation need be contained or destroyed: some of them can be domesticated and made safe by being brought up to date. Despite the apparent binarism of the division of the world into "civilised" and "uncivilised" nations, there are *two* figures who stand outside the reading of the history offered by "civilisation in-the-singular": as Foucault points out, we can understand the "other" of civilisation as either the "barbarian" or the "savage" (Foucault, 2005b: 194–197).

On the one hand, the barbarian "is someone who can be understood, defined and characterized only in relation to a civilization [...] There can be no barbarian unless an island of civilization exists somewhere, unless he lives outside it and unless he fights it" (Foucault, 2005b: 195). Although not disrupting the singular nature of civilisation – the barbarian is by definition, and in his belligerence, not the occupant of an alternative civilisation in a multi-civilisational world – he is both a warlike and a wicked figure and there seems little to be done with him: he can only be contained. The discourse of the "barbarity" of the attacks on London relates precisely to this irredeemable and warlike conception of the uncivilised other who co-exists with civilisation in time and space.

The barbarian has been a figure in political thought since Herodotus, but in contrast, the savage is of relatively recent origins, probably contemporaneous with the "discovery" of the Americas. The word comes from the Latin for a wood (*silvaticus*), and originally described people living in forests without the benefits of organised society (Salter, 2002: 20). The savage therefore exists prior to civilisation and can be understood as the ancestor of Western civilised man:

68 *Disordering histories*

> The savage – noble or otherwise – is the natural man whom the jurists or theorists of right dreamed up, the natural man who existed before society existed, who existed in order to constitute society [... and] that other natural man or ideal element dreamed up by economists – a man without a past or a history, who is motivated only by self-interest and who exchanges the product of his labor for another product.
>
> (Foucault, 2005b: 194)

As such, once the savage enters into the social and economic contracts of sovereignty and exchange that characterise Western civilisation, he is no longer a savage (Foucault, 2005b: 195), and consequently there is always the possibility that the savage may be domesticated, as Western man must once likewise have been.

Civilised and uncivilised gendering

This discussion of the civilised, barbarian and savage man is relentlessly, and deliberately, framed in masculine terms, and it is important to note that the figures of the savage and the barbarian are gendered in particular ways. The barbarian is on first reading exaggeratedly hyper-masculine (Ling, 1999): he is the soldier, defined only in terms of his military and fighting prowess. It is unthinkable that he might show mercy, love or understanding for others (virtues associated with the *de facto* caring roles of women): on the contrary, his only concern is to increase his strength (Foucault, 2005b: 196). The barbarian displays a wild and violent masculinity, however: his relations with women are those of the "rapist" (ibid.). He does not enter into the civilised, Enlightenment virtues of reason: his violence is total and as such it seems to be tinged with an emotionality that is uncontrolled and dangerous. If women need protecting from him, it is because he has refused the practices of masculinity associated with cool rationality, which assigns emotion to the safety of the feminine and domestic sphere. In contrast, the natural savage is feminised not only because of his contiguous relationship with nature and his apparently peaceable, noble existence in the forests, but also by virtue of being still immature and in need of tutelage: he is rather like a child, and therefore belongs to the feminine sphere.

It follows from this that the domestication of violent masculinity and the redemption offered by civilisation-in-the-singular is not so much about the emancipation of women from oppressive local practices (see Spivak, 1987: 297), as it is the proper re-alignment of gender relations in the civilised mould. The savage who enters the juridical social contract and the various contracting economic relations of the liberal governmental order, by that very fact, ceases to be a savage and is transformed into the traditional bearer of rights and the role of "*Homo economicus*" (Foucault, 2005b: 194).

It is precisely the gendering of this account of the sovereign and economic order as peopled by freely contracting, independent, autonomous men that has been much criticised by feminists. As feminists in the "ethic of care" tradition have pointed out, all human beings at some stage in their lives will require care and all have at least the potential to be enriched by participating in caring work (Gilligan, 1990; Gasper and Van Staveren, 2003; Robinson, 2006). We are, in this sense, not autonomous individuals, but rather *interdependent*. Thus, stories of *homo economicus* elide the complex relations of care and the reproductive work (usually provided by women) that enable interdependent human beings to grow into adults, and that feed, clothe, tidy up after them, and look after their sick or elderly relatives whilst they get on with the important business of politics and commerce (Fineman, 2004).

The entrance of the savage into history, then, inaugurates the division of the social world into the public and private spheres, and privileges the former. The ambiguous gendering of both the barbarian and the savage then serve as a foil to conventional gendered relations that implicitly upholds and legitimates them by equating them with civilisation. The savage is domesticated and ceases to be a savage when he enters the public sphere and founds a form of government that is recognisably liberal, thus constituting a private sphere in which women implicitly also participate in the work of civilisation by enabling men to appear autonomous and independent in public through their invisible caring work.

Why do these stories matter?

The reality or otherwise of real barbarians and savages in history is less at issue than how understandings of the past shape our practices of thought. I argue that they unreflexively enable us to identify current problems and envisage possible resolutions to them: this will "define where the center of the battle lies" (Foucault, 2005b: 197) in struggles over how to govern now and in the future.

How does the narrative of the barbarian and the savage relate to the civilisational discourse we find in the UK in the present? It sets up a *problem*, which is first of all a problem of knowledge. How will we know what to do when we encounter the barbarian or the savage? How will we know one from the other? What is the correct way of dealing with each? The civilisational discourse itself provides a certain answer to the problem. We know from this story that we must learn to distinguish between the two; we know that the barbarian must be destroyed or contained in order to secure civilisation; we understand that the savage might be domesticated by an entrance into history. As I argued in Chapter 2, however, the institutions of liberal democratic governmentality not only offer themselves as an endpoint of history, but also as an intricate and useful solution to the problems of knowledge that dealing with the savage and barbarian will entail. The importance of democracy for civilisation is reinforced – in a world where history never unfolds quite as it is expected to do – by the usefulness of democratic institutions in knowing and controlling an unruly world.

70 *Disordering histories*

Contemporary civilising missions

Tony Blair stated after the London bombings that, "the vast and overwhelming majority of Muslims [...] are decent and law-abiding people who abhor this act of terrorism every bit as much as *we* do" (Blair, 2005b; see Closs Stephens, 2008: 64). The "we" (British people? Civilisation?) invoked here clearly excludes Muslims, identifying them as in some sense foreign, but Blair does not put "the vast and overwhelming majority" beyond the promise of inclusion and domestication. Whilst the barbarian – in the shape of the terrorist – must be fought, it is this "vast and overwhelming majority" who rather resemble the savage.

The existence of parts of the world that are not (yet) redeemed by history, then, provokes the spectre of more barbarians. The FCO, for example, suggests that "terrorism" might be the consequence when "[s]ome parts of the world [...] are in danger of being left behind" (FCO, 2006: 4). This formulation explicitly evokes history and progress as the opposite of barbarism. However, democracy – as the endpoint of history – is also viewed as a crucial defence: Larry Diamond suggests that "[t]he enemies of democracy – such as the global jihadist movement of radical Islam – can win only if democrats defeat themselves" (Diamond, 2008: 13). This is echoed by Carothers who suggests – without denying the claim – that policy makers are convinced that "lack of democracy helps breed Islamic extremism", adding that "Pakistan is the most glaring case" (Carothers, 2004: 63–64). Indeed, it is Pakistan that is perceived as a particularly important "hard case" for democracy promoters (Swain et al., 2011: 2): the beginning of a backslide of the "third wave" of democracies is pinpointed by Larry Diamond as the 1999 coup by General Musharraf, which is itself understood as a failure of democracy to deliver on the promise of all the good things – development, good governance, human rights – that were meant to go with it (Diamond, 2008: 12).

The stakes, then, for ensuring that history takes its proper course in undeveloped or undemocratic places like Pakistan are understood to be very high: the consequences of failure are understood to be the encroachment of barbarism, the terrorist. However, and crucially, teleological time is something that is understood to be tractable to a push in the right direction and the institutions of liberal democracy are crucial tools to do so.

Civilisation and knowledge

For Democracy Promotion to function as a quest for knowledge, the participation of the "other" in the governmental order is required and it is here that we re-encounter once again the important issue of the formation of subjectivity. In order fully to participate in liberal democracy, the savage must become the freely choosing subject of modern governmentality. He must know himself and his interests and be able to make his choices and concerns legible in the democratic order. It is in entering into these modes of participation that the specific form of subjectivity of the modern citizen is formed.

A refusal to participate in liberal democratic governmentality will, by definition, constitute a subject as a barbarian: someone who cannot be integrated into the civilised structures of managing power and politics emblematic of a modern, developed society. On the contrary, the participation of the savage is what domesticates him and brings him to know himself in the ways that are required by liberal democratic governmentality. By knowing himself and then making his needs, desires and criticisms known through liberal democratic structures, he will become fully integrated into civilisation and any specific support required for bringing him up to date can be identified and rationally targeted.

Civilising missions have long been involved in projects to *know* the recalcitrant other. Edward Said draws on Foucault's work to demonstrate, in *Orientalism*, the ways in which very diverse narratives about cultures in the global "East" form together an orientalist corpus united by ways of knowing: "Orientals were [...] problems to be solved or confined" (Said, 1995: 207). He is thus able to show how "Orientals" have long been understood as "peoples variously designated as backward, degenerate, uncivilised and retarded", and as such are "linked thus to elements in Western society (delinquents, the insane, women, the poor) having in common an identity best described as lamentably alien" (ibid.). Note the way that domestic, or Occidental, identities are secured through this very same process. These alien elements wherever they are, it is implied, might also be contained if only they could be civilised, brought forwards in time. It was also, at least in part, the result of this narrative that people called "Orientals" came to exist at all, insofar as they came to understand themselves as such and became both subjects and objects of an orientalising form of knowledge.

Similarly, after the end of colonisation, as Escobar (1994) has shown, subjects come to *know themselves* as poor or lacking in development and in a political economy of representation in which development is the key currency, the key mode of understanding and making sense of the world, this becomes a decisive element in their identity – and often a useful means of making a living in the context of donor funding. Individuals' material, social and geographical positioning provides them with a means of knowing themselves and others as developed or developing.

Again, I have described these forms of subjectivity in masculine terms because the self-knowledge that is required assumes the autonomous, freely contracting, independent *homo economicus*. What impact does this have on the practices of gendering that constitute civilised subjectivities?

Civilised practices and gender

As I have suggested, to be civilised or developed implies an acceptance of the division of the public and private spheres, with a specific set of gendered relations that emerge as a corollary. Blair (2006) suggests that the terrorists' "positions on women [are] reactionary and regressive". The crucial point here

72 *Disordering histories*

is that in promoting particular institutions as progressive (rather than reactionary), the civilising practices recommended by Blair do not necessarily emancipate women, but rather aim at producing a particular re-alignment of gender roles and need to be understood within the context of the production of the public and private spheres so emblematic of liberal democratic governance.

The effects of the gendered constitution of civilisational narratives can be traced in the detailed projects undertaken in the name of the promotion of democracy and good governance overseas. As discussed in Chapter 2, for liberal democratic governmentality to function without distortion, so that the population can be adequately *known*, it is important that women are free and equal citizens with interests that are fully representable and legible, and which can therefore be managed and promoted:

> states require the capability and the political will to analyse gender equality issues objectively, for example by clearly identifying gender differences in survey data. States can then use this knowledge when developing and implementing policies that promote gender equality.
>
> (DFID, 2007b: 33)

There is, however, a curious tension in the construction of the category of women.

On the one hand, women are constructed as the autonomous, rights-bearing individuals of liberal governmentality, with one vote and the right to make free choices on an equal basis with other citizens in the public sphere. Governmental technologies that work through mobilising the free choices of individuals can even be designed with women's needs specifically in mind: for example, DFID "encourage countries to address issues of [...] how taxation impacts gender equality, such as enabling and constraining economic opportunities for women" (DFID, 2007b: 33), whilst the United Nations Development Programme (UNDP) advocates participatory mechanisms such as "gender responsive budget initiatives" (UNDP, 2002: 80), which require women to express their distinctive needs and interests to government the better to foster their economic and social flourishing and activity.

On the other hand, implicit in these specific mechanisms is the acknowledgement that not all individual citizens are equal or the same: that women tend to have different responsibilities from men and that they have a distinct social identity which may tend to constrain the exercise of their freedoms. This is because, as discussed above, women tend to take specific responsibility for caring work and this is an integral part of their identity. The governmental construction of all people as free and equal citizens has been much glorified for its promotion of gender equality and women's rights (DFID, 2007b: 33; UNDP, 2002: 23–26). However, it is precisely this construction with its in-built assumption of autonomy, that renders largely invisible the inter-subjective, interconnected domain of care – constructed as private and part of the set of processes in the "social" that can be managed but not directly controlled by the state – currently peopled largely by women.

A valorisation of a democratic practice that privileges individuality and autonomy not only tends to leave unquestioned the overwhelming responsibility on women for caring work, but also fails to value care, not least by placing emphasis on measurable indicators, such as economic productivity: this then contributes to women's low status. Conversely, a valorisation of care and interdependence would require a move away from thinking in terms of individual rights and freedoms, to a more intersubjective and relational approach. The latter approach would force a questioning of the constitution of masculine and feminine identities and thereby the notional universal bearer of individual rights, as premised on a subject (usually a man) who functions in a public space and whose private caring responsibilities and needs always already are, have been and will be met by others (usually women). As should now be obvious, such a questioning would explode the complex of practices of thought that posit the savage as the starting point for development. We would have to tell a whole new story about ourselves in order to achieve an alternative, intersubjective mode of thinking about women's rights.

Nowhere is the elision of power underwritten by contemporary narratives about history more evident than when women's rights are explicitly promoted. As I discussed in Chapter 2 – using the example of Spivak's subaltern – practices of femininity are the product of power, which both produces and constrains social roles and identities. This includes, for instance, cultural conventions that women defer to men, that it is their responsibility to perform caring tasks such as ensuring that their household is provided with water, or that they be more afraid of unsafe public spaces, not to mention the physical dangers of violence that are intimately linked to their low status. DFID comes close to acknowledging as much, when it suggests that the promotion of good governance must include intervention even at the level of the "relations between men and women in the household" (DFID, 2007b: 6).

However, its concrete strategies to intervene in the web of power that constitutes gender inequalities and identities do not resolve the tension between an assumption that all individuals are free and equal in the public sphere and the inegalitarian relations that constitute individual identity in private. Thus, it remarks that "women may not participate in a village meeting if it is held at a time of day when they need to collect water, if it is unsafe to get to, or if men dominate the discussion" (DFID, 2007b: 16). The implied solution assumes that the problem is a matter of when and where the meeting is held and how well it is chaired – but this does nothing to question the relations of power that produce what it means to be a man or a woman or how they might be reformed or transformed. A meeting held at a different time of day or in a safer place does not merely *accept* that there is little that can be done to intervene in the productive relations of power that create subordinate feminine identities, but also reinforces the very fear that might limit women's mobility and sense of security, not to mention the impression that it is their

74 *Disordering histories*

job to collect water. Thus, power relations do not merely *limit* the effectiveness of DFID's intervention; on the contrary, their intervention is itself *productive* of the power relations.

An insistence on a particular form of liberal democracy that privileges autonomy, then, actively constrains notions of what gender identities might be. Consider Gilmore and Mosazai's response to the complaints of village councils (*shuras*) that "'women's rights' are given too high a priority by donors as against issues like corruption and sustainable livelihoods": their suggestion is that "cultural sensitivities like this need to be factored in when development choices are explained to 'partners' in a recipient country" (Gilmore and Mosazai, 2007: 148). Leaving aside the breathtaking patronising arrogance of this remark and yet another attempt to save brown women from brown men, let us instead note that what is assumed is that "women's rights" are fixed, given and non-negotiable.

Note, too, that this non-negotiability is the case not *even* in democracies but *especially* in democracies, where the logic of human rights, as articulated with democracy and good governance, requires a particular gendered config-uration of citizenship. This is again underwritten by the assumption that the historical process by which women have won particular rights (and not others) in Western countries is the universal process that all people must pass through and which can thereby be short-circuited through a proper "expla-nation" that forecloses the possibility of struggle. The danger is that if women are bequeathed a set of already-established rights from a Western history, they are not democratic law makers, but rather – at best – merely litigants, and then only once their rights have already been violated (Mouffe, 2000: 42).

Again, this form of liberal democracy is taken to be universal because of an unspoken but insidious narrative about history, which assumes that the women's rights that we have in countries like Britain are the best we can do and therefore unquestionable. The vehement defence of "women's rights" in opposition to the Archbishop's lecture is instructive here. The widespread condemnation of the lecture is more often than not based on anxiety about the disastrous consequences for women's rights that would ensue if *shari'ah* law were accommodated inclusively in the British liberal democratic system. Widely expressed worries include "separate and impenetrable courts and schools", "extreme female segregation", "fully shrouded Muslim women" (Alibhai-Brown, 2008) and "a parallel system of religious courts" (Smith, 2008), although more outlandish concerns are voiced, such as a possible pro-hibition for women on coffee breaks (MacKenzie, 2008) or driving, as well as dark warnings about violent and barbaric punishments for sexual impropriety (Alibhai-Brown, 2008).

These worries proliferate despite the fact that the majority of cases heard by *shari'ah* courts are divorce proceedings, without which it would be impos-sible for some Muslim women ever to obtain a divorce (Khan, 2008a), thus arguably enhancing and not curtailing the possibility of women's rights. However, this point about *shari'ah* courts cannot be heard. The ferocity of the condemnation of the Archbishop shows how the very discussion of the role of religious institutions, or the practices constituting acceptable femininities, are in practice ruled out of the public sphere and therefore beyond the realm of democratic contestation. Indeed, he is attacked for having the temerity to bring up the subject at all. Thus, the *Independent* argues that:

> news has little room for the subtleties of academic gavottes [...] The problem comes when you ask what is meant by sharia. Most of us are clear. It is to do with the stoning to death of adulterous women [...] in a world where perception becomes its own reality, it is important for the leader of the Church of England not to create such fecund possibilities for misunderstanding.
>
> (Vallely, 2008)

As the precise content of *shari'ah* law apparently cannot and must not be publicly discussed, the resulting privatisation of such concerns appears to reinforce the possibility of exactly what these commentators fear: parallel and segregated lives whose self-evidence is put beyond debate. Indeed, the casting of these institutions as "foreign", other, stuck in an uncivilised past, is a very effective way of forcing a segregation by imposing the blackmailing logic of "your culture or your rights" (Williams, 2008b).

However, blackmail and segregation is the cost of maintaining the existing gendered status quo. Thus, when the *Sun* newspaper sends two "page three girls" (the young women who pose half-naked every day on page three of that newspaper for the purposes of male gratification) to the Archbishop's residence to play Rule Britannia at top volume (Wooding and Clench, 2008), this may be crass, but it cannot be condemned with a corresponding violence. The force of the *Sun's* intervention is that it reinforces fears that *shari'ah* law would compel women to wear the veil. The particular young women who besiege the Archbishop are perceived to have made the free choice to dress (or not) in a particular way. This is a right that could be contested only by bringing the subject of the constitution of gender identities into the public sphere. However, the civilisational narrative that suggests that the contemporary settlement of women's rights is the very endpoint of human evolution allows nothing further to be said. Contestation of the dress code begins and ends with the right of young, attractive women to get undressed in public, whether religious believers like it or not.

Thus the constitution of the private sphere as the proper location for the practices of both religious belief and relations of care emerges from the intersecting stories of civilisation, development and the spread of democracy. These stories are gendered and racialised in particular ways. They therefore *matter* because they inform the practices of thought that determine how an unruly and unknowable present is to be governed, down to the detail of what rights we have, what issues can be debated in the public sphere, what cannot be said and even what women might reasonably be expected to wear, particularly if they are to appear in the newspaper.

76 *Disordering histories*

It should be clear that I believe that some of these practices are ones we might want to change. How could we do so?

Telling different stories?

Development and its concrete practices have long been highly contested, and yet the overall project of development remains. Development interventions – particularly, in recent years, the ubiquitous structural adjustment programmes – have been controversial and widely criticised on their own terms for failing to achieve their stated aims of promoting growth, reducing poverty and inequality, and promoting good governance (Corbo et al., 1992; Mosley et al., 1991; Caufield, 1996; Chossudovsky, 2003; Cornia et al., 1987; Stewart, 1991; Moore and Unsworth, 2006; Unsworth, 2007). Various recent critiques that have captured the public imagination have taken issue with the ways in which development aid interferes with the proper functioning of markets, thus implicitly accepting the (neo)liberal status quo (Easterly 2006; Collier 2008; Moyo 2010). Meanwhile, proponents of more participatory forms of development, such as Robert Chambers, have documented the ways in which development interventions have wreaked havoc by ignoring the situated knowledge of local people and the complex systems upon which their livelihoods depend (Chambers 1997).

An especially perspicuous critique, Arturo Escobar's (1994) achievement in unmasking development as a teleological narrative has been significant: he de-naturalises a way of looking at the world which takes "development" as a universal process for granted by asking us to look again at the political consequences of development studies and practice and the way they constitute the undeveloped as subjects and objects of knowledge. Whilst the "post-development" school, of which Escobar is perhaps the most important thinker, has been subject to many justified (and some unfair) criticisms (see Ziai 2007 for a good summary of postdevelopment and its critics), this politicization of development *as a discourse* has been extremely important. It has been accompanied by others who have usefully demystified development as a teleological, depoliticising (Ferguson, 1990) project, caught up in historically specific and Western accounts of progress and science (Rist, 1997) and in the notion of "trusteeship", which is to say the idea that development professionals always already know which way the process of development is heading and what its goal is (Nustad, 2001; Cowen and Shenton, 1996).

Somewhat similarly, as we saw in Chapter 1, critical writers like Milja Kurki (2010, 2011, 2013), Alison Ayers (2006) and Rita Abrahamsen (2000) offer persuasive critiques of Democracy Promotion by pointing out that the narrow understanding of democracy that is promoted and demonstrating that it is based on a particular, Western, version of liberal democracy.

What all these critiques share, however, is an assumption described most pithily by postcolonial scholar Gayatri Spivak. Development, she suggests, can be "recognized as coded within the legacy of imperialism […] whose

Disordering histories 77

supposedly authoritative narrative production was written elsewhere, in the social formations of Western Europe" (Spivak, 1995: 164). She sees the development discourse, which draws so heavily on the assumed universality of the particular experience of the "West", as an example of what she calls "epistemic violence" (Spivak, 1987: 287). The pain and poignancy of inhabiting "widely different epistemes, violently at odds with each other" (Spivak, 1995: 163) might be illustrated by Hamid's evocation of the stark difference between narratives of a modern Pakistan of destitution and dependency and the proud and exalted history of the Mughal court, not to mention the elided but unmissable allusion to the various "civilising missions", colonial and developmental, that lie in between the two.

The problem with this account is not that it is wrong, but that it is partial. The corollary seems to be to assume that in the West we are *not* living with epistemic violence, but rather that the narrative production of our civilisation, our development, our democracy, is genuinely authoritative because it is, in some way, an authentic story about our real experience of history. Thus, accounts that focus on the Foreign Policy implications of these stories, including Democracy Promotion, fail to take the risk of challenging the stories that we tell of ourselves: the stories that legitimate civilising missions in the first place. This means that they do not challenge the basis of the power/ knowledge configurations that make Democracy Promotion an essential part of shoring up domestic/ated identities.

In contrast, I want to suggest that the stories we tell of ourselves are worth risking. In doing so, I take my inspiration from Michel Foucault's 1976 account of the importance of genealogy in his lectures, published in English as *Society Must be Defended* (Foucault, 2005b). I suggest that these lectures prompt us to disrupt the "narrative production" of development and democracy promotion.

Blood dried in the codes: Foucault on history

Foucault's sights in these particular lectures are firmly set on the systems and practices of thought and analysis that enable particular forms of *historical* knowledge to take shape. In doing so, he describes how ways of organising and thinking about the world have been enabled precisely because of modes of historical narrative.

Most accessible to an English-speaking audience is perhaps his discussion of how the narration of the history of the Norman Conquest structured political thought and dissent in the late sixteenth and early seventeenth centuries (Foucault, 2005b: 99). Foucault claims that a particular struggle over an understanding of the Conquest structures political discourse at this time, creating an understanding of the nation as split between an indigenous "Saxon" population and a conquering "Norman" monarch and aristocracy. This is found in competing myths, stories and legends: a cult of King Harold or the return of popular stories such as Robin Hood on the Saxon side, or the

78 *Disordering histories*

reactivation of non-Saxon, Celtic stories such as the Arthurian legends for the (Norman) aristocracy and monarchy (ibid.: 100). The struggle provides a framework for remembering and interpreting other, subsequent historical events, by means of a type of "coding" given by the Conquest: "conflicts – political, economic, juridical – could [...] easily be articulated, coded and transformed into a discourse, into discourses, about different races" (ibid.: 101). Thus, a story about history offered a binary schema of a society split into two races, which provided a whole way of understanding history and the world since.

This was a narrative that was explicitly concerned to discern "the blood that has dried in the codes" (Foucault, 2005b: 56, 65), the forms of struggle that had given rise to the ongoing divisions within society. Furthermore, the struggle was understood to continue on the very terrain of how history was understood and narrated. A systematic way of understanding society as a function of a history given by the Norman Conquest did not provide a "particular thesis", but rather was useful to a number of different groups in providing them with a means of formulating and making sense of their positions. That is to say, it enabled the development of a *politicised* understanding of historical narratives, one that challenged earlier "Roman" modes of historical writing which had sought to legitimate existing power structures by demonstrating their continuity with the laws, kings and power structures of the past (ibid.: 66). The different stories told by royalists, parliamentarians and more radical groups such as the Levellers or Diggers *about* the history of the Norman Conquest enabled them to use knowledge about history to advance their own struggles (ibid.: 102–109).

The English discourse of race war, then, "functions in both a political and a historical mode, both as a program for political action and as a search for historical knowledge" (Foucault, 2005b: 109). In their struggle over the interpretation of history, these groups are engaged on the terrain of power/knowledge, acutely aware that the historical narrative one accepts is crucial in determining political practice.

As Chris Philo points out, then, the purpose of treating history as having the structure of a battle between races is not:

> to prove in some once-and-for-all fashion that the "truth" of history is that politics is simply war by another name. Rather, it is to trace a process whereby scholars writing about history [...] began themselves to conceive of history in this fashion, and in the process composed a history that took war-like relations, the antagonisms endemic to struggle, conflict, combat and the like, as the model for what needed to be analysed.
>
> (Philo, 2007: 351)

In some sense, then, the factual accuracy of historical narratives is beside the point. What is of more interest is the function of these narratives: what are they *doing*? Foucault suggests that:

> I am well aware that I have never written anything but fictions. I do not mean
> to say, however, that the truth is therefore absent. It seems to me that the
> possibility exists for fiction to function in truth, for a fictional discourse to
> induce effects of truth, and for bringing it about that a true discourse engenders
> or "manufactures" something that does not yet exist, that is, "fictions" it.
>
> (Foucault and Gordon, 1980: 193)

The history that we take to be true – as we have seen – has material consequences, a concrete reality and existence of its own, and enables a political programme by which we can act.

This does not mean, however, that we should be indifferent to whether these narratives tell us anything important or accurate about the history of the world: "One 'fictions' history on the basis of a political reality that makes it true, one 'fictions' a politics not yet in existence on the basis of a historical truth" (Foucault and Gordon, 1980: 193). Thus the task of writing history is twofold. First, we need to discern the blood in the codes, and then second, we need to make visible and mobilise new narratives.

This first task is what we have achieved in this chapter. We have discerned in detail what version of history it is that enables the particular political programme of democracy promotion. This is the version of history that functions as true precisely because current politics depend on it. A passionate interest in the present, however, demands the mobilisation of new narratives: narratives that can be compelling not only because of their use of empirical and archival evidence, but also because they help to imagine an alternative political practice. The point of such histories is to disrupt the very codes through which we now know the world. Genealogy, then, is a method for disturbing complacency about the codes, the discourses, the stories we tell about ourselves.

Disorderly and tattered genealogies of democracy promotion

In this chapter, we have seen a variety of interlocking stories. Taken together they give us to understand that there is a universal logic to history, for all that the chaos of actual events may get in the way of its eventual, ineluctable progress. They constitute a particular regime of truth in which teleological time operates to produce particular subjects of history: the civilised, the barbarian, the savage. This then enables a whole political programme of detailed intervention, which is gendered and racialised in specific ways. Is it possible, however, to "fiction" an alternative political programme by re-coding these stories, or discovering new ones? One thing is now clear: if we are to embark on this work, then another seamless history will not do.

Genealogy, though, is opposed to the writing of seamless histories and universal teleologies:

> genealogy is, then, a sort of attempt to desubjugate historical knowledges,
> to set them free, or in other words to enable them to oppose and struggle

80   *Disordering histories*

against the coercion of a unitary, formal and scientific theoretical discourse. The project of these disorderly and tattered genealogies is to reactivate local knowledges.

(Foucault, 2005b: 10)

What follows in the next four chapters may indeed seem disorderly for any reader expecting a continuous historical narrative. However, its disorderliness is not random, but rather a deliberate attempt to disorder the neatness of the stories we tell of ourselves, taking the pivotal moments of those stories as starting points. Thus, we will ask, did democracy promotion really begin as a ruptural break with colonial practices? Did history end in 1989 with the beginning of a newly moral practice of democracy promotion? How do the continuities and the ruptures in these stories we tell of ourselves support a particular politics? What if they are not really continuities, or ruptures, at all? Are those stories merely useful fictions that provide a political programme, which we could, by telling other stories, change?

Although many readers of Foucault have characterised him as an historian of discontinuity (Philo, 2007; Thacker, 1996), this was not precisely his intention. In an interview he states that, "[t]his business about discontinuity has always rather bewildered me [...] My problem was not at all to say, 'Voilà, long live discontinuity, we are in the discontinuous and a good thing too'" (Foucault, 1991d: 53–54). He suggests instead that he is interested in changes in the regimes of truth and statements that appear to belie the "calm, continuist image that is normally accredited" (Foucault, 1991d: 54). The point is, as ever, to show that there are alternatives to the stories we tell of ourselves and potential to unearth alternative ways of knowing the past. It is therefore equally disorderly to discern the continuities where we took for granted rupture, as it is to show the rupture, where we thought to see only continuity.

In Chapters 4 to 6, we will see that almost everything about the seamless continuist stories we have seen above about civilisation, development and the spread of democracy is profoundly misleading. I will show that the British have been promoting democracy for much longer than the official history of democracy promotion suggests, and that decolonisation did not represent a ruptural break in which the iniquities of imperialism were replaced by a benevolent, but incomplete, Democracy Promotion. On the contrary, I will demonstrate that the civilising colonial mission has from the start been engaged in promoting versions of good government that have included various forms of representative institutions, which both precede and produce the movements for national self-determination in British India.

Moreover, whereas cautionary tales about the Cold War, or the discourse surrounding the London bombings, suggest that democracy is a remedy for, or alternative to, violence, I will show that the violence of the Partition of India and Pakistan was made possible, and provoked, by the promotion of "good government". Electoral democracy, representative institutions, the division into public and private spheres all enabled and enforced the particular solidification of religious identities that clashed catastrophically.

Finally, I show in Chapter 6 that far from vindicating the institutions of liberal democracy, another look at the events of 1989 – particularly the Salman Rushdie affair – can show us how democratic institutions enacted profound epistemic and physical cruelty and violence at that time. Chapter 7 shows how they continued to do so despite changing understandings of democracy promotion in the years of the "war on terror".

Most importantly, though, the next three chapters will demonstrate that the progressive, teleological understandings of time that provide the conditions of possibility for the precise stories outlined above have emerged in response to uncertainty about the present. They have therefore been successful discourses primarily not because they were accurate accounts of the past, but rather because they provided a useful means for orienting practical responses towards the future. This is why we should care about the stories we tell about ourselves, and this is why the stakes of showing why such stories are misleading are so high. We care about the past because it offers us a way of understanding how to proceed in the future.

Note

1 However, as Stuart Croft (2006) has pointed out, an account of history or society that was more closely based on the actual work of evolutionary scientists would look very different from this and would emphasise contingency, accident and chaos.

4 Authoring the codes elsewhere
Colonial governmentality and teleological time

> This is a common pattern in the history of thought: an idea becomes sharply formulated and even named [...] at exactly the moment that it is being put under pressure.
>
> (Ian Hacking, "How Should we do the History of Statistics")

This chapter goes back to the late eighteenth and early nineteenth centuries in order to unearth the emergence of some of the practices discussed in the preceding three chapters. I make two related points. First, I show that the teleological story we tell of ourselves that I presented in detail in Chapter 3 is misleading in a number of ways. Second, and more importantly, I demonstrate how this way of thinking about time and progress emerged in the early nineteenth century as a function of the problematisation of how to govern in a confused and unknowable India. Thus, I will show that whilst teleological versions of history are not a very good guide to what happened in the past, they did in the 1830s become a useful way of deciding what to do in the present. This is because they provided a way of thinking about the future. In other words, I show that history has not been produced by the logic of teleology; teleological narratives, however, have been produced by the specific unfolding of history.

The British have been worrying about the promotion of good government in what is now Pakistan, and devising representative institutions to help them, for much longer than is commonly thought. The very government of Britain *at home* was also profoundly changed by this experience. As Michel Foucault puts it in a rare reference to imperialism, this entailed a kind of "boomerang effect":

> It should never be forgotten that while colonization, with its techniques and its political and juridical weapons, obviously transported European models to other continents, it also had a considerable boomerang effect on the mechanisms of power in the West, and on the apparatuses, institutions and techniques of power. A whole series of colonial models was brought back to the West, and the result was that the West could practice something resembling colonization, or an internal colonialism, on itself.
>
> (Foucault, 2005b: 103)

Authoring the codes elsewhere 83

In the following pages, I will describe precisely how one instance of this boomerang effect took place. I show how it was that the quantitative technologies of liberal democratic governmentality that are now so familiar to us were implemented in the subcontinent, in the late eighteenth and early nineteenth centuries, *for the first time in the British Empire*. This was because they provided a means of knowing and controlling a population seen as unruly and a present that seemed uncertain.

Even more crucially, the teleological form of othering that constitutes British identity is also an invention that dates back to this precise period and its history is deeply intertwined with the emergence of liberal democratic governmentality. The word "civilisation" became established in the English language around the period 1772–1836 (Bowden, 2009: 31), at exactly the moment when ideas about time, temporality and progress were coming under new pressure in the way Ian Hacking describes in the quotation at the start of this chapter. In my discussion of these conflicting ideas about time, temporality and governing in this chapter, I am particularly indebted to Jon Wilson's excellent study, *The Domination of Strangers* (2008), although I take his ideas in a slightly different direction according to my purposes.

This pressure is most easily understood by considering how the different ways of thinking about governing respectively attempt to resolve the constitutive tension at the heart of liberal governmentality. This is a tension that emerges because governmentality brings together two rather different traditions. On the one hand is the notion of the self-governing polity of Ancient Greece, from which we draw our ideas about democratic participation on the basis of political equality as citizens: the city-citizen matrix. On the other, emerging out of a Christian tradition, is the idea of the shepherd and flock. It is this latter matrix, in which the community's leader is responsible for knowing and caring for each member of the "flock", and which – in an historical process that need not concern us here – has been displaced from the Church to the state, that underlies the understanding that it is the state's responsibility to know, understand, care for and enable the development of its population (Foucault, 2007; Dean, 2010: 90–101). The chapter proceeds in three main sections that each deal with a particular resolution of these ideas.

The first section explores ideas about governing that operated using a conception of time that was continuous and accretive, animated by the stadial notion of progress that was emblematic of eighteenth-century thought (Burchell, 1991: 137). Using Edmund Burke's work in particular, I show that eighteenth-century ideas about time had stressed an organic growth of wisdom, which was deeply involved with the place and people that were its subjects. Thus, the laws, procedures and processes of governing were unique to the time and place in which they had emerged and were emphatically non-transferable. Modes of governing that had evolved in India must, by this token, be respected in India. Meanwhile, British modes of governing that stressed participation and relationality were valorised as the precious inheritance of the past that must be preserved against the depredations of time.

84 *Authoring the codes elsewhere*

Here, the *pastoral role* of governance is privileged. Pastoral responsibilities are understood to be conferred by ownership of property, which brings with it the duty to care for and about the people connected to it, and who are tied to local landowners through historically constituted and inherited links of affection and obligation. This hierarchical and highly gendered polity is nevertheless highly participatory, not least because of electoral practices, in ways that enabled the British to see themselves as a peculiarly "free", self-governing people.

The second section shows that these ideas came into conflict with an India that was difficult to understand. It was for a long time accepted that the laws and customs that had evolved there should be respected, but in the everyday reality of trying to govern, this led to profound perplexity, which appeared to derive from the lack of a shared history. Concrete attempts to resolve the epistemological problems posed by India were justified (after the fact) by a Utilitarian perspective, associated with James Mill, which worked with a temporality that aspired to be ruptural. Given the "barbarous" and incomprehensible nature of India, the best thing to do was to break with past history, draw a line under previous customs and start again, using a rational and minute control of the population to instil a better governance founded on logic, objective knowledge and reason. The shepherd-flock paradigm was re-invoked, but in new terms: the flock would henceforth be known through objective categories and governed according to general laws.

The third section, however, suggests that – given the importance of freedom and the tradition of the city-citizen matrix for British ideas about governing – the new, abstracted forms of governmental rule created significant unease about the legitimacy of this new shepherd-flock configuration in India which did not appear to allow for the participation of the governed. This unease led to discussions, in the "Age of Reform" (the early 1830s), of how institutions could be used to represent India. The uneasy compromise that emerged of assuming that the East India Company could function as a kind of a representative institution was hardly democratic. Nevertheless, the debates at this time laid down the conditions of possibility for the liberal democratic institutions that are now so familiar.

In this period, two incommensurable sets of practices of thought about governing and time, characterised by Burke and Mill, were precariously resolved by the emergence of a set of governing practices based on teleology and a faith in progress. This resolution would have consequences long into the future. Thus Thomas Babington Macaulay and other thinkers who were concretely engaged in the difficult business of governing India took the emergence of scientific rationality and representative institutions in Britain as the endpoint of a process of organic development and upended this idea to imagine that India might, with help from its British governors, go through a similar process *in the future* and alight upon a similar endpoint. This, I suggest, marks the emergence of ideas about "progress" that is expected to be the same everywhere, as distinct from earlier ideas that progress would look different for different peoples and places: progress in the singular, rather than

Authoring the codes elsewhere 85

progress in the plural. By the 1850s, this new way of thinking about civilisation had become widespread, such that Henry Buckle's immensely popular *History of Civilization in England* was able to claim that human actions everywhere are likewise determined by general laws that are as fixed as those understood to govern the world of physics (Hacking, 1991: 188).

The British polity before the age of reform: affective ties and continuity

Governing relations

In late eighteenth-century Britain, the resolution of shepherd-flock and city-citizen matrices was achieved in a way rather unfamiliar to liberal democratic techniques of rule. The local landowner, who inherited administrative office along with, and inextricable from, his (and it was almost always his) other property (Wilson, 2008: 72), was deeply involved in highly decentralised practices of governing and this involved detailed narrative knowledge of the people. This knowledge could only be obtained through an ethical investment in the maintenance over time of the affective relationships that constituted political life. Within this framework, the existence of electoral practices, public hustings and some semblance of representative institutions provided a limited element of choice in whom to defer to, alongside an ongoing emphasis on participation and mutual accountability and responsibility.

This system of governance was taken as evidence of the widespread belief that the British political system was particularly conducive to freedom (Colley, 2009: 361–363). It was a belief that played a key role in constituting a sense of British identity and was buttressed by the popular practice, around election time, of crowds singing patriotic songs and waving Union Flags in order to demonstrate their support for the system of governing as "freeborn Englishmen", understood to form part of an historical narrative stretching back to Saxon England, the Magna Carta, the restitution of an ancient constitution in the "Glorious Revolution" of 1688 and so on (ibid.: 343, 352, 52).

Suffrage was, before the 1832 Reform Act, highly restricted, but it would be wrong to assume that the mass of British people were entirely excluded from political life. In comparison with other European countries, the British polity was, although hierarchical and highly gendered, also extremely decentralised, flexible and participatory in the late eighteenth and early nineteenth centuries.

It is perhaps Edmund Burke who gives the clearest account of the particular ways of thinking about governing at that time. His work has a particular relevance to any study of British India in this period, given his stinging attacks on the East India Company (Burke, 1991c, 1991d), and it is worth looking in some detail at his work, which gives important clues to the ways governing in India could be thought about just before the Age of Reform (see also Wilson, 2008: 28–33).

Burke was much more concerned with practical political skill and the management of relationships – described in affective terms – than abstract rules:

86 *Authoring the codes elsewhere*

> We Englishmen, stop very short of the principles upon which we support any given part of our constitution; or even the whole of it together [...] All government, every human benefit and enjoyment, every virtue and every prudent act, is founded on compromise and barter. We balance inconveniences; we give and take; we remit some rights, that we may enjoy others; and we chuse rather to be happy citizens than subtle disputants.
>
> (Burke, 1991b: 142)

Citizenship, here, is a whole tissue of complex relationships whose emotional resonances are more important than the cold rationality of the "subtle disputant". Instead, happiness, enjoyment and benefit are the outcome of being embedded in relationships in all their complexity and the never-ending negotiations they entail.

This is the antithesis of living by generalised rules. General rules lead to dispute, and rupture the very ties that hold the polity together. The happiness of a "happy citizen" has little to do with the Utilitarian "greatest happiness to the greatest number", because Burke's conception of happiness is not individualised but relational: it is therefore not tractable to quantification or measurement, but rather is something that must be maintained through ongoing ethical work. This implies that personal character, rather than codified law, is likewise of the utmost importance. Skill and tact in managing relationships, disagreements and ongoing events were the crucial political attributes: "Whilst *manners* remain entire, they will correct the vices of the law and soften it at length to their own temper" (Burke, 1991a: 152). Crucially, the relationships that cemented the political community are taken to be constituted by the ownership of property (Langford, 1991: 50–51; Wilson, 2008: 32), and it is thus the character of the local landowner as the practical and skilled arbiter of the compromises and judgements of everyday life, that is centrally important for the management of the affective life of the community.

Hierarchy and deference are also valued in electoral practices: on the face of it, the outcomes of elections might seem like a foregone conclusion, given the many-faceted influence of local landed families with long histories of ruling particular constituencies. Indeed, many seats went uncontested. However, it is important not to over-estimate this tendency, because that would be to disregard the complex networks of responsibility and accountability that accompanied relations of deference: "the voters demanded, indeed anticipated, paternalist services of many kinds in return for their loyalty" (O'Gorman, 1989: 225–226). The process of making these demands was highly participatory. Elections would go on for days (somewhat curtailed by the Reform Act) and formed a kind of rowdy, public carnival in which a powerful emphasis was placed on the practices of the hustings, at which people of all social classes, including women, held the much-valued and -vaunted right to "have their say" (Lawrence, 2009: 30, 5). In the event that demands and expectations of paternalist services were not met, it was by no means unheard of for seats to change hands.

Authoring the codes elsewhere   87

MPs were accountable not just to the electorate, but to the crowd more generally. Furthermore voters were also understood to be accountable to one another and to non-voters. Voting took place in public and even when the secret ballot was introduced – not until 1872 – it was tellingly widely denounced by Parliamentarians as "un-English" (Lawrence, 2009: 46). Voters were expected to be able to explain and stand by their decisions. Thus elections were fully implicated in complex networks of affection, patronage and mutual responsibility. The development of British institutions, then, was perceived quite differently from the way the same history of the same set of events is used today.

Government and chivalry

As this discussion suggests, political relations were gendered in ways that, despite some obvious continuities, nevertheless differ importantly from the configurations of liberal democratic society. I argued in Chapter 3 that a valorisation of care, relationality and the emotions would explode the complex of gendered practices of thought that emerge from the narrative of the savage and the barbarian. In this section, my reading of Burke suggests, by way of illustration, that a radically different way of thinking about time and history necessarily entails an alternative ethics of gender relations.

None of what follows should be taken as an invitation to idealise Burke's thought. Eighteenth-century Britain was a world in which paternal benevolence was valued alongside "manly" courage in leaders, and the public sphere of the hustings was often violent and hyper-masculine (Lawrence, 2009: 14–20). Nevertheless, the highly partisan presence of women at these events – for all that they were valued in part for their "decorous role in the proceedings" (ibid.: 21) – signals that they were never quite excluded from participation. The gendering of political relations requires some teasing out.

Burke, then, takes the familiar Enlightenment view that a society can be judged by observing the way its women are treated and he makes regular appeal to the ancient virtues of "chivalry". On these grounds, he is outraged by the brutal treatment of Marie Antoinette at the hands of French revolutionaries and likewise the perceived violation of Begums of Oudh, when Company servants raid their palaces to take possession of disputed revenue (Colley, 2009: 258; Fidler and Welsh, 1991: 30, 48, 55).

There are various elements to Burke's horror at the Oudh incident that are worth examining in detail. The first is the lack of "reverence paid to the female sex in general" (Burke, 1990: 4.5.99), a breach of traditional gender norms of chivalry that extends to "a rapacious and licentious soldiery in the personal search of women" (ibid.: 4.5.101). This violating failure of the important virtue of good manners is compounded, second, by the fact that these are women of "high rank and condition" (ibid.: 4.5.99). The importance of this is signalled by the origin of the fortune allegedly plundered by the Company under Warren Hastings:

88 *Authoring the codes elsewhere*

> This prince (suspicious, and not unjustly suspicious, of his son and successor) at his death committed his treasures and his family to the British faith. That family and household, consisted of *two thousand women*; to which were added two other seraglios of near kindred, and [...] of about fourscore of the Nabob's children, with all the eunuchs, the ancient servants, and a multitude of the dependants of his splendid court. These were all to be provided, for present maintenance and future establishment, from the lands assigned as dower, and from the treasures which he left to these matrons, in trust for the whole family.
>
> (Burke, 1990: 4.5.83, emphasis in the original)

Burke has no problem with the idea of a woman owning property, then. However, it is not thought about as a personal fortune that is hers to dispose of. Rather, property brings with it a whole web of inherited and future responsibility and dependence, including particularly the well-being of the family's women and others in need of protection. In the Company's act of forcible confiscation, they are not merely dispossessing the princess, but also disrupting, not only for now but for future generations, a series of hierarchical relations of trust and dependence on which the well-being of a whole community depends.

Perhaps the worst element of the Company's actions, for Burke, is that the instrument of the prince's dispossession is "*her own son* [...] It was the pious hand of the son that was selected to tear from his mother and grandmother the provision of their age, the maintenance of his brethren, and of all the ancient household of his father" (Burke, 1990: 4.5.83, emphasis in the original). The most immediate of familial ties that are founded upon and vested in the bodies of women are severed through a violent and highly intimate violation of the bodies of a mother and a grandmother, and in the process an entire family, household and broader society are imperilled in the work of a moment. The familial model of a Burkean polity, then, with its basis in affection, trust, paternal authority and provision, is dependent on particular gender relations, in which the figures of fathers, sons and brothers engage in the political work of ensuring that mothers and grandmothers, the elderly, the eunuchs and the dependants are provided for. A disregard for gendered codes of behaviour is, then, potentially catastrophic – and not only for women.

Feminist scholars of international relations have long remarked the litany of differential binary oppositions that litter the discipline (Thapar-Björkert and Shepherd, 2010: 275; Campbell, 1998: 195–205). Just as the masculine is privileged over the feminine, the public is given primacy over the private; universality and abstraction over the cultural, the local and the specific; spatial relations over temporal; morals over ethics (Gilligan, 1990); rationality over sentiment. The former terms in each case are linked through their association with the public world of men, whereas the latter are feminised and confined to the private, domestic sphere.

Whilst Burke's thought is populated by the "figure of the lady in distress" (Zerilli, 1994: 60) in ways that are highly problematic for any present-day feminist, we can nevertheless now see that it is possible to read his work as putting these binaries radically in doubt. Indeed, he suggests that culture, affection, care, ethics, and domestic and familial relations are constitutively important for the very possibility both of the nation and therefore the international. Burke alerts us that there is nothing inevitable about our gendered discursive economy. On the contrary, I suggest that it was recently forged along with other techniques of governing that sought to abstract politics from the day-to-day management of relationships and affective ties.

History, time and preserving continuity

Inseparable from this idea of the political community as a set of pragmatic, familial relations is Burke's sense of temporality, as underlined by the importance of the "ancientness" of the Oudh estate: he views the nation as "an idea of continuity, which extends in time as well as in numbers, and in space", and the relationships amongst the political community as a "partnership not only between those who are living, but between those who are living, those who are dead and those who are to be born" (quoted in Fidler and Welsh, 1991: 40–41; see also Wilson, 2008: 33). Thus the guiding conception of time was one of continuity – literally borne through the bodies of women – in which accumulated wisdom, sensitivity to context and practical skill and experience, were of the highest importance (Fidler and Welsh, 1991: 11). This bears important similarities with Adam Smith, who, in his *Theory of Moral Sentiments* (Smith, 2010), laid out a view of the political community as a complex, interconnected organism which functioned according to sentiment and affective ties (Rothschild, 2001).

Dramatic change, then, was dangerous because these relational processes by definition could not be thought up or contained within a single mind or moment, but rather were the emergent property of a set of temporal and spatial relations that exceeded any attempt to capture, codify or abstract them. This was, of course, the basis for Burke's fierce opposition to the French Revolution (Fidler and Welsh, 1991: 29–36): "Rage and phrenzy will pull down more in half an hour, than prudence, deliberation and foresight can build up in an hundred years" (quoted in ibid.: 30). As there could be no map, blueprint or set of rules that could encompass the complex practical wisdom built up over continuous time, once lost, they would be gone perhaps forever.

For this reason, Burke is horrified by the idea that the British in India might be destroying ancient ways of doing things, customs and traditions that had evolved locally and were highly adapted to the environment and people who had produced, and been produced by, them (Burke, 1991d: 209). He was committed to the idea that political practice was a matter of local culture and had to be approached in all its specificity: "I could never conceive that the natives of *Hindostan* and those of *Virginia* could be ordered in the same manner" (Burke, 1991a: 161). The problem of the cultural distance of the Company from those they are ruling is furthermore compounded by the fact that:

90 *Authoring the codes elsewhere*

they are separated from the Country that sent them out and from the Country in which they are; [...] there is no control by persons who understand their language, who understand their manners, or can apply their conduct to the Laws of the Country.

(Burke, 1991d: 211)

Thus lacking in the appropriate relational ties, it is impossible for them to rule appropriately. Culture – understood as both language and ethical "manners", as well as specific, not universal, "laws", all of which are temporally constituted – is what founds good government and enables the accountability of rulers.

Modes of governing were changing in the first third of the nineteenth century in very important ways. This was the "Age of Reform" – often vaunted in the stories we tell of ourselves about the history of British institutions – which had already by 1833 seen Catholic emancipation, the abolition of the slave trade and the extension of the parliamentary franchise to every adult male who owned a house worth £10 or more (Colley, 2009: chapter 8), whilst in India, the burning of widows had been formally abolished in 1829 (Wilson, 2008: 167).

However, such reforms were an attempt to reconfigure complex relationships within the context of a present thought to be linked intimately with the past. The supporters of the 1832 Reform Act were not intending what might be perceived as a damaging break or rupture of the affective and temporal links that constituted the polity. On the contrary, attempts by Utilitarians, like Bentham, to codify the complex web of unwritten laws had long been marginalised and resisted (Wilson, 2008: 29–35). Despite the fact that industrialisation, urbanisation, scientific discovery and Enlightenment philosophy were changing patterns of governing across Europe, Britain continued to function in ways that made it look almost ungovernable according to the rational principles becoming fashionable in continental Europe at the time (Hilton, 2006). However, it was the experience of governing India that would, in important ways, change much of that.

Uncertainty, abstraction and the machinery of government

The assumptions of how to rule in Britain were in some respects translated to the business of governing in India, at least at first. There was never any question, in the eighteenth century, as the Company gained ever more political power through battles and treaties: the local population should be ruled according to "ancient customs and usages of the country" including the "ancient Mughal constitution" (Wilson, 2008: 51–52).

What these laws concretely were was not a matter of particular interest for Company servants, so long as they could be established and enforced. The important thing – for the Company as much as for Edmund Burke – was to rule legitimately through the institutions that constituted a link to the past

Authoring the codes elsewhere 91

and not to allow invasion and conquest to rupture the delicate web of continuity that held the polity together. Thus, in the late eighteenth century, Company servants were writing long explanations in prose to substantiate and explain their decisions and actions, making reference to historical precedent and the advice of local judges and scholars (Wilson, 2008).

By the 1830s, however, there had been a very significant change. By now, Company servants were filling in forms. This process required them to classify local inhabitants according to a restricted number of general categories (Wilson, 2008: 129). India experienced bureaucratic governmentality for the first time. This was not because it had been imported wholesale and fully formed by a foreign force: as we have seen, governing at home was a question of narrative, precedent and judgement based on specific pastoral knowledge built up over time. Rather, it became necessary because of the discursive encounter of the British with the particular challenges and puzzles thrown up by the novelty of colonial rule (ibid.).

The difficulty involved in governing India was a very practical one. Company servants working in courts and revenue offices simply did not know what the laws and customs of the land were that they were required to uphold. Wilson's archival work – using documents from the courts of late eighteenth-century Bengal – describes trials that dragged on for years in the attempt to establish who owned what and just what local custom ought to dictate. Local leaders and lawyers – not unaware of the opportunities opened up by British uncertainty – gave conflicting opinions on the correct course of action (Wilson, 2008: 83–91). This was taken by Company servants to be evidence of "despotism" in India, a term connoting arbitrary and uncertain governance. This was taken to reflect particularly badly on the character of the Indians who interacted with Company servants, who were understood to be lacking in the "public virtue" and "honour" that would enable the proper management of the community (ibid.: 65).

This characterisation is only comprehensible in terms of the particular resolution of governance that was current in late eighteenth-century Britain, with its emphasis on relationship management *as* politics. The perceived incomprehensibility of local manners and behaviour led to the conclusion that local governance was devastatingly poor: "For most Britons [as for Company servants in 1780s Bengal], the word 'despotism' simply conjured up an image of a society so disorganised it was almost impossible to think about how it was able to exist at all" (Wilson, 2008: 65).

Attempts to manage this uncertainty began with tentative attempts to write down and enforce a set of strict principles, such as the "permanent settlement" to introduce stable, heritable property rights and fix rent revenues implemented by the Marquis of Cornwallis in 1793. This system was understood to be abstract and generalisable enough that it could be transferred to Madras and Benares without making any allowances for local circumstances. This bespeaks a genuinely novel way of thinking about property, which would have been quite alien to the Burkean conception of ownership as constitutive

92   *Authoring the codes elsewhere*

of political relations, inseparable from the specificities of local context and affective relations. The new "Bengal system", then, constitutes a way of thinking about a fully formed, private economic sphere that is distinct from the public practices of governing, creating the autonomous, contracting *homo economicus* of liberal governmentality perhaps for the first time in the British Empire. Note, too, that the development of this abstract system of rules and a separate public sphere in which they apply emerges not as a deduction from rational first principles, but rather as an entirely pragmatic response to the challenge of working out who owned what in an unfamiliar terrain (Wilson, 2008: 69–74).

Around the same time, the usefulness of abstract rules and categories extended into a movement to write down and translate local codes of law into English, so that there would be some steady point of reference for decision making. However, these Indian texts did not offer a codified set of rules, but rather elaborated the practices and principles "created by the active participation in a sphere of customary activity outside the court" (Wilson, 2008: 83), which might and did vary greatly from place to place. As such, these sorts of texts were of little practical use in dispute resolution since, "if an official was able to trust the logic of Bengali jurisprudence [which involved a particular style of reasoning, rather than an abstract set of rules] well enough to make sense of the text, he would have no need for the work in the first place" (ibid.: 83).

The frustration and uncertainty of being unable to make enough sense of India to be able to govern leads by the 1820s to sets of pithy rules being written down by William Hay Macnaghten in his *Principles and Precedents of Mahometan Law* and *Principles and Precedents of Hindoo Law*, published in 1825 and 1827, respectively (Wilson, 2008: 96). As the author of these works was well aware, he was not merely writing down pre-existing rules, but rather creating *for the first time anywhere in the British Empire* (including Britain itself) a body of positive, abstract, textual laws that were expected to govern the conduct of an entire population (ibid.: 97).

The new ways of ruling that came to prominence in India, then, included the use of abstract rules, the delineation of categories of people, the separation of the public and private spheres, and the introduction of a disinterested, rational system of decision making in which personal ties were less important than general principles. A form of rule was instantiated in which the state took on the pastoral role of the disinterested shepherd who knows the flock not according to a sentimental or narrative relationship with each, but rather according to the categorisations and statistics that are the indispensable science of modern governmentality.

Governing began to be perceived less as the skilled exercise of wisdom in the management of relationships and more like the running of a machine, in keeping with changing times and the innovative new inventions that emerged from the Industrial Revolution. However, such perceptions did not emerge fully formed out of progressive, rational reflection in domestic institutions, but were rather the product of perplexity and attempts to deal with what was perceived as chaos in colonial India. In a strange environment where the

Authoring the codes elsewhere 93

assumptions, mutual obligations and taken-for-granted understandings no longer necessarily held, governing turned out to pose profound epistemological problems, as expressed by Thomas Babington Macaulay when he describes the experience of governing India as one of "walking in darkness" (Macaulay, 1833). It was the encounter of Company servants with a polity who did not resemble them, with whom they felt no long historical associations or ties and with whom they shared little mutual understanding, that changed ideas about ruling and about time.

As Wilson argues, although the changes in Indian government around this period have been read as influenced by Utilitarian thought propounded by Jeremy Bentham and James Mill (see Stokes, 1959; Said, 1995: 214–215), the growing abstraction, rationalisation and codification in India *precedes* the influence of Utilitarianism (Wilson, 2008: 136). This is not to deny the importance of Mill's work on India, but rather to suggest that theory and practice inform one another in complex ways. Mill's prescriptions for India and for Britain were at least in part based on his reading about the difficulties faced and the practical muddling-through that had been exemplified by Company servants in India, whilst also laying down an intellectual rationale for them.

Utilitarian codes

James Mill's *History of British India* – first published in 1818 and still in print – is perhaps the most important source on colonial Utilitarian thinking. It would lead to the author's appointment as examiner of correspondence at the Company, would function as a textbook at Haileybury – the college for future East India Company servants (Gilmour, 2007: 13) – and was described by Macaulay (1833), no great admirer of Mill's thought in general, as "the greatest historical work that has appeared in our language since that of Gibbon". It is important because, in synthesising the problems of governing India and the abstract solutions that had been proposed for them in this influential text, he elaborates a theoretical account of the concrete governing practices we saw above. Thus, the ad hoc muddling through of administrators becomes a generalised prescription about how to govern that is understood (by Mill) to be universally applicable.

What is particularly important for my purpose here is to note how governance in India has been re-problematised on the basis of an entirely different reading of history. Rather than attempting to discern the customs and traditions from the past in order to manage the present, Mill wants to make a ruptural break with the past. He did not elaborate a theory of civilisation that understood history as evolution towards civilisation. Rather, he viewed societies on a more or less binary schema as either "civilised" or "barbarous", with Britain – by virtue of its uncodified laws – occupying a rather ambiguous position between the two (Pitts, 2005: 129). In order to contain the barbarity, a single, heroic effort of law making was required by which a rational mind

94 *Authoring the codes elsewhere*

could draw a line under the past and provide a full, precise and rational codification of the Indian legal system (Wilson, 2008: 140; Pitts, 2005: 128).

This is not to say, however, that even Mill hoped to impose European practices wholesale into India; rather the codification of Indian law would provide a rupture with the corrupt practices of the present, but would take as its basis local rules and principles that could be tidied up and made into a logical and consistent body of positive law. Paradoxically, every attempt to produce a rupture by producing a code of Indian law would refer back to Indian practice.

Thus an impulse towards rational abstraction was not itself the consequence of logical deduction, but rather the result of entirely inductive, rooted and contingent negotiations with the difficulties of the present. Mill's solution and the locally specific variations on it that emerged *derived from*, as well as feeding back into, the anxious and tentative response by Lord Teignmouth and others in Bengal who first attempted to manage uncertainty by establishing and writing down some principles according to which it would be possible to proceed (Wilson, 2008: 57–63, 136).

The 1833 Charter Act

In the context of this wide-ranging attention to the proper practices of good government, public attention was drawn to the East India Company's anomalous position as both commercial trading company and the *de facto* ruler and sovereign of British India, which began to appear increasingly troublesome beyond those with a direct interest in free trade. When its Charter came up for renewal in 1833, it was ripe as the next target for reform.

The 1833 Government of India Act, known as the Charter Act (House of Commons Parliamentary Papers, 1833), not only finally ended the Company's right to trade by abolishing its monopoly on Chinese imports of tea, but also created what Henry Tucker – member of the Court of Directors and future Chair – called a "new constitution for India" (quoted in Wilson, 2008: 149). From now on, the sovereign power of India would formally reside in the British Parliament, ending the nominal authority of the Mughal Emperor, and would be delegated to a unitary Legislative Council, which would have powers over all India. This appears, on the face of it, to be a triumph for Mill and his advocacy of a single set of laws devised by an efficient legislature that would break dramatically with the confusion and uncertainty of the present.

The 1833 Charter Act did indeed establish a unitary legislative authority in India that, it was hoped, would provide a single legitimate source of generalised, abstract law. The hopes of both Mill and Thomas Babington Macaulay, who led the first commission to codify the law in India, were that India could now be governed according to rational principles, rather than the capricious, arbitrary will of the Oriental despot (Kolsky, 2005: 652).

This radically new resolution of the city-citizen/shepherd-flock problematic – in which the role of the shepherd is emphatically enshrined and the participatory practices of the city-citizen tradition marginalised – was for many in Britain deeply alien to the prevailing understandings of how a society should be governed. The ways in which it was reconciled with governing practices at home rebounded in important ways on British modes of thinking about how to govern.

Teleology and reform

James Mill's advocacy of a fully codified legal system for India has rightly been read as much as a critique of British governance as it was of India's (Majeed, 1992). Drawing attention to attempts to contain the "barbarism" of governing practices elsewhere, he deliberately and inevitably drew attention to the perceived deficiencies of government at home, where there was an equal dearth of codified law.

However, the critique of British institutions was not necessarily shared by the majority of reformers, who were proud of British institutions and modes of governance. Unlike Mill, they discerned a troubling tension between the "free government" enjoyed in Britain – with its representative institutions and traditions of widespread participation – and the "good government" to be instituted in India – with abstract rules and a centralised, unified government. This final section shows how they resolved this tension by tacking between the two conceptions of time – Burke's organic and Mill's mechanical time – that came with these different modes of government. A precarious combination of the delicately continuous, accumulative time of the Burkean polity, and the once-and-for-all rupture of Mill's end to barbarism, gave rise to a specific teleology that prefigures present-day practices of temporal othering.

The negotiations and debate that preceded the new Charter were bound up in Britain's sense of its own identity and place in the world, articulated through its supposed superior and benevolent governing practices. The Company's General Court, for example, were at pains regularly to stress:

> their anxious wish to concur with His Majesty's Government and with Parliament, in every way in their power, to promote the welfare, prosperity and happiness of the Natives in India, alike important to the cause of humanity as to the power and to the commerce of Britain.
>
> (India Office, 1833a: 8)

Similarly, Charles Grant of the Government's Board of India stated that:

> the establishment of a just and benignant system of administration over the territories of British India, an object of the last moment to the nations who inhabit them, is, at the same time, not only most important to our national honour, but must, in several views, reflect back on us the benefits which we bestow.
>
> (India Office, 1833c: 11)

96 *Authoring the codes elsewhere*

It is notable that these statements appear in confidential documents that were not for public consumption. These arguments, then, are not merely rhetorical devices to appease a critical public, but rather integral to the discourses employed by powerful men at the time: what counted as a good argument for these men debating over the future of millions of people thousands of miles away, was expressed in terms of national values and purpose. The moral superiority of British governing, then, is already seen as a crucial element of British identity.

This discourse of good government and national pride is echoed in Macaulay's speech in favour of the Bill in Parliament: "I compare [the government of India] with the government of the Roman provinces, with the government of the Spanish colonies; and I am proud of my country and my age" (Macaulay, 1833). Here we see the legitimation of a particular British practice of governing as integral to national identity and standing. Note also that here we have another example of temporal othering: British modes of governing now, as they have (organically?) emerged over time, are superior to the civilisations of the past. In linking "my country and my age", Macaulay is explicitly noting that he believes that, with the passage of time and the accretion of wisdom, contemporary civilisations have gone beyond what was to be expected in the past: even Ancient Rome. Given the pride taken in British forms of rule, it remains surprising that more serious consideration was not given to the establishment of some form of genuinely representative institution in India on the British model. A closer explanation of why not will enable understanding the specific mode of temporal othering that was emerging.

Mill famously believed that representative government was "the grand discovery of our times [in which] the solution of all difficulties, both speculative and practical would be found" (quoted in Held, 1996: 119). Alongside his close friend, Jeremy Bentham, he viewed it as a machine-like technology that would solve the problems of governance, as the panopticon would solve the problem of crime and punishment. Yet he does not even want the English people represented on the legislative body of India, in the guise of a councillor appointed by Parliament rather than the Company. At a House of Commons select committee in 1832 he is asked whether he considers "representation as entirely out of the question", and he simply replies "I conceive wholly so", without any further explanation (House of Commons Parliamentary Papers, 1831d).

Yet the fact that the question is asked at all suggests that his answer is not self-evident and it is not that the idea never seriously presented itself. On the contrary, it was very much one of the alternatives on the table at the time, although this "counter-knowledge" has now been largely forgotten. Robert Rickards – a liberal reformer who published a series of popular pamphlets on India following his long residence in the subcontinent – gave lengthy evidence to the select committees in which he condemned the lack of engagement between government and Indian people, laying out proposals for the establishment of "native councils" at the various presidencies:

What I consider of paramount importance, the appointment of a permanent native council or committee, either with or without a European
president, to revise and amend, alter or repeal, existing laws and to assist
in the formation of new ones, and to watch with unceasing vigilance such
as may be consequently confirmed so as to be able to report to government, as the superior legislative authority, such amendments, modifica-
tions, or repeals, as circumstances shall appear to render expedient or
necessary. The power of originating laws should also be extended to this
committee or council, who would submit the same to the government for
confirmation; and no new law should be put in force that had not
received the approbation of the said committee.

(House of Commons Parliamentary Papers, 1830a: 277)

This, for Rickards, is the optimal solution for solving the vexing epistemological problems faced by India: mirroring Macaulay's remarks on the problem
of knowing India, he suggests that, "without it we shall still be wandering in
the dark in India" (House of Commons Parliamentary Papers, 1830a: 278).
Whilst there is obviously no suggestion here of elections or genuinely popular
participation, and the (British) government would still hold ultimate sovereignty, this proposal is quite clearly informed by a sense that local people and
their knowledge can be represented by means of a law-making institution.

Less "visionary" (House of Commons Parliamentary Papers, 1830a) is Sir
Henry Tucker, who had also lived in India for many years and as a Tory and
conservative took a rather different view of most matters than Rickards would
(Prior, 2004). His way of thinking is more obviously in the Burkean mould, and he
is wary of "untried theory" and the hazards of novel ideas that may not export
easily (Tucker, 1833b: 138, 141). Whilst he does not advocate representative
institutions, he is at great pains to advocate that small deliberative bodies, or
councils, are maintained at the sub-presidencies and that the wisdom of servants who know the customs, traditions and languages of a local area is fully
brought to bear in decision making (Tucker, 1833a). This highly paternalist,
but nevertheless rather participatory argument no longer holds sway.

Rickards's and Tucker's very different proposals for how to incorporate the
city-citizen matrix better into the governance of India are both argued in
detail, yet they are not acted upon. Instead, Mill's view that representative
institutions for India would simply not be possible is upheld, without further
elaboration. The question remains: why?

To understand the answer, I first need to show that Mill did not win the
argument as convincingly as this account might suggest. He did obtain the
unitary legislative council that he wanted for India – but not because his ideas
about mechanical governance and ruptural time had been universally accepted. Mill's ideal of government as a machine that would make a rational and
ruptural break with the past to clear away the corrupt despotism of India was
not necessarily shared by men whose faith in reason and science was more
cautious.

98 *Authoring the codes elsewhere*

Governance as a machine?

The metaphor of the government as a machine was something new, an idea that had emerged with the Industrial Revolution's faith in science. It would have been anathema to a late eighteenth-century sensibility that viewed government rather as an organic process. A generation of men who had been brought up in a more Burkean age frequently employed metaphors of machines breaking down or running out of control.

Macaulay, for example, worries that absent the governing structures of the Company then "the whole machine of state would stand still" (Macaulay, 1833). For Henry Tucker, the idea that governing the whole vast Empire could be done by one centralised body is "visionary and impractical": "The machine will be overloaded and will not move" (Tucker, 1833a: 344). Meanwhile, the prospect of government from a distance in London, abstracted from the everyday concerns of life in India, would, he states, "make us something like a steam engine, which the hand of the engineer is wont to stop or put in motion at pleasure [...] unlimited power without responsibility" (India Office, 1833c: 129). This is echoed by the Court of Directors, which worries about the Company being reduced to a "mere machine" (India Office, 1833a: 63). This is not to say that they reject the metaphor of government as a "whole [...] complex machine" (India Office, 1833c: 41), but they are wary of the dangers machines bring with them.

For Macaulay – *contra* Mill – representative institutions are desirable not because they function mechanically and make a rational break with a confused present. This is because reason for Macaulay is not a disembodied, ahistorical force, but rather an organic process, rooted in a particular history, that reminds us of the Burkean polity in which he had spent his whole life. British institutions, he says, are the product of "all our habits, all the reasonings of European philosophers, which all the history of our own part of the world would lead us to consider as the one great security for good government". If "[r]eason is confounded" in India, then it is not because there is no adequate machinery, but rather because history gives no guidance as to how to proceed: "We interrogate the past in vain" (Macaulay, 1833). Representative institutions are, by this account, the endpoint of a long history: a history that has evolved organically, accumulating wisdom through *time*.

Intriguingly, Holt Mackenzie, who played a key role in drafting the Charter Act, uses a tellingly different sort of metaphor to talk about governance: "to disjoin the several parts of government, in a country which is not self-governed, is like placing the different members of the body in the charge of different physicians" (Wilson, 2008: 134). Whilst Wilson claims that this is analogous to a mechanical trope, it is actually different in important ways. A body is a self-regulating system that grows, develops, heals and revitalises itself without conscious direction. This metaphor of the body bespeaks a sort of uneasy reconciliation between the two temporalities of Burke and Mill. On the one hand the body is a kind of machine: it is a self-regulating system that does not require conscious direction to function. On the other, it is fully organic: it grows, heals, revitalises itself and *develops*.

Macaulay and Mackenzie, then, are not uncritically accepting the need for a ruptural break, but are beginning to enunciate a new temporality. Rather than assuming, like Burke, that the wisdom that accumulates over time is specific to context and linked to the relationships that are understood to exist between the living, the dead and the not-yet-born, Macaulay is speculating about whether "our habits [and] history" might not be more widely applicable. The suggestion is there in Mackenzie's metaphor that the best mode of governing might be just as universal as the human body and its operations. However, this metaphor emerges at just the time when the political problem emerges that not all bodies are equal: some are constituted as free subjects who participate in their own self-government, whereas others – children, women, the poor, colonial subjects – require tutelage, discipline and training (Foucault, 1991f). For colonial subjects (alongside children) in particular, they need to grow up and be educated before they can be entrusted to make the free choices that will enable them to govern themselves. This will entail leaving behind the private sphere of the nursery and entering into the public sphere of rational men.

India and the public sphere

Just as two very different conceptions of time that we saw above were being articulated onto each other in this period, so were the different ways of thinking about the public and the private.

Macaulay's answer to the question of why India cannot have its own representative institutions can be discerned in his qualified defence of the highly participatory, negotiated judgements that form the uncodified common law in England. These are still just about tolerable in a country like Britain:

> where there are popular institutions; where every decision is watched by a shrewd and learned audience; where there is an intelligent and observant public; where every remarkable case is fully reported in a hundred newspapers; where, in short, there is everything to mitigate the evils of such a system.
> (Macaulay, 1833)

This is a vision of representation and the familiar institutions of liberal democracy as "protective" against tyranny (see Held, 1996: 78–99). Democratic engagement depends upon the existence of a clearly defined "public". Representative institutions can be understood as the linking technology, or means of making legible and aggregating, the interests and opinions of the population. Something important has changed here: this is a different view of the public from the localised negotiations characteristic of Burke.

The faith in the importance of the existence of "a public" pervades the political discourse surrounding the negotiation of the Charter Act. For

100 *Authoring the codes elsewhere*

example, there are only two very serious sticking points on which the Company and the government cannot agree by the summer of 1833. One of these is a quibble about money, but the other is the Company's insistence that they should be able to seek "publicity" in Parliament in case the government asks them to implement a decision with which they disagree (India Office, 1833c: 57; India Office, 1833a: 24–26). Charles Grant, whilst he disputes the necessity for any special arrangements, does not disagree in principle, he merely reminds them that they already have the right to petition Parliament and thereby seek "the judgement of the Legislature and the arbitration of public opinion" (India Office, 1833b: 28).

However, the problem of "absolute government" means that a participatory system of law, justice and dispute resolution in *India* "is a scandal and a curse". This is because despotic rulers cannot set their private interests aside from their objective public duty. Their lack of ability to act in the proper ethical manner means that they will make capricious judgments. Worse, the failure of a public ethics and accountability more generally implies that a rational, objective public will not subject them to scrutiny. In India, the trouble is that there is "no public" (Macaulay, 1833): only a messy and indissociable chaos of contending private interests compounded by a lack of publicly accountable good manners. It is through the practice of comparing a freely governed Britain with a despotic India that the importance not only of correct manners in public but also of a completely separate private sphere emerges. Thus, the superiority of the separation of public and private spheres characteristic of liberal democratic governance becomes an important feature of British identity through an othering practice that invokes India.

To see how widespread this way of thinking was becoming, it is informative to look at John Wade's *Extraordinary Black Book*. This was a pro-reform text that articulated the cause of reform and the construction of a more representative and inclusive public sphere with patriotism and national pride. The popular appeal of the text, which comprised a collection of essays on all the major institutions of the day and presented the case for reforming them, is evidenced by the fact that it was used as a script from which activists made public speeches as the debates about the various pieces of reforming legislation took place (Tony Taylor, personal communication).

Not a radical text – it endorsed the property qualification on suffrage – it nevertheless advocated representative institutions and claimed that at home the Reform Act would produce for the first time "a national government responsible to 500,000 electors, every one of whom has an interest in domestic peace, order, and prosperity" (Wade, 1832: 607). The book is critical of the East India Company and current governing practices, particularly perceived abuses of property rights in India, but the solution it offers is a tellingly domestic one:

> Such improvements in the national representation, as would insure an honest and enlightened government, would render unnecessary any great

changes in the scheme of our Indian administration [...] [P]rovided that the people of England had an adequate control over [government ministers in charge of India], there would be little risk of misgovernment, either in Great Britain or her great dependency [...] Hence, the happiness of the vast population of Hindustan, no less than that of the United Kingdom, is identified in the great question of parliamentary reform.

(Wade, 1832: 418–419)

This is a wonderful example of the boomerang effect of colonisation. The author implies that India has no public and therefore must be represented by Britons. This makes the case for the expansion and consolidation of the public at home even more acute, so that India can be well governed. The dangers embodied by the other thus contribute to the urgency of securing a representative public at home.

Furthermore, though, the danger of a private sphere that emerges ungoverned into the public is here viewed as particularly emblematic of Indian governance: "disposition to pervert justice [...] is the great political vice of the East." Again, however, this forms the basis for understanding the virtues of British society:

Corruption will never triumph over true patriotism – a mock representation over one that is real – private interests over the public weal – a mere faction over the king, his ministers, the public press, and the nation!

(Wade, 1832: 608)

British identity itself, through an othering of India, is articulated and defended in a narrative that advocates not good manners and the constant negotiation of relationships, but rather the side-lining of such concerns into a private sphere. "Private interests" and the relational ties of the "faction" are no longer understood to be the legitimate stuff of politics.

It is important not to over-simplify. This is a complex change in ways of thinking that came from many directions and had many causes. What it is possible to state, though, is that one of the means by which the superiority of the public–private divide could be established in contemporary discourse was by comparison with an inferior India: this might remind us of just the way British liberal democratic practices are legitimated now. Yet only 50 years before, Company officials had assumed that Indian modes of governance were entirely appropriate for India precisely *because* no strict division between the public and private existed.

Technologies of representation

Macaulay and Grant are less sanguine than John Wade about the ability of the British public to represent India. Whilst an all-male Parliament could represent women, whose interests were understood to be bound up with theirs

102 *Authoring the codes elsewhere*

at the private, domestic level of the household (Wade, 1832: 602; Held, 1996: 97–99), the British Parliament was too far from Indians to be a "faithful representative": parliamentarians had not the time, the inclination, the knowledge nor the correct incentives to solve Indians' problems rationally and well (Macaulay, 1833).

Thus, they devise the ingenious solution of using the Company, that anomalous accident of history, which does have the necessary closeness to Indian affairs, and "binding up [their financial] interests with the country they are to assist in governing" (India Office, 1833c: 57). Nor, it should be noted, is this an entirely unsuccessful endeavour at the level of the workings of the technology, so to speak. As early as July 1833, when directed to appoint an additional bishop, the Court of Directors responds that, "convert[ing] the Natives to the Christian faith […] is undoubtedly an object most interesting to the civilized world, but it is one for which it cannot be right to tax the Natives" (India Office, 1833a: 66). The bruising lesson of "no taxation without representation" in the colonies may have already been learned, though not in a guise recognisable to twenty-first-century democracy promoters. Highly exclusionary, and unaccountable to Indians, the Company nevertheless provides India with a representative institution of sorts.

The beauty, though, of pinpointing the reason why India cannot have its own representative institutions so specifically and concretely is that there is now plenty to do. If a public sphere does not exist, it can be created through time, development and maturity:

> I see the public mind of India, the public mind which we found debased and contracted by the worst forms of political and religious tyranny, expanding itself to the just and noble views of the ends of government, and of the social duties of man […] Consider too, Sir, how rapidly the public mind of India is advancing […] It may be that the public mind in India may expand under our system till it has outgrown that system.
>
> (Macaulay, 1833)

This future-oriented project implies certain quite specific interventions: notably for Macaulay the spread of education and a free press. It is thus of great *use* in deciding what to do and orienting attitudes towards the future.

What India needs, then, is entry into a teleological history of civilisation: note the language of "advance", "expansion" and "growth". Bringing together the ideas of a European present that is constructed historically from the ties and accumulated wisdom of the past, and the urgent need to contain what is understood as a despotic barbarism, Macaulay employs the novel language of "civilisation" to suggest that British history might be an example of a general history. Macaulay's preference for English-language education, too, is based on a teleology for India that is expected very closely to mirror actual British history. He poses the following question when defending a preference for teaching Indians using English texts to ancient Indian philosophy:

Authoring the codes elsewhere 103

[H]ad [our ancestors] confined their attention to the dialects of our old island, had they printed nothing at the universities but chronicles in Anglo-Saxon and romances in Norman French – would England ever have been what she is now?

(Macaulay, 1835)

Thus, India is expected to travel the same historical path to develop its own public sphere and separate autonomous, private sphere that would contain and power the economy.

The legacy of 1833

Democracy promotion in what is now Pakistan, then, did not begin in 1945 with the concrete negotiations around decolonisation. This is not to say that there was any intention to promote democratic institutions in India in 1833: at least not in the immediate future. As we will see in more detail in the next chapter, the reforms that were put in place on the contrary functioned to limit political participation by creating a separate private sphere in which the workings of economic, social and family life would be confined, away from intrusion by government.

However, the conditions for the possibility of liberal democratic governmentality were put in place by these reforms; for the first time in the Empire, a form of rule was instantiated that, it was hoped, would enable the management of whole populations. It would function according to general rules, abstract principles, the creation of distinct social categories, and the delineation of separate public and private spheres. These features would have been unimaginable as "good government" to the vast majority of British or Indian people just a generation before.

The law in India was never fully codified, despite the best efforts of an enquiry led by none other than Thomas Macaulay. However, the impulse to produce written codes and categorisations has proliferated ever since, and many of the legislative codes that emerged in the nineteenth century remain on the books of South Asia today (Kolsky, 2005: 638). As James Mill hoped, codification in India also provided something of a model for London. Indeed, in 1877, James Fitzpatrick Stephen was invited by Parliament to bring to bear his experiences in India on the ongoing problem of codification in Britain, as London was felt to be developmentally lagging behind Calcutta in this important endeavour (ibid.).

Meanwhile, in the same period as the Charter Act, we also see the beginnings of Utilitarian ways of knowing at home, marking a break with the old affective modes of governing based on continuity and personal ties, *after* this break had occurred in thinking about governing in India. In 1833 the Royal Society of Statistics was founded in London in order better to understand "others" like the poor, women, the insane and colonial subjects using these sorts of abstract, governmental techniques, so that the population could be

104 *Authoring the codes elsewhere*

managed, fostered and made healthy (Royal Statistical Society, n.d.). The Society's founding members included Thomas Malthus and Charles Babbage, who brought to bear their experiences as tutors at Haileybury. Only a year earlier, a Royal Commission was established to investigate the workings of the Poor Law that had been in place since 1601. The Commission, much influenced by the Utilitarian ideas of Bentham, Mill and Malthus, sought to understand the problems of domestic poverty by creating abstract categories of people (the aged, the infirm, children, able-bodied men, able-bodied women, the deserving and undeserving poor). They furthermore located responsibility for poverty firmly in a private sphere of work, economic activity and family life (Carabine, 2000).

The precise links between these new ways of knowing in Britain and modes of governing in the Empire are worthy of much more detailed research, but what is clear is that the modes of governmentality that emerged in British India quickly made the reverse journey to effect an "internal colonisation" of othering processes.

What I do not want to do here is to posit 1833 as an alternative ruptural moment. As we have seen, the teleological resolution that emerged in response to the clashing temporalities of British and colonial forms of government contained many continuities with the past, just as it transformed our orientation to it. Nor – despite my obvious preference for a more relational, negotiated, narrative and historicised approach to democracy – would I wish to idealise the period leading up to the 1830s, which – as we have seen – was patriarchal, hierarchical and in many respects extremely exclusionary.

I do, however, want to use it to suggest that there was nothing natural or inevitable about the changes that did take place. Rather, the very narrative of "progress" as a natural and inevitable process itself emerged as a form of temporal othering which served an important purpose in the historical moment in which it arose. It served to legitimate ruling practices at home by drawing on, but also transforming, notions about temporality and history in ways that were rather contradictory. Political community had been understood in the eighteenth century as the outcome of the accumulated relationships and wisdom of the past, but this had never, until now, been viewed as a teleological process. The encounter with India, however, transformed ideas about British institutions, which were now seen as an idealised endpoint and a projected future for the Indian other, even as an encounter with that very other was transforming British governance in entirely novel ways. The present in India would now be found wanting in comparison with an imagined future with idealised European institutions.

It became possible to understand civilisation – a new concept at the time – as a process inaugurated by the division of the public and private spheres emblematic of the story of the savage's entrance into history. This marked a new way of thinking about India, which – unlike the New World – had hitherto been considered a separate polity in its own right and not a land of savages. This change in modes of thinking was furthermore understood to entail the need for detailed intervention. The future trajectory that India was now to be guided through might be understood to look a lot like Britain's history, but only by virtue of changing dominant narratives about what British history had been, what it meant and how it related to the present and the future. Thus, in a sense – in Britain and in Pakistan – the codes we all still inhabit were authored, at least in part, elsewhere.

5 Blood in the codes
Liberal governmentality, democracy and Pakistan

To paraphrase Michael Shapiro slightly, even to speak of Pakistan is:

> to license a forgetting of the history of struggles through which such entities have come to be domesticated within modern international space. Such a forgetting is not a psychological but a textual phenomenon, for it is a scripted or institutionalised forgetting.
>
> (Shapiro, 1989: 15)

In this chapter, I examine those struggles.

In researching and writing this book, a question that has often arisen in conversation and questions is how far I am able to account for the complex and different postcolonial trajectories of India and Pakistan, in which India is understood as "the world's largest democracy" and Pakistan as its undemocratic other. There is a literature on how a colonial history has led to very different types of regime in India, Pakistan and Bangladesh: for example, work by scholars as diverse as Maya Tudor (2013), Ayesha Jalal (1995b) and Matthew Nelson (2011). I agree with Jalal and Nelson that there is not a simple dichotomy of democratic and authoritarian rule in these countries, but rather complex patterns of different kinds of governance at a range of levels. Nevertheless, an understanding of India as a successful democracy and a foil to Pakistan is ingrained in common-sense understandings of the region (Mohan, 2007).

My aim is not to revisit those debates, but rather to unearth the conditions of possibility for their thinkability by examining the logic of Partition. In doing so I make two related, overarching points. First, the emergence of Pakistan in 1947 did not inaugurate democracy there for the first time. Rather, the British had already been promoting liberal democratic institutions in what is now Pakistan for a long time. Indeed, as we saw in Chapter 4, the beginnings of such institutions have their roots as early as 1833. Thus, the struggle of British Indians for representative institutions was already coded through a logic of democracy promotion: nationalist campaigners demanded representative institutions because colonial ways of thinking had enabled an understanding that that was what democracy *was*, even though politics in the

Blood in the codes 107

subcontinent had not been understood in these terms prior to the colonial encounter.

Second, I argue that violence did *not* erupt in British India in 1945 because of the failure or absence of democracy, but rather because violence was inherent *in its very practice*. Representative institutions, broadly understood, provoked the violence by constituting two communities, understood to be separate, in the first place. This separation was made possible by a rigid division of social life into public and private spheres that would have been entirely alien to late eighteenth-century Indian jurisprudence.

The argument I make here about violence is extremely important because one of the great selling points of liberal democracy is that it is understood to be a *remedy* for violence. By talking and by voting, it is thought that citizens can resolve their differences peacefully. Thus, when Larry Diamond talks about military coups and democratic breakdown in Pakistan, he pins the blame on the *failure* of the specific institutions of liberal democracy, such as the justice system and the rule of law (Diamond, 2008: 58). By implication, the function of all the institutions of liberal democracy is together to prevent violence, and violence will only ensue if they are not working. This assumption about democracy's role in *preventing* violence is also inherent in Democratic Peace Theory: the theory – supposed to be the nearest thing we have to an empirically provable "law" in International Relations – that democracies do not fight each other (Russett, 1993). This is assumed to be because the peaceful norms of tolerance and rational discussion, eschewing violence, are understood to be incorporated into the Foreign Policy of states in their dealings with one another (ibid.; Owen, 1994). Democracy is understood as the *opposite* of violence.

Naturally, it is well known that in some highly divided societies, democracy is not able to prevent conflict and that majoritarian voting systems may even provoke it (Huntington, 1968; Chua, 2004; Hawksley, 2009). Thus much effort has gone into designing institutions that would minimise this risk (Lijphart, 2004). Nevertheless, this understanding does not cover the possibility that the logic of representational democratic practice *creates* a divided society in the first place, by constituting divisions amongst people. It is the latter claim that I make here, and I suggest that it should give us pause.

The argument in this chapter will proceed in three main sections. First, I will trace the emergence of a separate Muslim identity as it was enabled through British colonial practices of representation. Second, I will explain how an election was in particular responsible for the disaster of Partition because of the representations it produced and enabled. Finally, I will briefly bring the story up to date, showing that the representative institutions and practices inaugurated by colonial rule and democracy promotion continue to have a malign effect on Pakistani politics. It is worth noting that although this chapter aims to link the events of 1833 and 1945–47 with the present, it does not provide an exhaustive history of the years in between which would fill many volumes. Rather, it is my intention to license a remembering of the

108 *Blood in the codes*

struggles that have constituted Pakistan. In doing so, I disrupt the story we tell of ourselves about colonialism, rupture and the failure of peace because of the absence of democracy, and show that the structures of colonial governmentality are still felt in Pakistani politics to this day.

Coding religion

First of all, we need to explore how the constitution of a separate Muslim identity was enabled by British colonial practices. In doing so, I will take seriously Ian Hacking's suggestion that "[t]he bureaucracy of statistics imposes not just by creating administrative rulings, but by determining classifications within which people must think of themselves and the actions open to them" (Hacking, 1991: 194).

Of course, Hindus and Muslims existed in India before the arrival of the British. They understood themselves as having a religious identity and made legal judgments according to the dictates of their religion. However, religious commitments had existed alongside customary and tribal practices (Nelson, 2011), ties between people of the same class, linguistic and spatial communities, and intricate webs of patronage and loyalty that had always been accompanied by mutual interaction and dialogue (Khan, 2008c: 20–22; Sen, 2006: 16–25). It is likewise notable that Hindus as well as Muslims offered their loyalty to the Mughal Emperor, religion not being seen as the only defining element of political life, but rather one element in its complex negotiations (Dalrymple, 2006: 12). The pre-colonial workings of local law and jurisprudence had never worked according to a strict separation of Hindu and Muslim law, but rather relied on the resources of both and were continually adapted to meet the demands of a specific present, rather than relying on adherence to ancient texts (Wilson, 2008: 84).

With the new forms of colonial governmentality introduced by the British in the early nineteenth century, however, religion became a particularly important category. This was because – as described in Chapter 4 – the British were both keen to govern according to local customs and traditions, and also deeply uncertain about what these were. Consequently, great epistemological hope was invested in religious categories. Religious laws and customs were known to exist. Thus, by concentrating on them, East India Company servants hoped to discern a set of procedures by which they could govern.

This focus on religion had three related consequences. Let us look in a little more detail at each of them in turn.

Codifying identity

First, religion came to be the chief defining characteristic by which subjects could be known and could know themselves. As particular communities were understood to have the right to be governed according to their own traditions, the colonial state took a particular interest in how Hindus and Muslims respectively constituted themselves as separate groups abiding by different rules. The usefulness of this sort of sociological category for the British has been extensively discussed by Bernard Cohn (1996), who shows how – through myriad technologies including legal codes, the army, the collection of statistics and census data and so on – the colonial state was able to manage the population through practices of enumeration and bureaucracy. The existence of religious categorisations also enabled the establishment of communal leadership figures understood to speak for, or represent, that whole community (as defined by the census): this representational technology supported colonial rule, then, by working through the participation of the governed populations.

Muslims and Hindus were also understood to have emerged out of quite separate histories: James Mill's book, for instance, divides the history of each into separate volumes (Mill, 1858). This assumption of a long-standing historical division is reflected in the anxious search for a set of written legal principles for each group, which tended to focus around a search for the "pristine" ancient texts that would reflect practices that had been stable for thousands of years and could yield an original source on which to base legitimate law (Wilson, 2008: 93). The notion of the ancient civilisation of India, which was historically Hindu, sat alongside a narrative of Muslims as relatively recent conquerors whose rule was in decline.

Meanwhile, extensive questioning at the various select committees in the early 1830s was not only organised around the specific religious and legal practices of Hindus and Muslims, but also the differences in character, population distribution and proportions of each group in the employment of the British administrative system (House of Commons Parliamentary Papers, 1831d, 1831a, 1831c, 1831b, 1830b, 1830a). Understandings of India as fundamentally divided into Muslims and Hindus are shared by thinkers as different as Robert Rickards, James Mill, and conservative Company Director Henry Tucker.

The impact of ideas about governance as analogous to the running of a machine also intensified the drive to categorise populations. Nowhere was this more true than in the part of the world that is now Pakistan. When the British finally took over the Punjab and Sindh in the 1840s, the annexation of this territory created a huge administrative problem for the British, bringing the familiar characters of the local barbarians: "a wild martial people", who had to be pacified (Stokes, 1959: 243). In response, John Lawrence set up the "Punjab system of government":

> Control was achieved on the best Benthamite principles – personal responsibility, accountability and inspectability. A rigid system of recording and reporting was enforced [...] The union of all judicial and executive authority in the hands of a single officer might seem to give him well nigh arbitrary power, but [...] he was obliged to adhere to a rough code of criminal and civil law.
>
> (Stokes, 1959: 245)

110   *Blood in the codes*

Benthamite or not, the civilising and disciplining of the Punjab and Sindh by the British was attempted through an almost frenetic mapping, surveying and documenting, the filling in of standardised forms, which went into setting out the categories by which Punjab could be governed and discerning how the local population fitted into them (Nelson, 2011: chapter 1).

Codifying the law

Second, the codified law itself became a key principle of politics in a way that it had not before. The point of all this careful categorisation was the aspiration to master the uncertainty of how to govern in India for once and all, by writing down some abstract principles. As has been established, the intention was to "uphold native institutions and practices as far as they are consistent with the distribution of justice to all classes" (Lord Dalhousie, Governor-General of India, quoted in Nelson, 2011: 17), but only insofar as these could form a stable and rational set of general principles. However, it is important to note that stable and rational general principles were themselves unfamiliar to Indian jurisprudence. W.H. Rattigan, attempting to codify property law in Punjab in the late nineteenth century, was still of the opinion that, "Indian customs are of a very flexible and bending character" and did not easily admit of general rules (quoted in ibid.: 309, n.11).

Matthew Nelson is absolutely right to suggest that particular laws, such as the disinheritance of women, were not "merely a legal fiction invented (or exaggerated) by an array of inflexible imperial jurists" in colonial Punjab (Nelson, 2011: 32), but rather emerged from accounts taken directly from local people. Nevertheless, his claim leaves out something important, which is that a particular fixed principle that women could not inherit property would have been unintelligible in local traditional law, which was rather "rooted in a complex, practical understanding of the specific context the dispute emerged from within" (Wilson, 2008: 169). The resolution of disputes would, in this way, entail a good deal of detail about ties of family, kinship and would take the form of complex negotiations. The emergence of general abstract rules to the effect that women did not have the right to own or inherit property in India (House of Commons Parliamentary Papers, 1830a: 38, 68; Mill, 1858: 248) – which would have surprised Edmund Burke and the Begums of Oudh, and is contrary to the provisions of Muslim *shari'ah* law – did not so much reflect local customary norms, as ossify a principle that would previously have been negotiable.

One important consequence of this is that it altered conceptions of how the law related to everyday practices. The legislative framework of the state became the main arena for political contestation: the goal of state activity, in other words, was to produce a positive body of legislation. Thus the everyday power relations of kinship, say, that might have been negotiated in court on the basis of a complex set of local and specific circumstances, instead became invisible to the law.

Blood in the codes 111

Thus, whether the law is made by democratic representatives or by unelected administrators, law in this sense functions *tactically* in two related ways. First, the law positively and actively regulates the conduct of conduct. It does so not least by reproducing those categories and abstractions that enable concepts like family and kinship to be understood, often reanimating them in new ways. Therefore, inheritance patterns already existing in nineteenth-century Punjab were made intelligible by reference not only to similar patterns the British had observed elsewhere in India but also to entrenched ideas about what constituted a "property right" that could be inherited in the first place. The result of this encounter, as I show in more detail below, was paradoxically both to preserve existing power relations, but also to transform them. Indian men not only maintained but also strengthened their claims to cultivate the land in preference to women. Furthermore, they also obtained new claims to benefit from its commodification: specifically, the right to mortgage it.

Second, the law functions negatively. The whole business of politics is understood to be reducible to the question of lawmakers "[attempting to] transform local economic and political demands into new or more appealing laws" (Nelson, 2011: 5). This is a rather common way of thinking about what the job of democratic politicians is. It establishes the legitimate sphere of contestation as legislative activity in the public sphere, whilst marginalising and privatising concern with other relations of power away from the democratic domain. As such, then, we can think of law as a depoliticising tactic.

Although an abstract approach to the law was new, this did not mean that local people did not take up these discourses and use them for their own ends. Indian resistance to British rule was, on the contrary, regularly articulated around demands for a uniform, textual criminal law and equality under it (Kolsky, 2005: 682). Thus, Indian resistance to colonial rule began to take on a distinctively liberal flavour, as local people participated in the new discourses enabled by novel modes of governing. This impacted significantly on the types of institutions that were ultimately demanded and acquired by the struggle for Indian self-rule, and to understand this it is important to return to the topic of the public and private spheres.

Public and private coding

Third, religion became not only a defining category, but also a key arena in which Indians had some autonomy. Rammohan Roy, known as the "father of modern India", argued in the 1830s that "ancient" Indian (Hindu) society had been governed by a fixed, stable and written set of rules (Wilson, 2008: 167), a proposition which would have been unimaginable a few years earlier. He furthermore suggested that society had at that time been characterised by a "sphere of unfettered social conduct autonomous from the dangerous and corrupt realm of power politics" (ibid.: 168). He used this argument to contest the colonial legislation against *sati* – despite being vehemently opposed to

112   *Blood in the codes*

the practice – on the basis that it was an illegitimate intrusion of the state into the private sphere of family and religious practice. As such, he was appealing to liberal ideas about a separation of public and private spheres which would have been entirely incompatible with earlier forms of dispute resolution in their emphasis on negotiation rooted in all the detail of domestic and familial ties (ibid.: 84). Roy was strategically using the space carved out by the codifiers who, according to Elizabeth Kolsky, were from the outset keen to make a distinction between a public sphere in which crime would be punishable and commercial contracts enforced, and a "private sphere of difference". It was by means of the creation of this private sphere that Indians were subject to their own religious or customary norms in matters of family and faith (Kolsky, 2005: 637, 660).

This is a notion that clearly informs John Lawrence's vision for Punjab of "a country thickly cultivated by a fat, contented yeomanry, each man riding his own horse, sitting under his own fig tree, and enjoying his rude family comforts" (quoted in Stokes, 1959: 244). Although the image functions through an idealisation of a romantic past, it was also radical in its utopianism and modern in its individualising logic. It aimed at the delineation of a gendered private sphere, untouched by all that Benthamite bureaucratic control, in which the concerns of family and domesticity could be managed by the male head of household. Not a description of an existing situation, this seeming nostalgia is a future-oriented project.

The project was the creation of a separate economic sphere of activity and regime of private property, understood as independent from government intervention so that freely choosing landowners would maximise their revenue and create wealth that could be taxed. As a revenue manual in 1844 put it, "the first step [...] towards the creation of a private 'right' in land [...] was to place such a limit on the demand of government as would leave to the proprietors a profit which would [...] constitute a valuable [right]" (quoted in Nelson, 2011: 15).

Thus, the threefold logics of the proliferation of categories, the codification of previously unwritten law and the delineation of hitherto inseparable public and private spheres intertwined and enabled Indians to think quite differently about how to govern. Two communities were now understood to have emerged from two different histories and religious traditions. Importantly, these histories were taken to be antagonistic because Muslims were understood to have conquered a much older Hindu civilisation. Two communities were rigidly categorised and expected to abide by the laws of their own tradition, in a world where the law was now framed in abstract general rules that formed the key arena of political contestation and which were governed at first by unelected British administrators. Thus, quite logically, Indians started to campaign for the right to play a role in making those rules: legislative power had become, as they say, the only game in town.

In the meantime, however, the newly created private sphere had become the one arena for autonomy and self-government that Indians did have. Thus, from Roy onwards, this division was not only accepted, but vigorously defended. Roy's conception of an autonomous civil society can be discerned

Blood in the codes 113

in Mohandas Gandhi's notion of *"swaraj"* (self-rule), for instance, which advocated dismantling the bureaucratic apparatus of the state – a "soulless machine" (quoted in Singh and Sundaram, 1996: 167) – in favour of village-level organisation, self-help and community support. Again, the paradoxically modern discourse of referring to an ancient, idealised past is remobilised against British interference, precisely by invoking the private sphere that colonial power had done so much to create.

Sir Alfred Lyall (former Lieutenant Governor of the North West Provinces and Chief Commissioner of Oudh) sardonically remarks in 1910: "thus we have the strange spectacle, in certain parts of India, of a party capable of resorting to methods that are both reactionary and revolutionary [...] preaching primitive superstition in the very modern form of leading articles" (in his introduction to Chirol, 1910). What is important to note here is that *both* of these methods would have been unimaginable in late eighteenth-century India, where appeals to a primitive past would have been perhaps yet more alien than reading an editorial. The division of society into public and private spheres, with democratic institutions like a free press functioning as a link between the two, was re-written as a crucial aspect of Indian history and identity. As ever, then, forms of resistance are highly delimited by the relations of power in which they are intertwined.

Gender, the law and the private sphere: coding inheritance

To give another example of how these three logics of categorisation, legal codification and the delineation of public and private spheres worked in practice, it is useful to look in a little more detail at the disinheritance of women that took place in rural Punjab under British rule.

It is difficult to know just how decisions were made about who should cultivate the land in Punjab prior to British annexation. However, it is certain that there was no such thing as a legally enforceable property right that entailed, for instance, the ability to sell or mortgage the land. This is not to say that no one had previously had the right to cultivate particular areas of land to the exclusion of others in pre-colonial Punjab. However, the right to cultivate land, the right to inherit it, the right to sell it and the right to borrow money against it, these had not been thought of as bundled together into a single "right to own" it (Nelson, 2011: chapter 1).

Rather, an emphasis seems to have been placed on keeping the land under the cultivation by families – or the *biraderi* – who resided in the village, *including* widows and women who had married endogamously (staying within the village). Thus, rather than a regime of private property rights, there was a complex set of negotiations about who would cultivate the land, based on detailed knowledge of circumstance and kinship, which were not conceived of as private matters beyond the purview of the courts. Rights of cultivation might, for example, especially for women, be in the form of a "lifetime interest" rather than any right to bequeath or sell it (ibid.).

114 *Blood in the codes*

The colonial governors did not arrive with the intention of transforming property relations. However, they did arrive with a set of assumptions – provided by their own experience and set out on those ubiquitous bureaucratic forms – that private property rights of the type described above must exist in an abstract, enforceable and – above all – stable sense. The problem was not framed in terms of asking how private property rights might be established; rather, administrators wanted to know who already owned the land.

However, this turned out to be an extraordinarily complicated question: Matthew Nelson quotes reports of British administrators on the annex of Punjab having to march villagers in and order them to lay claim to the land. This happened because they recognised that land ownership would lead to taxation, but had not yet discovered the benefits of private ownership in a British regime and the access to credit and, sometimes, legally enforceable sale that it implied. This situation changed rather quickly, of course, as some of the opportunities offered by the British property regime were rapidly grasped in the Indian population, leading to some rather dramatic changes of reports of custom, ownership and practice the next time the land was surveyed, much to the consternation of the administrators, who were expecting to find sets of stable practices (Nelson, 2011: 37–41, 53).

British attempts to codify property law had a particular impact on women. As the British continued their detailed work of recording, codifying and abstracting, village by village, Indians provided information about ownership and inheritance practices, not according to religious law, but rather the structures of tribe, or *biraderi*, that already prevailed in that area (Nelson, 2011: Chapter 1). These practices seemed to the British rather similar to Hindu inheritance practices they believed they had encountered elsewhere, with their prohibition on female inheritance.

This had consequences that had by no means been the intention of the British colonial governors. First, the law that ended up on the statute books related to tribal, rather than religious, custom and practice. This was not a matter they found particularly troubling, as they intended to refer initially to local custom and practice whatever that might be. However, it did have concrete consequences. First, contrary to some claims that, as we have seen, are still made about *shari'ah* law, its adoption would in fact have significantly *advantaged* women. Second, though, the new regime of property rights did have communal consequences. Mortgaging land and risking its loss to (Hindu) urban moneylenders had never before been an ordinary practice. Nor, when that option was introduced, did it work in the rational way expected. It had been anticipated that landowners would borrow to invest in their land and increase its value. However, there instead transpired a worrying tendency to spend the loans on such things as expensive weddings and other status symbols. This created a political crisis, as British administrators worried in the late nineteenth century about a "crisis of rural indebtedness" that might cause loss of land that had been cultivated by particular families for centuries, rioting and huge rural poverty. The crisis was only exacerbated by a concern that rural Muslim landowners were falling into debt to urban Hindu moneylenders, causing worrisome social antagonism (Nelson, 2011: Chapter 1). This is an antagonism, furthermore, that has to be understood alongside all the other myriad ways in which Muslim and Hindu identities were set against each other as never before.

To recap, then, the colonial state did not invent the two religious groups: Hindus and Muslims. However, as part of an ongoing process of managing uncertainty, colonial governors categorised individuals, codified the laws by which they lived and created a separate private sphere. Indians in the Punjab and elsewhere took advantage, as they could, of the novel practices of the British to consolidate and transform their existing claims to land to their own perceived advantage (short or long term), all of which altered relations between the genders, between families and between religious groups. Overall, the creation of particular categories of difference between religions did not help the British produce knowledge that could describe Indian society. Rather, it dynamically produced and reproduced the practices of religion, *biraderi* and gender that divided society, in ways that offered important resources not only to help the British solve their epistemological problems, but also to enable Indians to resist colonial rule.

Coding Pakistan

We will next move on to how these new demands for the democratic right to formulate the law played out in the Indian struggle for self-determination. In this section, we will – necessarily rather briefly – remember those struggles to show how they were structured by colonial ideas about governing and democracy. There are very many good histories of the Indian nationalist movement, the debates over the creation of Pakistan and the eventual Partition, and it is not my intention here to provide another one (for example, see Khan, 2008c; Jalal, 1994; Talbot and Singh, 2009; Wolpert, 2006, for a variety of perspectives and approaches). Instead, the point is to show in a focused way that the violence of Partition and the beginnings of democratic self-rule were not ruptural, but rather were produced by and continuous with the representational practices of colonialism.

The people of British India, of course, did demand the liberal representative institutions characteristic of some parts of Europe as early as the 1830s. This was partly as a function of the demand for greater autonomy in the private sphere that emerged with a particular Indian liberalism. However, following the final violent overthrow of the last Mughal Emperor – the last visible rallying point for earlier modes of governance – in the rebellion of 1857 or, perhaps, the "First War of Indian Independence" (see, for example, Dalrymple, 2006 for a vivid account), resistance to British rule also became a matter of obtaining representation through liberal democratic legislative institutions.

Through political parties, campaigning organisations and the relatively free press, India's nationalist movement gradually fought for and won increasing

116　*Blood in the codes*

political representation. With the Indian Councils Act 1892 (House of Commons Parliamentary Papers, 1892), a limited number of Indians could vote for their representatives for the first time, and the franchise and scope of Indian democracy was expanded, following Indian demands, in subsequent reforms in 1909 and 1919 (House of Commons Parliamentary Papers, 1909, 1919). Despite some resistance to these moves in Britain (see, for example, House of Commons Parliamentary Papers, 1918), British administrators also found the ability to gather information through electoral processes *useful* in governing the population. For example, in early twentieth-century Punjab, it was agreed that the best way to confirm and ratify local attempts to codify (and preserve) the bafflingly diverse practices of property ownership and inheritance was to put it to a "majority vote" (Nelson, 2011: 74).

Thus the introduction of democratic practices is best understood not as a process of the gradual ceding of power in the face of principled resistance. Rather, the very resistance itself was produced by the structures of colonial power. Indian nationalism enabled the emergence of the freely choosing subjects who could ensure that liberal democratic governmentality could function. This is not to downplay the courage or sincerity of those who struggled for years in the Indian movement for self-determination, but to suggest that this is an example of what Foucault calls the "strategic reversibility" of power relations: "the ways in which the terms of governmental practices can be turned around into focuses of resistance" (Gordon, 1991: 5). Power – rather than violence, or oppressive force – *requires* individuals who are free to act in one way or another. Nevertheless, although this means that there are always new opportunities for novel resistance, and the position of subjects in the field of power may very well change (British rule is transferred to Indian voters), power relations will not cease to carry their history with them. This is evident when we look at the history of the emergence of a Muslim majority state called Pakistan.

Voting for Pakistan

The *usefulness* of electoral practices can be seen perhaps most evidently in the important general election in India that took place in 1945–46:

> how best to find out, at the end of empire, who to hand over power to? [...] For those engineering the transfer of power, in keeping with the British ideal of democratic decolonisation, the answer was an Indian general election [...] It was most useful to the British government who needed to rubber stamp any future constitutional settlement.
>
> (Khan, 2008c: 30–32)

The contest was thus quickly understood as a plebiscite on the constitutional future of British India after independence, and local leaders immediately understood that their strength in the contest would determine their negotiating position in regard to the final settlement, particularly whether India would be divided. No province was more important than Punjab in this process: without Punjab there could be no Pakistan (Talbot, 1980: 65; Gilmartin, 1998: 420).

It is easy now that the entity called Pakistan is such a taken-for-granted feature of our international scripts, to imagine that the election result in Punjab was a foregone conclusion. The separation and distinctness of Muslim and Hindu populations was inscribed everywhere in the colonial system: separate canteens at railway stations and separate drinking taps co-existed with an official calendar that revolved around separate holidays and festivals. Government censuses, statistics, maps, rule books and the law all relied on the notion of completely distinct religious communities (Khan, 2008c: 20–22). Most importantly of all, on the basis of Muslim demands that – again – would have been unthinkable a century earlier, the reforms of 1909 and 1919 introduced Muslim-only electorates and quotas for seats. From now on the two religious communities would also have their "own" political parties and politicians (Das, 1964).

Nevertheless, there was nothing inevitable about the Muslim League victory in 75 of the 85 Muslim seats. On the contrary, only in 1937 the Punjab Unionist Party, which appealed to tribal ties of *biraderi* and gained votes across communities from Hindu and Sikh, as well as Muslim, agriculturalists, had won a convincing majority in these seats. By contrast, the Muslim League had fielded only seven candidates and won just two seats (Talbot, 1980: 65). What changed in 1945–46?

As David Gilmartin has convincingly shown using the pamphlets and posters from the 1946 elections in Punjab, the existence of separate electorates was crucially important. However, his most startling insight is that it was "not only that they were *separate* but also that they were *electorates* that defined a new form of public arena" (Gilmartin, 1998: 418). In other words, not only the specific voting system in place in Punjab, but also the very logic of electoral democracy itself was crucially important in the election result that inaugurated the violent partition of British India. This was because of the way that quantification simplified and divided up a complex set of ideas and preferences.

I am particularly concerned here to show how the structure of colonial elections produced and interacted with three interlocking elements of Muslims' resistance to British rule. This interaction, I suggest, produced particular tensions between liberal democratic practices, military rule, Muslim nationalism and the politics of *biraderi* that are characteristic of Pakistani governance even to this day. First, the existence of Muslim seats produced an othering practice: Hindus were identified as foreign in ways that shored up a Muslim identity. This discursive othering relied on the threat of Muslim disunity in which "collaboration" with Hindus – long the absolutely normal everyday way of living – was seen as a particular threat. Second, and relatedly, this othering practice depended upon a narrative of Islamic history as

118 *Blood in the codes*

one of the coming of unity, which brought with it a particular conception of time. Third, the articulation of these two elements depended upon, and reproduced, the existence of separate public and private spheres. Let us look in a little more detail at each in turn.

Coding Hindus: electoral practices and foreign policy

First, then, the structure of the electorate into separate religious blocks meant that Jinnah's All-India Muslim League was competing for votes with other parties seeking to appeal to Muslim voters. This meant that the opposition, by and large, were other Muslims. Thus the Muslim League was forced overtly to campaign on the basis of a Muslim identity defined in opposition to British and Hindu "others" that, by the same token, they produced. Both the British and Hindus were cast as oppressors, adversaries and even enemies of Muslims, and they were linked in the electoral rhetoric: voters were asked "whether they wanted to trade slavery to the British for slavery to the Hindus" (Gilmartin, 1998: 421). Activists were furthermore encouraged to go to villages, find out what the local social and economic grievances were and – whatever the matter – give the solution: "Pakistan" (Talbot, 1980: 75, 79–75, 80). By suggesting that Pakistan would be both Muslim and independent, campaigners articulated social and economic problems with two linked sources of domination: the Hindus and the British (Gilmartin, 1998: 421).

The Muslim League campaign also drew explicitly upon Islamic identities: they recruited the influential *pirs* (holy men in the Sufi tradition thought to be descended from saints) to their campaign, used mosques as campaigning centres, attended Friday prayers and held election meetings directly after-wards, as well as parading with the Holy Qur'an and asking voters to pledge their support on it (Talbot, 1980: 77). These sorts of direct appeal to religious identities and values constituted an "excruciating choice" for male agri-culturalists. The choice seemed to be, on the one hand, "voting with their purse strings", that is voting for the Punjab Unionists who favoured tradi-tional practices, particularly of inheritance, associated with *biraderi*-based loyalties. On the other hand, they could vote in accordance their religious commitments, which included some rather more generous terms of inheritance for women (Nelson, 2011: 110).

So far so unsurprising, but what is less expected is that a rather different "Other" is invoked even more prominently in the election literature: "the specter of internal dissension and disorder among Muslims themselves" (Gil-martin, 1998: 422). In particular, the Unionists' politics of the *biraderi* were characterised as divisive, putting ties of family and neighbourhood above an over-arching Muslim solidarity. Crucially, the Muslim League linked the Unionists to the two external enemies, Hinduism and colonial rule: Jinnah suggested that they were "the primary enemy [...] backers of *naukarshahi* (oppressive bureaucratic rule)" (quoted in ibid.: 423). In another poster, they are accused of preferring to work together with "bigoted sectarians and

Mahasabhites [the Hindu nationalist movement]" (ibid.). Division *amongst* Muslims, then, is understood to be linked to British strategies of divide and rule, which privilege narrow interests and loyalties, as well as collaboration with future Hindu oppressors, over a broader Muslim solidarity. Thus, although not yet formally a nation, the structure of separate electorates enables the Muslim League to identify internal threats to a solidaristic Muslim identity and make them foreign, linking them discursively to the supposedly external threats of Hindu and British domination. This move then legitimates a separate Muslim nation, by constructing threats to it as alien forces alongside which it is impossible to live.

The stories Muslims told of themselves

Within this othering narrative about Hindus, and the British, as foreign oppressors, second, a particular vision of history prevails. The feared disorder, confusion and divided loyalty amongst Muslims is linked to the time of "*fitna-i-jahiliyat*", or ignorance and moral chaos, before the coming of Islam (ibid.). Gilmartin describes a poster telling the story of Musa (Moses) and Harun (Aaron) from the Qu'ran in which Musa returns from receiving God's covenant, having left Harun in charge, and is furious to discover the people have started to worship a golden calf. Asking why he had failed to put a stop to this, Harun replies that he had not wanted to cause division; the poster uses this story to suggest that division is even worse than idolatry (ibid.: 426).

Although, this cautionary tale is set in the ancient past, its invocation is clearly rooted in the present, with division, disorder and, pointedly, cow worship articulated in opposition to the moral clarity of a unified submission to God. This intervention creatively marshals and rearticulates the discursive resources of the British narrative of a pristine ancient *Hindu* civilisation that had slowly degraded over time, as well as a reminder of Mill's ruptural, eschatological time. Even the name Pakistan (literally "land of the pure"; Khan, 2008c: 39) resonates with the pristine connotations of *swaraj*, but reinvents it not as a legitimation for a free India but rather for a separate Pakistan.

However, the future-oriented and utopian narrative of *Pakistan* as a solution to all contemporary problems and a symbol of unity that would overcome the dangers of *fitna* roots the community in a linear temporal trajectory in which they are moving together towards an imagined future. This temporality is reminiscent of the teleologies of civilisation and thus rather different from traditional, cyclical Muslim conceptions of time in which key events from the life of the Prophet would recur and form the basis of an ongoing struggle (Gilmartin, 1998: 433). This rewriting of history, then, is made possible by the colonial temporality of civilisation. Thus a temporal othering is adopted and re-inscribed. Now it is cow worship and dissent that are understood to be features of an undesirable past, legitimating a future-oriented project in which Indian Muslims constitute a unified nation: Pakistan.

120   *Blood in the codes*

Public and private coding (again)

Third, these two related modes of othering are appealed to in terms of a clearly delineated public and private sphere and the freely choosing subject of liberal democratic governmentality. Voting is characterised as an individualised activity in which every citizen must interrogate his or her own private and equal conscience before casting a vote. This vote, by aggregating the private passion, faith and commitment of those thousands of individual consciences, would constitute a transcendent, honourable and unified Muslim community in the public sphere: Pakistan (Gilmartin, 1998: 430).

Thus, the constitution of the public sphere is made possible through making legible the interests and desires of freely choosing, fully constituted individuals in private. The structure of the election reinforced this public/ private dichotomy: although religious symbols were certainly mobilised, it was forbidden to suggest that any particular choice of party or candidate was divinely sanctioned. This would count as "corruption" under electoral law (Gilmartin, 1998: 428). Thus, religion is understood as, first and foremost, a private and individualised matter.

The Muslim League made full use of individualised understanding of the Islamic faith, by putting forward their vision of a Pakistan made up of the sincere, combined individual will of free voters as an attractive alternative to the hierarchical and collective politics of *biraderi*. Jinnah declared that voters should "vote according to the voice of your conscience; give your vote without fear to those candidates to whom you *want* to give your vote" (quoted in Gilmartin, 1998: 429), thus attempting to delegitimise a vote for the Unionists, who made appeal to the traditions of *biraderi*, not faith.

In practice, electoral politics regularly operated through "matters of [...] connection, questions of family relations and disputes of faction". However, it was precisely these sorts of divisions that were understood to reside squarely in the private and domestic sphere and had no place in the idealised public domain of the utopian, idealised Muslim community (Gilmartin, 1998: 434). Thus, the claims of the Unionists were marginalised on the basis that they were engaged in a type of collective politics that simply had no place in the public sphere. This now-familiar strategy is a common means of using liberal democratic structures to rule certain issues out of contestation, as the Archbishop of Canterbury found out in 2008. That this technique can be used both to marginalise a discussion of *shari'ah* law in twenty-first-century Britain and to marginalise opposition to an independent Muslim state that would live by the provisions of *shari'ah* law in the twentieth, shows the flexibility of this strategy of power – its contingency, but also its pervasiveness.

The election in Punjab was won by the Muslim League. The specific discursive strategies that enabled this victory were premised on the technology of an election. That is to say, a negotiation premised on more deliberative and less quantitative techniques would have played out very differently. That is not only because the structure of the electoral system meant that Muslim identity itself became a salient issue. Also, and more importantly, the delineation of public and private spheres meant that individuals could be encouraged to set aside their complex relational identities and instead consult their individual preferences not only as Muslims, but also as *voters*. This stark individualisation was the culmination of many years of the forging of separate and individualised subjectivities through colonial representational practices. The consequences of this severing of a complex, relational, multi-layered subjectivity in favour of a privatised individualisation that prioritised a religious identity were dramatic and catastrophic.

Violence and Partition

The historian Yasmin Khan argues that a vote for the Muslim League in 1945–46 was often viewed by voters themselves as an expression of a desire for protection for Muslim rights and solidarity with a broader Muslim community, rather than any explicit desire for a separate Muslim nation-state (Khan, 2008c: 38). Whilst elections aim at making private interests legible in the public sphere, there is often more than one reading available: "The British thought in terms of territory. The grey margins between territorial nationalism and other forms of patriotic, emotive expression – not so easily linked to land – remained imperial blind spots" (ibid.: 39). Not natural and inevitable, but rather produced by the contingent intersections of local and colonial power, Pakistan would be created as an independent nation-state after independence.

The tragic violence that accompanied Partition resulted in the loss of perhaps a million lives (estimates vary wildly, but see Khan, 2008c: 6; Tunzelmann, 2008: 265), along with systematic terror and torture. It was a violence that was horrifically gendered. As is not uncommonly the case (Okin, 1999), women's bodies were understood as vessels for religious, and therefore national, identity, by virtue of their role in giving birth to and educating future generations within the sacrosanct private sphere of the home. Women were repositories of national identity, guardians of the private sphere of religion, family, kinship and honour, from which the nation drew its power and identity. Their public violation, brutalisation and murder were ritually coded in quite specific ways.

Systematic rape was widespread and at times accompanied rituals of forced religious "conversions". Women were abducted, killed, and their bodies mutilated or sold on "flesh markets" (Khan, 2008c: 69, 76, 134). The slogans "*Jai Hind*" and "*Pakistan Zindabad*" ("Long Live India/Pakistan", still shouted every day at the Wagah border that separates and links Indian and Pakistani Punjab) were frequently branded on the faces and breasts of women and girls, so that those who survived would be symbols of terror, the new nations of South Asia literally inscribed on their bodies (ibid.: 134).

122 *Blood in the codes*

Liberal democratic beginnings

In another sense, though, the violence of partition failed to effect a rupture: if British shepherding of India towards freedom and democracy had had catastrophic consequences, Pakistan's new leadership still nevertheless celebrated liberal democratic ideals. In common with others who have noted the propensity of electoral practices to flare into violence (such as Chua, 2004), Mohammed Ali Jinnah's response, in the midst of the crisis, was to propose more thoroughgoing liberalism.

Indeed, Jinnah's inaugural presidential address to the Constituent Assembly of Pakistan on 11 August 1947 contains several echoes of Macaulay's words on the Charter Act more than a century earlier. Like Macaulay, he begins by suggesting that the new state of Pakistan is an anomaly: "there is no parallel in the history of the world" (Jinnah, 1999). Thus ruling out any appeal to – or analysis of – historical continuity that might form the basis of a critique of liberal democracy as a mode of governing Pakistan, he draws instead upon the history of Britain as a model to which to aspire. This is framed specifically in terms of religious identity and draws upon familiar notions of progress:

> The Roman Catholics and Protestants persecuted one another [...] The people of England in course of time had to face the realities of the situation and [...] they went through that fire step by step. Today, you might say with justice that Roman Catholics and Protestants do not exist; what exists now is that every man is a citizen, an equal citizen of Great Britain and they are all members of the nation.
>
> (Jinnah, 1999)

Regardless of the dubious merits of this historical characterisation of Britain (more on this in Chapter 6), what Jinnah is referring to here is not the desire to eradicate religious belief and practice, but rather the continuing ideal of a separate private sphere in which religion is a matter of the "personal faith of each individual", which has no bearing on their "political" life as "equal citizens of the state".

Alongside the hope for "progress", Jinnah also re-affirms the arena of legislative and electoral politics as the key legitimate terrain of contestation: "the first duty of a government is to maintain law and order, so that the life, property and religious beliefs of its subjects are fully protected by the State" (Jinnah, 1999). This invocation of the protective role of government, enabling individuals to associate and accumulate property in the private sphere, then, rearticulates the concerns of colonial governmentality as well as prefiguring the efforts of democracy promotion in the years to come.

A democratic Pakistan?

In the narrative of the Muslim League in the 1946 elections, we saw appeals to a national unity and homogeneity, which denied claims to particularistic

Blood in the codes 123

loyalty and disavowed local power relations. These founding narratives of Pakistan can be traced through the country's subsequent long periods under military rule (Gilmartin, 1998: 435; Jalal, 1995a). It is through a similar narrative of a broader national interest that the army still legitimises its position as a ruler capable of behaving rationally and instilling the order and discipline alongside a commitment to national unity and homogeneity, still highly valued in a country where identity constitution is generally articulated around the identification of an other which is Indian (Cohen, 2004: 93). Meanwhile, the constant refrain that the country's civilian leadership are "squabbling politicians" (see Masood and Rosenberg, 2011; Sethi, 2012a; *The Economist*, 2011), also characterises them as corrupt: incapable of putting aside the petty disagreements and personal interests that should rightfully belong in the private sphere. I suggest that this is not because of a *failure* of liberal democracy in Pakistan. Rather, the way Pakistan has had liberalism coded into its very constitution from the beginning has depoliticised everyday power struggles in ways that have been deeply unhelpful to its politics.

However, in contemporary Pakistan, the possibilities for contestation in this public sphere are even further severely curtailed by two intersecting logics that take the law to be fixed in advance. For Muslims in Pakistan – as Matthew Nelson has shown – the law is understood to be already fixed in advance by the provisions of the *shar'iah* (Nelson, 2011). Meanwhile, the efforts of democracy promoters are curtailed by an understanding that various legal provisions – particularly a given conception of inviolable human rights – are also non-negotiable.

Returning to the specific issues of tribal ties, the politics of the *biraderi,* and related gender inequality, in Pakistan these remain profound concerns. They are understood by practitioners of Democracy Promotion as a way of inhibiting genuine public democratic participation. Attempts to cast the politics of kinship and tribal loyalty into a private sphere so that they would not taint the public process of elections in 1946, and the subsequent enactment of *shari'ah* law with its more generous provisions for women, did not eradicate the customary practices of *biraderi*: on the contrary, they remained "exactly the same" (Nelson, 2011: 111). Thus, as Nelson has shown in detail, local power networks now focus their efforts in electoral politics on getting leaders elected who will enable them to evade the provisions of the law, particularly in terms of women's inheritance, rather than engage in making new law (ibid.).

For the purposes of Democracy Promotion, the crucial difficulty with this is that it means votes are controlled by the collective, rather than the result of individual decision making. This is perceived to corrupt the whole process. The Department for International Development (DFID) is concerned that "[s]ocial hierarchy and power structures [by which is meant 'tribal' organisation] especially in rural areas strongly shape the numbers and types of voters" (DFID, 2006a: 9), and its country governance analysis states that:

> it is the patronage of local leaders rather than responsiveness to public opinion that generates votes for mainstream parties. Thus for the

124 *Blood in the codes*

majority, electoral choice is less about selecting a suitable representative than a means of purchasing goodwill and services from their customary leaders.

(Coffey International Development, 2011: 5)

Here we have another attempt to police the divide between public and private: patronage, goodwill, local affective ties of responsibility and obligation, duties of kinship, family and honour are illegitimate concerns in an election, belonging as they do in the private sphere. Instead, what needs to be established is "public opinion", so that a representative can act effectively as a legislator, re-enacting the transparent will of the public in a fully legible code of law.

If elections are a problem in this context of the collapsing division of public and private, however, the solution turns out to be: elections. The policy recommendations in this report strongly privilege "refreshing the electoral system", including "using elections" to highlight issues of legitimacy and "shape a democratic process that offers real potential for positive change" (Coffey International Development, 2011: 9–11). Understandings of local politics, then, continue to be articulated around the assumption that freely choosing individuals are able to leave the intertwined power relations and hierarchies that structure their everyday lives in the household and community behind them as they fulfil their idealised and individualised duty in the polling station, making legible their individual interests as though they could be abstracted from the private sphere power relations.

They cannot. The assumption by democracy promoters (local and international) that the everyday negotiations of kinship, religious duty and gender relations are only relevant to democratic contestation insofar as they can be codified by elections into individualised/totalised public opinion and translated into rational legislation paradoxically *creates* an undemocratic situation. These collective norms are simply wished away in an insistence on more elections as a solution to the problem created by the very logic of the election and the public–private divide that it inaugurates. Crucially, what is never up for democratic contestation is the very division into public and private on which liberal governmentality depends and which it constantly reproduces.

This chapter has linked the story of the emergence of colonial governmentality, which we saw in Chapter 4, with contemporary practices of Democracy Promotion. Along with Chapter 4, it has left very little of the story we tell of ourselves about democracy still standing. To recap, we have seen that liberal democracy is not a guarantor of women's rights against a violent Islamic *shari'ah* law, but rather in Pakistan has been the opposite. We have seen that democracy is not the remedy for violence, but rather that its very individualising logic can be violently divisive. We have seen that the inauguration of national self-rule in 1946/47 was not the rupture of colonial rule nor the beginning of Democracy Promotion in Pakistan, but rather entirely continuous with the structures of colonial representational governmentality in all its detail. We have furthermore seen that those structures continue to this day with consequences that remain depoliticising. The only rupture we have seen in these two chapters has arguably been the one that took place in the early nineteenth century. This was a rupture that appeared to sweep away forever the narrative, relational, contextualised political ethics, which brooked no sharp divide between the public and private, that had existed in both Britain and India.

6 Twelve months that shook the world
1989 and the Salman Rushdie affair

> [T]wo images – the burning book in Bradford, the crumbling wall in Berlin – came in the following years to be inextricably linked in many people's minds.
> (From *Fatwa to Jihad: The Rushdie Affair and its Legacy*, by Kenan Malik. © Kenan Malik, 2009, published by Atlantic Books Ltd)

In Salman Rushdie's 1983 novel, *Shame*, the narrator says that: "[E]very story one chooses to tell is a kind of censorship, it prevents the telling of other tales" (73). Taking seriously this observation, in this chapter I want to ask what other stories a triumphalist narrative about 1989 has prevented us from telling about democracy and what significance they might have for our understandings of democracy promotion.

To start with the telling of a tale: Hanif Kureishi was a prominent supporter of Salman Rushdie (BBC, 2009) and his darkly comic novel *The Black Album* (1995) is a subtle and wide-ranging fictionalised account of the "Salman Rushdie affair". Written in the early 1990s, it is set in a 1989 in which the fall of the Berlin Wall and revolutions in the former Communist countries of Eastern Europe form a backdrop to a story of social dislocation and upheaval in London. In the novel, the "third wave" of democratisation is a matter of particular distress for Dr Andrew Brownlow, the "Marxist-Communist-Leninist" history lecturer, who develops a stutter in response. As one of his students describes it, "it come on since the Communist states of Eastern Europe began collapsing. As each one goes over he get another syllable on his impediment, you know [...] By the time Cuba goes he won't even manage [to say hello]" (Kureishi, 1995: 32). The joke about Cuba underlines the sense of teleological certainty that sooner or later (not "if" but "by the *time*") all Communist states will alight upon the end of history. For Brownlow, however, this collapse of former certainties does not lead to a new commitment to the values of liberal democracy. Rather, he involves himself in the campaign by a number of British Muslim characters against an unnamed blasphemous book, which is said to insult the Prophet Mohammed (ibid.: 169). For Brownlow, there is a clarity in the "combustible freedom" of the struggle of British Muslims (ibid.: 214–215).

Twelve months that shook the world 127

For Shahid, though, the principal character in the book and a young British Muslim student, the last thing 1989 seems to presage is any kind of clarity or certainty:

> He couldn't begin to tell the sane from the mad, wrong from right, good from bad. Where would one start? None of this would lead to the good. But what did? Who knew? What would make them right? Everything was in motion; nothing could be stopped, the world was swirling, its compasses spinning. History was unwinding in his head into chaos, and he was tumbling through space. Where would he land?
>
> (Kureishi, 1995: 220)

By unteasing these related logics of teleology and uncertainty, in this chapter I make four related arguments. First, I show that far from being a time when Britain was secure in its democratic identity by dint of having "won" the Cold War, 1989 was a time of great uncertainty, in which a new "foreign" other appeared to emerge for the first time: the British Muslim. Second, I suggest that such understandings are a form of democracy promotion which asserts the value to liberal democracy of a free press in a public sphere unencumbered by censorship. This argument is heavily reliant on an understanding of earlier arguments about the repressive hypothesis of power and a division of public and private spheres. It may be best read in conjunction with Chapter 2. Third, I show that Muslims who supported banning or censoring Salman Rushdie's *The Satanic Verses* were accused of being foreign, undemocratic, misogynist and violent, and that these characterisations are difficult to sustain. On the contrary, as is now a recurring theme, the practices and institutions of liberal democracy were fully implicated in silencing certain forms of debate and objectifying women. Above all, the institutions of the liberal democratic state and society, such as the police and the free press, were engaged in vicious violence, casting radically into doubt the notion that democracy is the opposite of, or remedy for, violence. Finally, I argue that the usefulness of the "end of history" narrative during this year was primarily not because it described the present accurately. It did not. However, in a time of great uncertainty, it did provide a much-needed guide to future action. It may be worth noting that this is *not* a chapter about the philosophical issues raised by the Rushdie affair about free speech and its limits, secularism, religion and blasphemy (for a very good treatment of these issues, see, for instance Asad et al., 2009), but rather a specific discursive analysis of the modes of othering that emerged in 1989 in Britain.

The year that ended history?

1989 is an important year for the stories we choose to tell about ourselves, particularly when it comes to stories about democracy. As we saw in some detail in Chapter 3, 1989 heralded not only the "third wave" of

128 *Twelve months that shook the world*

democratisation (Huntington, 1991, 1996), but also – as Francis Fukuyama (1989) would have it – the "end of history". As one of the third wave of democratising countries, Pakistan seemed domesticated at this time in a way that it has not for a long time since. This was apparent particularly in the election of Benazir Bhutto, the world's first female Muslim leader, who was noted not only for her aspirations for the "creation of a democratic and free society", but also – as Baroness Ewart-Biggs put it in the House of Lords – for "fulfill[ing] her role as a wife, mother, politician and public figure with distinction and elegance" (Hansard, 1989e).

Pakistan appeared to have made its entrance into history right on cue, then, complete with a set of well-ordered gender relations in which a commitment to democracy and freedom went alongside an unthreatening, feminised version of Islam that was compatible both with a proper devotion to caring work in the private sphere and Westernised norms of appearance (for more on Bhutto as an idealised and gendered figure for democratic values in Pakistan, see Elliott, 2009). Whilst there was still need for development and "social reform" (Hansard, 1989e) in Pakistan, then, this seemed to be more in the way of continuing the historical progress of what was no longer "savage" than of taming and containing an enemy "barbarian". The British High Commissioner in Islamabad suggested that "the only issue causing me problems at present" (Barrington, 1989a) was the widespread offence and anger amongst Muslims at Muslim – and Indian-born, British novelist Salman Rushdie's novel *The Satanic Verses*.[1] As various documents obtained from the Foreign and Commonwealth Office (FCO) using the Freedom of Information Act reveal – many of them still tantalisingly redacted more than two decades later in the interests of "maintaining trust and confidence between governments" – the situation strained relations between Britain and Pakistan (FCO, 2012). This situation was, of course, deeply exacerbated by the Ayatollah Khomeini calling for a death sentence on Rushdie. Even more important, though, was the way that the perceived threat to the core liberal democratic value of freedom of expression seemed to create threats to national identity *within* the conventional borders of the UK.

Freedom of speech and the price of visibility

In a speech in Birmingham's Central Mosque on 24 February 1989, ten days after the Ayatollah Khomeini had issued his infamous *"fatwa"* inciting Muslims to kill Salman Rushdie, UK Home Secretary Douglas Hurd laid out to British Muslims why *The Satanic Verses* could not be banned under British blasphemy laws and appealed to them to renounce violence:

> It is not the job of ministers in this country to go about banning books. I tell you that very strongly. Once you start on that I promise you it is a slope you would regret having pushed us down.
>
> (Seton, 1989)

This was a speech that was particularly welcomed by the British High Commissioner in Pakistan, who felt that it was "likely to be appreciated by many Muslims" (Barrington, 1989b) and encouraged its dissemination in Pakistan; this appeal appears to be based on the explicit link made between the right of Salman Rushdie to publish his novel and the rights of Muslims to practise their own religion under the broader democratic category of the right to freedom of expression. Hurd explicitly spells it out:

> It is the law which permits freedom of worship for religious minorities [...] It is the law which punishes racial attacks and harassment [...] It is a shield and a refuge, perhaps more for religious and ethnic minorities than anyone else.
>
> (Hurd, 1989)

The choice that lies before British Muslims, by the British government's account, is that they might either accept the liberal rule of law that acted as the guarantee of their religious freedoms, or push for a repressive set of powers that might one day result in their own beliefs, practices and texts being outlawed.

As we saw in Chapter 2, liberal democratic governmentality operates with the notion that the state's role is to provide a guarantee for a public sphere free of censorship so that individuals can freely reflect on their interests and populations can become fully legible to governments. However, the sorts of things that are, or are not, sayable are constrained by the very flows of power that constitute the public space as neutral, secular, rational and divorced from the concerns of the private sphere. Thus, by assuming that if they are not actively – repressively – censored, then people have the right to say whatever they like, the repressive conception of power foregrounds coercive relations of censorship, but elides the productive power by which particular discourses become possible, particular arguments count, particular types of claim are taken seriously, particular stories are told.

It may be a fairly obvious point to suggest that the press do not present a neutral version of events and therefore that to enshrine the right to freedom of expression is not at all the same thing as equalising the relations of productive power. In other words, the right to speak does not imply the opportunity to be listened to, nor yet – as we saw in the discussion about the silent subaltern – that everything can be said. Obvious or not, when it comes to discussions about censorship, it is a point worth exploring here, because it illustrates how deeply the values of freedom of expression are implicated in the production and reproduction of existing power relations. British Muslims managed in 1989 to disrupt the relations of power that dictated that matters of religion should remain in the private sphere, lest they threaten the very secular edifice that protected those beliefs in the first place. To achieve this, however, they had to pay the price of being understood as *outsiders* or even enemies of that liberal state edifice.

130   *Twelve months that shook the world*

When news of the content of *The Satanic Verses* first became widely known amongst British Muslims, in December 1988, 7,000 people from all across Britain marched in Bolton to register their anger, an impressive display in a town whose Muslim population numbered just 10,000 (Malik, 2009: 4; BBC, 2009). No one paid any attention. The protest went unremarked in the press: the demands of British Muslims were therefore unrepresented in the national public sphere.

The protest that took place in Bradford on 14 January 1989 was different, however. Whilst news of the large march in Bolton did not reach me just five miles away in Bury, I remember watching television with my family, aghast at the images of a book on fire over the Pennines in Bradford. Kenan Malik claims that the book had also been burned earlier in Bolton, although this is difficult to substantiate, given the lack of press coverage, and the fact that he does not provide a reference (Malik, 2009: 4). What is certainly true is that the burning book created a story the press were eager to run. Furthermore, the leaders of the Bradford protests were more "media savvy" and somewhat better organised (Malik, 2009: 5): they understood that a burning book was a good story and that it needed to take place right in front of a journalist.

This leads to a rather entertaining story, related independently both by Liaqat Husain of the Bradford Council of Mosques and Peter Chapman, a journalist from the *Bradford Telegraph and Argus* newspaper, to a BBC documentary in 2009 (BBC, 2009). As Husain puts it, "[b]ooks are very difficult to burn": the whipping Yorkshire wind "kept undermining us". This was by no means a relief for Chapman, despite the fundamental importance of the right to freedom of expression for his trade and democracy more broadly, of which a free press is such an important part. Rather, he recalls saying, "[c]an you get on and do it so I can get it in the paper?" At his prompting, a helpful demonstrator ran to buy some paraffin. The pictures were quickly transmitted around the world and the rest is history.

The point is both that the press are fully implicated not in neutrally reporting the news but in subjectively in creating it, and also that what counts as a good story emerges from flows of power that far exceed any given instance. In purchasing and then setting fire to a bound set of printed papers, the demonstrators in Bradford were committing no crime. They were, however – several weeks before any threat to Rushdie's life – doing something astonishingly provocative. They were participating in a whole history of book burning that enabled them to claim visibility in a regime where visibility is all.

Thus, Salman Rushdie was able to say on 30 January on *Daytime Live* on BBC1: "There are laws in a civilised society that are not written on the statute books. The point is the burning of a book always means the same thing" (rebroadcast, BBC, 2009). The burning book in Bradford conjured up images of books being burned through history by past enemies such as Nazi Germany (*The Times*, 1989), Communist regimes (Garton Ash, 1989) and the Catholic Church (Sardar and Wyn Davies, 1990: 14–19). It invoked the very notion of a civilisation that had been struggled for against the forces of oppression, a democracy that had been wrested from numerous threatening others, a struggle for freedom of expression that saw Enlightenment texts prosecuted and books by free thinkers burned as "blasphemous" by the public hangman (Nash, 2007: chapter 2). Douglas Hurd makes explicit reference to this idealised history in his speech, remarking that freedom of speech and expression are "ideals to which the British people are firmly committed, and for which they have made many sacrifices over the years" (Hurd, 1989).

Peter Sissons perhaps put forward what is at stake here most clearly of all in a *Channel 4 News* broadcast on 17 February that brought him some fame: "[the freedom to express any opinion] is the *bedrock* of what we believe in just as the Qu'ran is the *bedrock* of what you believe in. If you offend against that, the offence to us is very great" (rebroadcast on BBC, 2009). In order to obtain the attention of the world's media, then, the Bradford demonstrators are in a sense *committing blasphemy* against that most sacred of Enlightenment – and Protestant – symbols: the book.

The protesting Muslims appear to be setting themselves against the liberal democratic values that are constitutive of being British: proclaiming their foreignness by disturbing the notional boundary that is supposed to keep religion in the private sphere. This is a forced move dictated by the very terms of liberal democratic neutrality. Because of the way that liberal democracy is understood to have emerged from a particular history of opposition to organised religion, religious claims are – on the face of it – questions of "personal preference and minor matters of conscience" (Sardar and Wyn Davies, 1990: 3), relegated to the private sphere. They can therefore be made publicly only at the cost of entering into an opposition to the liberal democratic order overall.

Indeed, Hurd may have been offering a form of advice in saying, "I have read the book. In my personal opinion it is not a great book" (Hurd, 1989). If Muslims had done the same thing to Salman Rushdie as the media had done to them in Bolton – ignored his book – it would have been read, in private, by a small and politically irrelevant readership. Public blasphemy against democratic values, he implies, is not the best way to obtain what they are demanding. His plea to Muslims, then, is to "express your protests, peacefully and with dignity" (ibid.), which appears to be a direct intervention against both the book burning and violent slogans that had been the price of their visibility. This shows a rather subtle understanding of the usefulness of relegating dissent to the private sphere, where it can be quietly ignored. As Sardar and Wyn Davies acidly remark, "you can have any belief you want, so long as it is not useful in negotiating the future of society" (Sardar and Wyn Davies, 1990: 12).

Foreign policy and civilisation

On the face of it, then, there is in 1989 a clear binary choice to be made, a choice that comes down to an acceptance or rejection of civilised British values and their insistence that religion, along with emotional and relational ties, belongs in the private sphere. The protestors in Bradford were described

132 *Twelve months that shook the world*

in Parliament by MP Tony Marlow as "alien people with little commitment to our country or way of life" (Hansard, 1989d), whilst the very citizenship rights of some of Rushdie's most stringent critics were also queried in Parliament (Hansard, 1989b).

For some this is an explicit question of pitting civilisation against barbarian outsiders. For the widely read and populist *Sun* newspaper, for instance, the very integrity of Britain is understood to be at stake. Alongside calls physically to deport those making death threats against him, they also seek to externalise the problem by focusing on Iran:

> If we allow a blood lust hooligan like [British citizen] Sayed Abdul Quddus [to] walk the streets, the Ayatollah will have beaten the British race more surely than if he had dropped an atomic bomb on Westminster.
> (Macdonald Hull, 1989: 9)

Note that democracy, as symbolised by Westminster is, as ever, at the heart of understandings about Britishness. Similarly the *News of the World* (the *Sun*'s then sister paper on Sundays) raises the stakes of individual Muslims breaking the law by inciting murder, such that it becomes not an individual instance of criminality, but rather a matter of national security and even survival: "Fanatical Muslims breaking the law must stop. Otherwise it'll no longer be Britain" (*The News of the World*, 1989c: 8). Elsewhere, specifically invoking the Second World War as "the last time Britain faced a wicked dictatorship", the *Sun* proposes that a bombing raid on Iran by the Royal Air Force (RAF) would be the most effective means to "persuade the Mullahs of the wrongness of their ways" (*The Sun*, 1989e: 6). Meanwhile, the externalised enemies of democracy are characterised as "medieval crackpots" (ibid.), bringing in a familiar temporal dimension alongside a distinction between Western rationality and Islamic insanity.

Outside the pages of the tabloids, a temporal othering is likewise invoked in the name of civilisation and democracy, with figures from the high-profile cultural commentator Melvyn Bragg to the heroic figure of Václav Havel proclaiming that Britain and the world could not be civilised if Salman Rushdie could not be free to express his opinions (Winder, 1989; Havel, 1989). Casting the protestors as the barbarian other of civilisation is the obvious corollary of this move, as happened most vehemently in the House of Lords when Lord Stoddart rhetorically asked:

> Is it not a fact that book burning, threats to publishers, threats to organisers of proper and legal meetings, and incitement of a mob to murder a fellow citizen is not Moslem fundamentalism; it is naked, brutal and primitive fascism?
> (Hansard, 1989c)

In this conflation of legal book burning and illegal threats and incitement, a primitive and violent imagined past and the more recent fascist (book-burning) others of Britain, he brings together a whole complex of fears.

Twelve months that shook the world   133

Malise Ruthven, former professor of Islamic Studies, wrote one of the first books to discuss the Salman Rushdie affair and, in an extract that seems to sum up the complex web of modes of othering that are circulating around the protestors, he opens with the following description of the large demonstration that took place on 27 May 1989:

> They came in their thousands from Bradford and Dewsbury, Bolton and Macclesfield [...] They wore white hats and long, baggy trousers, with flapping shirt tails. Most of them were bearded; the older men looked wild and scraggy with curly grey-flecked beards – they were mountain men from Punjab, farmers from the Ganges delta, peasants from the hills of Mirpur and Campbellpur. After decades of living in Britain, they still seemed utterly *foreign*: even in Hyde Park, a most cosmopolitan part of a very cosmopolitan city [...], they were aliens [...] they seemed like men from the sticks, irredeemably provincial.
>
> (Ruthven, 1990: 1)

The externalisation of these protestors is taking place on three inter-related levels, here. They are, first, "foreign" by dint of their backgrounds in Pakistan. Second, they are out of step with the times, harking back to a rural or traditional past that can be accommodated only uncomfortably in that icon of the disorderly post-modern, the "cosmopolitan city". This highlights the third mode of othering, which is to suggest that they are "provincial" – here, I mean not only that their concerns come from a distant, disconnected part of the world, but also that they are redolent of an English industrial past that is in decline in the face of modernising history. The northern mill towns of Bolton and Bradford seem to be as much an anachronistic relic of Britain's colonial past as the Empire that bought their products, and so too do the immigrants who came to work in their now derelict factories.

Such forms of othering populate perceptions of Bradford, the Yorkshire mill town that hit the headlines in January 1989. Although the 1991 census suggests that the city's Muslim population (which was overwhelmingly of Pakistani heritage) was significant but still very much a minority of around 13 per cent (Valentine, 2006: 9), Conservative MP John Townend caused consternation among anti-racist activists by stating that the city had become "another Pakistan" (Wintour, 1989).

The term "the Bradford book burners" quickly sprang up as a shorthand for the more provocative Muslim protestors, as epitomised by the Bradford Council of Mosques (see, for example Neuberger, 1989; *The Independent*, 1989; Rosenthal, 1989; *The News of the World*, 1989a: 8), whilst the *Independent* suggested that "[r]eligious trouble involving Islam always has the potential to become racial trouble. Ask Bradford" (Brown, 1989). Meanwhile, the *Sun* criticises a decision by Channel 4 to dedicate six hours of broadcast time to a dramatisation of the classic Hindu text *The Mahabharata* by speculating "it must have got them their highest viewing figures ever – in

134   *Twelve months that shook the world*

Bradford", adding that "not even the maddest mullah" in that city could have enjoyed it in its entirety (*The Sun*, 1989a: 17). Leaving aside a bizarre ignorance about the different religions of the Indian subcontinent, this intervention is particularly interesting for the remedy it suggests: "perhaps they could use it as a springboard for a series closer to home – about King Arthur or the Crusades" (ibid.). A reassertion of the more usual stories we tell of ourselves, then, is the remedy for foreign practices of thought.

Anxiety about the Muslim protests, then, became focused on Bradford as a site of foreignness threatening the very integrity of British borders with its spectacular propensity for seemingly barbaric behaviour. Bradford appeared to be located in a precarious position that seemed neither quite inside nor outside. This is an important point because it once again demonstrates that as concerns about identity became increasingly salient following the uncertainty provoked by the "end of history", the border between the UK and Pakistan is increasingly understood to be located not in airports or even immigration queues, but in the minutiae of daily life in the northern mill towns, including the shared history promoted by television broadcasts.

It is also important to note that whilst it took a death sentence from the Ayatollah Khomeini for the *Sun* to hail Salman Rushdie as a "genius" (*The Sun*, 1989c: 6), support for him was not always so wholehearted. A certain disapproval of bringing religion into the public sphere appears, at least for some, to apply to Rushdie as much as to his Muslim critics. Thus Geoffrey Howe, the Foreign Secretary, is able to state on the BBC World Service that "we understand why people of the Muslim faith, which we respect, resent what is said about their faith" (rebroadcast in BBC, 2009). Other politicians, including Prime Minister Margaret Thatcher, joined in this distancing from Rushdie, with Norman Tebbit (former Chair of the ruling Conservative Party and prominent ally of Thatcher) going so far as to call Rushdie "an outstanding villain" (Malik, 2009: 33). Whilst Kenan Malik views this reaction from British Conservative politicians as a lamentable moral quiescence to illiberal demands, in fact this ambivalence towards Rushdie is entirely in keeping with the logic of liberal democracy. Blasphemy, like religion, is a matter for the private sphere.

The consequence of this is that Rushdie is also caught up in the modes of exclusion circulating at the time. Geoffrey Howe suggests that "[Rushdie] is a man who comes from a world of which he was part [and therefore] must have known what would happen" (rebroadcast on BBC, 2009). Tebbit went on to ask: "How many societies, having been so treated by a foreigner in their midst, could go so far to protect him from the consequences of his egotistical and self-opinionated attack on the religion into which he was born?" (quoted in Malik, 2009: 33). This is an impression that appears to have been rather widespread, at least judging by Andrew Brown's observation in the *Independent* that:

> One has only to look at the Salman Rushdie jokes circulating to realise that the aspect of the affair which really appeals to popular humour is

Twelve months that shook the world 135

not that he is a writer, a blasphemer, or a standard bearer of free speech, but that he is a Pakistani of some sort.

(Brown, 1989)

This suggestion that Indian-born Rushdie is Pakistani would appear odd to any reader unfamiliar with the appallingly abusive racist term "Paki" – which might refer indiscriminately to anyone of South Asian appearance or descent – but the reference is immediately recognisable to anyone who lived in Britain in the 1980s. Rushdie, too, is cast as an outsider, a foreigner, from a separate "world" of Islam.

Democrats/Muslims

The binary opposition at the very core of the modes of exclusion we have explored was that between Muslims on the one hand, and committed democrats on the other. This distinction, however, was a deeply unstable one, even leaving aside the possibility that not all Muslims were involved in protests against the book. Although Salman Rushdie may have claimed that to burn a book "always means the same thing", there is good reason to believe that the meaning of book burning is deeply entwined with the context in which it takes place, as with any discursive performance. In general, the anti-Rushdie protestors' primary stated aim was to get the British law changed in order to widen the scope of blasphemy laws that protected only the Anglican Church, and to get the novel banned. It is worth noting at this stage that these blasphemy laws were far from anachronistic anomalies left on the statute by an oversight: calls to repeal them were regularly rejected during the furore (see, for example Patten, 1989), and they were used in 1989 to ban a film called *Visions of Ecstasy*, which was allegedly blasphemous against Christ (Nash, 2007: 4674).

Muslim lobbying on this matter took place in a number of ways. For example, as we have seen, large peaceful protests and marches were held throughout the UK, including the large "march on Downing Street" on 27 May 1989 (Ruthven, 1990: 1); petitions were organised, signed and sent to MPs (Wahhab, 1989b); public meetings were held in which the issue was put to the vote (Roy, 1989) and a new political party was even set up avowedly to provide conventional political representation so that British Muslims could press their claims (Wahhab, 1989a). Many protestors were furthermore keen to lay claim to Enlightenment and democratic credentials, brandishing banners that quoted Jean-Jacques Rousseau and George Bernard Shaw on the merits of Islam (Ruthven, 1990: 1). Shabbir Akhtar, from the Bradford Council of Mosques, is adamant, furthermore, that "[t]he book burning in Bradford was not Nazi style. We merely burnt one of Rushdie's books" (Lister, 1989). The book burning, in other words, takes place not as any attempt to institute an alternative, despotic form of governance, but rather as a deliberately shocking, yet entirely legal, performance within a much broader

136 *Twelve months that shook the world*

set of actions that demonstrate not only a deep understanding of the rituals of democratic representation, but also a genuine commitment to them.

Matthew Nelson argues, in respect of (liberal) democracy in Pakistan, that "[d]emocracy is not about supporting or avoiding ostensibly inaccessible laws. It is in fact about supporting or opposing the law – and, *if opposing*, seeking perchance to change it" (Nelson, 2011: 230). If that is what democracy is, then the actions taken by the Bradford Council of Mosques and other Muslim protestors are *quintessentially* democratic. It may be that many liberals would not agree with the changes to the law being proposed, but it is part of a commitment to democracy that one sometimes has to engage with others' opinions in an atmosphere of profound disagreement.

Curiously, though, every attempt by Muslim protestors to obtain democratic representation for their attempts to extend *already existing* blasphemy laws to cover their own beliefs met not so much with democratic engagement and debate specifically on the merits of this deeply felt issue, but rather with equivocation and the accusation that bringing this demand to the public sphere at all was in its own way undemocratic. For instance, Max Madden MP of Bradford West attempted to bring the demand to the House of Commons to be debated in the ordinary way. Not only could no parliamentary time be found for the debate, his proposal to discuss the matter in the primary democratic deliberating chamber of the land in order to "see what fresh initiatives can be taken to defuse this dangerous and difficult situation" is dismissed by the Leader of the House in the following terms: "The Government have made themselves very clear on this matter, and I am surprised that the hon. Gentleman phrased the question as he did" (Hansard, 1989a). The implication is that the matter is not up for debate.

The *Sun* newspaper, meanwhile, notes the reluctance of the Labour Party to condemn the protestors and sarcastically asks: "Why so coy? [...] Surely they can't be worried about the effect on the Muslim vote?" (*The Sun*, 1989d: 6). In a curious paradox, then, it seems that the legitimate debate of particular legislation and the public representation of particular voters and their stated interests cannot be allowed in the very name of democracy. Here we have a particularly clear example of the limits of democracy promotion: what is to be promoted and defended is implicitly liberal democracy, with its constitutive and necessary separation of the public and private spheres. This issue, because it is assumed to belong in the private sphere, is put beyond the reach of democratic contestation even as any kind of censorship is decried.

A further paradox is that the resistance that seemed to be posed within and to the liberal democratic state and its current system of law by Muslim protestors is not, on closer inspection, independent of that state itself. On the contrary, the very existence of a population called "British Muslims" who can exert themselves as a group is wholly dependent on the everyday practices of governmentality. In the 1980s, in an atmosphere of racial tension, mistrust and violence, the Conservative government operated through local authorities to fund particularistic civil society organisations, often based on narrow ethnic or faith differences, in order to draw people from ethnic minorities into the democratic process and develop a leadership with whom democratic representatives could deal (Malik, 2009: 58–71). One of these state-funded organisations, designed to be a "channel of communication" between Muslims and the local authority, was the Bradford Council of Mosques (ibid.: 73).

This pursuit of a politics of "multiculturalism", in which faith identities were particularly privileged, was fully implicated not only in managing communities, but also in *creating* attachments to particular kinds of identity, which were by no means inevitable. On the contrary, an attractive alternative source of identity in the 1980s for many Muslims and other ethnic minorities was the politically inflected identity, "black". This did not mean, as it does in the United States, people who could trace their heritage at some point to Africa. Rather, it was a self-consciously political call to arms, which attempted to bring people together in opposition to a state and society that was understood to be profoundly and institutionally racist, discriminatory and violent (Malik, 2009: 51).

The ultimate failure and eventual disappearance of this attempt to forge a solidaristic identity based on politics rather than faith or ethnicity was not only because of state-based multiculturalism, but rather owed something also to a disquiet around the flows of power *within* this movement. "Two of us were officially 'black'", says Karim, the narrator of Hanif Kureishi's *The Buddha of Suburbia*, "(though truly I was more beige than anything)" (Kureishi, 2009: 167), betraying an anxiety that subsuming a range of histories and commitments into a unitary politics might bring with it its own forms of oppression and exclusions. Without idealising this political alternative, however, it is important to note that:

> It is difficult to get the council's attention by insisting that your area is poor or disadvantaged. But if you were to say that the Muslim community is deprived or lacking, then council coffers suddenly open up – not because the council is particularly inclined to help Muslims, but because being "Muslim", unlike being "poor" or "disadvantaged" registers in the bureaucratic mind as an authentic identity. Over time, you come to see yourself as a Muslim [...] not just because [that identity] provide[s] you with access to power, influence and resources, but also because those identities have come to possess a social reality through receiving constant confirmation [...] It is how you are seen, so it is how you come to see yourself.
>
> (Malik, 2009: 69)

Not innocent of power, then, nor the neutral arbiter of demands made in the public sphere by individuals and groups who might freely associate in private, the liberal democratic state is fully complicit in the contradictory flows of power which both enable the creation of a British Muslim identity and then rule out of the public sphere the democratic demands made by this faith-based

138 *Twelve months that shook the world*

community, effectively censoring them. This leaves British Muslims in a painfully difficult position which has nothing to do with being for or against democracy.

Women's rights/Islam

A familiar set of anxieties can be discerned in Malise Ruthven's account of the large London protest against *The Satanic Verses* on 27 May 1989:

> the marchers suddenly saw a group of Asian female demonstrators holding aloft a banner proclaiming their membership of Women Against Fundamentalism. History does not reveal what taunts or jibes the women threw at the marchers [...] What is certain is that the Muslim psyche was bruised at a tender spot: relations between the sexes. Thereafter the organisers, the stewards and the police lost control. Muslim youths tried physically to assault the erring females. When the police went to protect them, they started a running battle.
>
> (Ruthven, 1990: 5)

The Asian women depicted here are perceived to be not "Muslim" themselves: women in all these accounts appear to be victims of Islam rather than practising Muslims.

The group Women Against Fundamentalism was set up by Southall Black Sisters and was actively interested in promoting a solidaristic "black" feminist identity in contradistinction to the more communal Muslim identity that was emerging so strongly through the process of these protests (Gupta, 2003: 17). Nevertheless, the fiasco of a group of white police officers protecting "Asian women" from "Muslims" seems an archetypal example of the colonial commonplace of "white men saving brown women from brown men" (Spivak, 1987). This episode draws on one of the most regular anxieties expressed about Islam, in 1989 as now, and as in colonial India: that it is a religion that is somehow inimical to the women's rights that have been hard won through the civilising process of history in Britain and other Western societies.

The *Sun* meanwhile, depicts the Ayatollah Khomeini in a cartoon as surrounded by women wearing veils: this cartoon shows him tearing up *The Satanic Verses* in a rage and the caption runs: "This is nothing. You should see him when he can't find his car keys" (*The Sun*, 1989b). The uncontrolled emotion in a domestic setting, with perhaps an undercurrent of domestic violence, hints at a gendered ordering at the centre of Iranian power which is out of joint and therefore laughable, whereas the outrage in the accompanying article is played absolutely straight. The Iranians, we are told, are men "*WHO* allow guards to rape girls in prison yet stone people for adultery; *WHOSE* teachings force women to wear veils and be treated like animals" (*The Sun*, 1989e: 6, emphasis in the original). Here, state and sexual violence, religious modes of dress and the policing of sexual behaviour are woven together in an intervention that seeks to externalise abrogations of "women's

Twelve months that shook the world 139

rights": the oppression of women is understood to be a matter that is *foreign* and it further underlines Iran's status as an enemy. Islam overall, then, is portrayed as a foreign, violently masculine and intolerant religion, without the gentlemanly restraint, the rational tolerance, or the autonomy and freedom for women of the implied self, the rational, democratic West.

How useful is this caricature for a feminist approach to democracy promotion, however? Many Muslim women and men, of course, strongly contest such caricatures and suggest that the practice of some more radical forms of Islam are particularly attractive to women because they encourage education and political participation for women (Mahmood, 2005), as well as opposing arranged and especially forced marriages (Malik, 2010: 45). In this way, women can escape some of the more patriarchal practices associated with the practices of the *biraderi*, which we encountered in more detail in the previous chapter.

Ruthven oddly compares Islam to Christianity by suggesting that the latter "gives some acknowledgement to the female principle in the Virgin", but suggests that "Islam tends to suppress it altogether" (Ruthven, 1990: 6). This is curious not just because Jesus and his mother, Mary, are key figures in the Qu'ran, but also because one of the particular scenes in *The Satanic Verses* that caused great offence took place in a brothel in which the prostitutes were given the names of the Prophet's wives. Whilst one might argue about the political usefulness of any of these figures for women's everyday lives in the late twentieth century, it is difficult to defend the view that the Virgin Mary is a more emancipatory figure than the Prophet's energetic and active wives, whose autonomy was far greater than would have been expected by the standards of their time. There is no particular reason to believe that Islam is *particularly* inimical to women and their rights.

Part of what is at stake, here, however, is as usual what counts as "women's rights" and how we might go about deciding. What is perhaps most pernicious about contemporary democracy promotion is that in comparing Islamic practices with those of the Western liberal democracies, the values of the latter are unreflectively upheld as an idealised model to which other societies should aspire. As Ruthven's remarks about Christianity – and the idealisation of Benazir Bhutto's Westernised gendered role as wife and mother – attest, we run the risk here of shielding liberal democratic practices from proper critical reflection if we divert attention onto the perceived oppressiveness of Islam.

To illustrate this, I want to look briefly at how the *Sun* newspaper, which was so angry in its defence of women's rights in Iran, saw fit to celebrate the much vaunted third wave of democratisation in Europe. Delighted to be witnessing the beginnings of a free press in the newly liberalising Czechoslovakia, the *Sun* prints a Czech-language edition, which is distributed amongst the pro-democracy protestors in Wenceslas Square. This is the newspaper's expression of solidarity with the activists, and it is keen to remind its British readers that by successfully obtaining liberal democratic reforms, Eastern Europe is entering "our world, the world of freedom", emphasising the familiar story that "Britain has a thousand-year tradition of democracy" (*The*

140   *Twelve months that shook the world*

Sun, 1989f: 38). Czechoslovakia, then, is becoming altogether more civilised and less foreign, a development that can only reinforce commitment to the UK's liberal democratic institutions.

The Czech edition is accompanied to Prague by none other than a "Page Three girl". Page Three, we may remember, is something of a dubious British institution: another immediately recognisable phrase, it denotes the young female models who pose topless on the third page of that newspaper – sold in every newsagent on the bottom shelf – each day. The triumphant victory of democratic values – which rely so heavily on the freedom of the press, for which reason Rushdie is so vigorously defended by the paper – are summed up as follows:

> For more than two decades, miserable Czechs have only been allowed boring Communist newspapers. Instead of reading fun-packed stories they had to wade through long tirades against democracy. Instead of Page Three the sour Soviets made them look at pictures of party bosses.
> (*The Sun*, 1989f)

The article is, of course, intended to be light-hearted, but nevertheless betrays rather clearly the terms of the status quo that democracy promotion upholds. Women's rights, here, can be read off from the dress code and a "free" and democratic society is almost parodically symbolised by the freedom, mainly, to take one's clothes off, especially if there is money to be made in the activity. There is no space here to discuss in detail the politics of wearing the veil for Muslim women, but in this context, one can perhaps feel much sympathy for those who assert that this decision is a self-confident feminist statement that disrupts the objectification and commodification of women's bodies (Ahmed, 2011).

The broader point is that whether it comes to political representation, violence, modes of dress, poverty, equality or respect, there is plenty to criticise in the liberal democracies when it comes to women's lives, and the pitting of democracy against Islam, as continually evoked by the image of white men protecting brown women from brown men, positively inhibits a genuine engagement with these issues by upholding existing freedoms as the best we can do. As ever, this is effected not least by the repressive hypothesis of power, which focuses the attention on "censorship" as the force that says "no" and therefore detracts attention from the flows of power that produce the sorts of things that *do* get printed as equally a matter for democratic concern.

Rationalism/violence

What may have appeared to be missing from my account up to this point is a robust condemnation of violence. After all, the anxiety provoked by book burning and the history that accompanies it is partly, but not only, that the regimes that once burned books often did not stop there. As Rushdie's supporter Lisa Appignanesi put it, "first the book, then the man" (BBC, 2009).

A condemnation of violence is not difficult to provide. The Ayatollah Khomeini's pronouncement of a death sentence against Salman Rushdie

Twelve months that shook the world 141

(along with a reward for carrying it out) was reckless and dangerous in the extreme. Salman Rushdie was put through many years of terror, humiliation and extreme inconvenience, when he had committed no crime. His colleagues were tragically yet more unfortunate: Japanese translator Hitoshi Igarashi was stabbed to death, and Ettore Capriolo, the Italian translator, was severely wounded in 1991, whilst in 1993 37 people died in Turkey in a fire that had been targeted at Aziz Nesin, the Turkish translator, who himself survived (Malik, 2009: 17). Also in 1993, William Nygaard, Rushdie's publisher in Norway, was shot three times and was seriously injured (ibid.: 15). These were each terrible acts, for which there can be no excuse.

Against this horrifying backdrop of violence, the UK's Conservative government of the time are rather to be admired for disdaining the advice of the *Sun* newspaper pre-emptively to send in the RAF against a Middle Eastern state, and rather expressing admiration for Islam and its enshrined values of tolerance and mercy (Hurd, 1989), providing police protection for Rushdie at no small state expense, and endeavouring to maintain some form of diplomatic channel of communication open with Iran, as well as with British Muslims (ibid.; BBC, 2009). The values of liberal democracy look rather attractive against the mob violence that might have directed itself against Rushdie. Indeed, as Peter Mayer of Penguin, Rushdie's publisher, put it when first faced with the distress caused by the novel: "One relied on the sanity of secular democracy – that people met together, discussed their differences and sorted them out" (quoted in Malik, 2009: 11). Democracy is again understood precisely as the remedy for violence.

A condemnation of violence is not difficult. This is probably why the vast majority of Muslims who were angered by *The Satanic Verses* did not resort to or condone violence, but instead – as discussed above – protested in legal and peaceful ways, using the democratic channels open to them. It is probably why polling suggested that less than 30 per cent of Muslims – even in a highly hysterical and polarised environment of great peer pressure and bravado – would at any point even *say* to a pollster that they supported the death threat, much less act upon it. Why such polling evidence was reported as "Muslims back Rushdie action" by the usually responsible *Guardian* newspaper is simply baffling (*The Guardian*, 1989).

A condemnation of violence is not difficult to provide. That is why it is so distressing, even after all these years, to read about the story of "Ramesh K" and his family, who were in 1989 hounded from their shop, livelihood and home as a consequence of a degrading series of violent, racist attacks, which resulted in broken bones and internal injuries as well as racist slogans and posters daubed on their premises over the course of two years (Rose, 1989). Mr K showed great courage and forbearance in continuing in his work: "We couldn't let them win. We could have put the shutters up, but they'd have said, 'yeah, we got the Pakis out'" (quoted in ibid.). The last straw came on 17 August 1989, when two men entered the shop and insisted that Mr K display a photograph of Salman Rushdie along with the slogan: "Rushdie in, Pakis out" (ibid.). "Would

142 *Twelve months that shook the world*

you stay there when you were getting attacked night after night?" asked Mr K (quoted in ibid.). Meanwhile, a Mrs Bagwell from the local residents' association and Chief Superintendent McLean of the Metropolitan Police were in agreement that the ongoing attacks were not racially motivated, but rather the result of a "personal vendetta", on the basis that when told to "fuck off", Mr K had the temerity to "tell you to fuck off right back", described by local police officers as an "attitude problem" on Mr K's own part (ibid.).

The detail about Salman Rushdie (perhaps) aside, this is not an isolated story. The depressing, relentless, quotidian violence faced by British Pakistanis in the 1980s is almost impossible to quantify, given the under-reporting that is hardly surprising in light of this kind of police response. However, there were 2,366 *recorded* racially motivated incidents in the UK in 1988 and the vulnerability of "Asians" in particular increased over the course of the 1980s, such that these kinds of attacks were understood by the Home Affairs Select Committee to be "a feature of the lives of Asians in Britain" (House of Commons Parliamentary Papers, 1989: v–vi). This is more vividly evidenced by Kenan Malik's memories of mobilising with other young British Muslims to protect vulnerable families in the face of police indifference. It is evidenced in the memories of anyone living in the northern mill towns in the 1980s, as I did, who will be fully familiar with the phrase "Paki-bashing", from those who viewed perpetrating racial violence as some kind of enjoyable and entirely normal "national sport" (Malik, 2009: xviii).

It is evidenced in the press in the casual way that even television reviews dismiss programming for people interested in the subcontinent with: "They're more likely to be planning Singh Something Simple or Curry-nation Street [than programmes on 'British' history]" (*The Sun*, 1989a: 17). Or when the Sunday tabloids condemn the Commission for Racial Equality for preventing people of "Asian origin [from] understand[ing] they're now supposed to be British" (*The News of the World*, 1989c: 8). Or when the same tabloids suggest that "coloured immigrants" should be given financial help to "return to their country of origin [unless] they become genuinely British. Not like the book-burning Bradford Muslims" (*The News of the World*, 1989a). With such racist complicity from the democratic free press, little wonder perhaps that Mr K's neighbours felt he had no right to answer them back.

Lest we congratulate ourselves on how much better things became later, Zaiba Malik tells the story of running a corner shop – a vulnerable and exposed occupation undertaken by many British Muslims – for an undercover film in 2001, and the constant racial abuse and intimidation she suffered:

> pretty much all the abuse I got was from normal white people in the town – men, women and children. So then I stopped liking and trusting white people. Because I thought they all thought I was a piece of shit […] Even though I had a security man with me, I was petrified the whole time.
>
> (Malik, 2010: 258)

Twelve months that shook the world   143

A condemnation of violence is not difficult to provide. However, for Foucault, "[p]racticing criticism is a matter of making facile gestures difficult [...] It is a question of making conflicts more visible" (Foucault, 1988: 155–156). What is _difficult_, but worthwhile, is challenging a story of ourselves as a rational, evolved, civilised liberal democracy that has grown out of 1,000 years of specifically British history.

When we focus on the productive power that flows through the institutions of liberal democracy, rather than the repressive power of censorship that says "no", we can see that what can and cannot be represented in a liberal democratic polity is dependent on the repressive hypothesis itself. Violence against liberal values is vividly visible, because this is violence that appears to be repressive: the protesting Muslims were demanding direct censorship. Peaceful democratic protests by a beleaguered and invisible minority, violence against individuals in private spaces, the pain caused by an endless litany of racist remarks that are casually perpetuated and legitimised in the free press – these can be more difficult to see, because they require us to take notice of the web of productive power in which we are embedded and which makes some things more sayable than others.

Let us be particularly careful of the facile stories we tell about the violence to which liberal democratic values are subjected, when it behoves us to tell a more difficult story about the violence that is perpetrated against the "other" that our liberal democratic institutions of the free press, civil society and the rule of law are fully complicit in creating, upholding and perpetrating.

Democracy promotion and the end of history

Any confidence that 1989 was a year in which liberal democracy was discovered as the one best way to govern is misplaced: the Salman Rushdie affair makes visible a flux of uncertainties that affected more than just Marxist history lecturers like Andrew Brownlow in the weeks and months that followed the collapse of the Communist regimes and the end of the Cold War. For many commentators, it is the very pervasiveness of doubt and uncertainty that creates a serious problem in 1989. No less a mind than Edward Said's diagnosed "[t]he virtual exhaustion of grand systems and total theories" (Said, 1989). This concern invaded even the satisfaction at the demise of an old enemy. According to the Dean of Emmanuel College, Cambridge:

> Our self-satisfaction has been confirmed at the end of the decade by the sudden tottering of the East European regimes. We think we are in comparatively good shape; but we are not. We have our own spiritual crisis. We may not like the fundamentalist diagnosis and remedy, – but it may prevail over us, unless we get down to producing something better for ourselves.
>
> (Cupitt, 1989)

What is the narrative that might provide a satisfying riposte to the "fundamentalist diagnosis and remedy", that might re-galvanise Western forces and

144 *Twelve months that shook the world*

offer a certain moral clarity? For journalist Amir Taheri, it is democracy that provides an answer and an alternative. In an oddly haunting plea, he suggests that in the absence of democracy, "[p]eople led into despair by an oppressive system are always in danger of choosing something much worse, just as a man caught in a skyscraper fire might jump out of the nearest window" (Taheri, 1989).

As a new "other" to liberal democracy is identified in English towns, as the Salman Rushdie affair presented an opportunity – according to Inayat Bunglawala of the Muslim Council of Britain – "for the forging of a more confident Islamic identity among many British Muslims" (quoted in Malik, 2009: 123), as Muslims offer up religious belief as a corrective for a world in which "the supreme value of doubt" is epitomised by Rushdie and the kind of artistic work that privileges "duplicity, truthlessness, doubt and ambiguity" (Sardar and Wyn Davies, 1990: 10–11), the narrative available for a secular alternative to doubt is that of liberal democracy.

The "end of history" narrative paradoxically came in useful in the way it could recommend an *answer* to all this uncertainty. The teleological narrative, then, is not the explanation of recent events; rather recent events make this narrative particularly attractive: "Professor Fukuyama (whom God preserve)", suggests the *Times*, "has suggested that now the clash of ideologies in the world has been resolved, history in the future will be a relatively anecdotal affair [... But] new threats always hatch to keep life interesting" (Hill, 1989). If the civilising course of history is now complete, leaving no more than anecdotal events, and if threats are no longer really a matter of ideological disagreement, then the uncivilised others of democracy can be easily understood and dealt with: they are either barbarians to be contained or savages who can be civilised through democracy promotion.

Although the *Sun* recommends the military destruction of liberal democracy's barbarian enemies, in the more sensitive hands of Douglas Hurd the problem is rather how an unruly population might become civilised. He sets out in some detail in his speech at the Birmingham Central Mosque how "the Government wants a country where all citizens, whatever their origins, have a sense of belonging to Britain". This is to be achieved in a variety of ways of which obedience to the law is the most important, but which also includes learning English and "playing [a] full part in the mainstream of our national life" (Hurd, 1989). What this means in practice is spelled out in some detail. Muslims are to have "a clear understanding of the history and institutions of Britain, of its democratic processes – at both local and national level, its system of Government, its police and judicial system" (ibid.). Not only knowledge of British democracy, however, but also participation is the ideal:

> Whether you look at police officers, magistrates, local councillors or Parliamentary candidates, men and women from the ethnic minorities can now be seen in growing numbers. In both our economic and cultural life they are making a welcome and positive contribution to the nation.
>
> (Hurd, 1989)

Democracy promotion, then, can be understood to operate through a series of ethical practices. It operates through the stories we tell of ourselves in which various undemocratic (and book-burning) others have been defeated (Nazi Germany, the Soviet Union) or civilised (the Catholic Church in England, out-dated and undemocratic forces associated with despotism and absolutism). It functions through history books at school, through the narrative constantly reinforced by the television broadcasts and newspaper articles the imagined community are understood to be reading together, through participation in elections (as voters and candidates), through interactions with the police and judicial system, through engaging with the capitalist economic system and through speaking the national language. In all these detailed ways, the precise practices that are required for belonging are laid out, with liberal understandings of democracy pre-eminent amongst them.

It is important to note that Hurd expresses a perfect ease with the idea that languages other than English might be spoken at home and also suggests that "[n]o-one can or should object to those who come to settle in this country or their children being brought up faithful in the religion of Islam and well-versed in the Holy Koran" (Hurd, 1989). This is a sentiment shared by *The News of the World*, which remarks that "coloured citizens [...] can speak and do as they like at home" (*The News of the World*, 1989c: 8). Hurd goes further than this, indeed, and suggests that "[t]here is much to admire about the way in which British Muslims centre their lives around their religious faith, and about their continuing regard for family" (Hurd, 1989). However, in keeping with the requirements of liberal democratic governmentality, the point is that these religious and linguistic practices are to be confined to the gendered private sphere of home and family, and are not to intrude into public national life. Even then, the precise ordering of gender relations is considered to be a legitimate matter for intervention for those who have not yet fully entered history, with a clear emphasis put by Hurd on the entrance of both men *and women* from ethnic minorities into public, liberal democratic life.

In a context of resistance and public blasphemy, then, the established order of liberal democratic governmentality asserts itself firmly to establish, in a number of social locations both through and beyond the state, that belonging and inclusion are conditional on participation in democratic rituals and an acceptance of the public–private divide on which liberal democratic governmentality relies. The usual history of democratic Britain and its undemocratic others is reinforced by a victory over the Cold War others who would limit freedom of expression. This is a version of history that both creates the protesting Muslims as a new enemy and also provides the remedy.

After the end of history

The end of the Cold War gives the triumph of liberal democracy a particularly victorious slant, but its intersection with a "1,000-year" imagined national history and the tropes of civilisation that go with it means that it is a

146 *Twelve months that shook the world*

narrative that has considerable flexibility and appeal. Considering these events 20 years later, Kenan Malik suggests that "the burning book in Bradford to the burning towers in Manhattan on 9/11 and the burning bus in London on 7/7" are intimately linked through the emergence of an Islamic identity that is alienated from democracy (Malik, 2009: xii). In response, he advocates a more robust liberal democratic narrative (ibid.: 130). If the problem is doubt and uncertainty, then the answer is democracy promotion. This is a response that, as we have seen, offers a useful solution which entails plenty to be done when disaster strikes in 2005. The end of history began as a future-oriented civilising project, as it continues to be.

In this chapter, I have shown that democracy promotion is not innocent of the power that makes certain things unsayable, that censors, that oppresses women and that perpetrates violence, but is rather fully complicit in the power relations that constitute these things. This has been an attempt "to escape the dilemma of being either for or against", as Foucault (1988: 154) would have it, showing that a choice between a rational, liberal, civilised, secular British democracy and an emotional, violent, misogynist, barbaric, foreign Islam is a false one. This is a theme that will continue into the next chapter.

Note

1 For a discussion of why great offence was taken, see Sardar and Wyn Davies (1990).

7 The art of integration
Representing British Muslims

> A solitary image cannot testify to what is revealed through it, but must be attached to another image, another piece of information, another assertion or description, another grievance or piece of evidence, another broadcast, another transmitter. An image is only ever another statement in a regime of statements.
> (Ariella Azoulay, *The Civil Contract of Photography*)

In some ways, things did improve for British Muslims after 1989. The common law offence of blasphemous libel was finally repealed in Britain in 2008, by which time a law against incitement to religious hatred had been introduced, offering protection to Muslims as well as Christians and other major faiths (Nash, 2007: 138). Racist violence against British Asians also decreased somewhat (Malik, 2009: 236). From my long hours in the newspaper library, I can also report that the tone of the populist tabloid press became considerably less overtly racist in the intervening years: I have no examples of crass jokes about curry or offers to send Muslims "home" from these papers in the period of the London bombings.

At the same time, however, the circulating discourses that had emerged at the time of the Salman Rushdie affair – the fears that Islamic religious identities might be in some way incompatible with Britishness and its democratic values that had been hard-won through the civilising process of its history – intensified. Following the bombings, increasing anxiety about belonging, identity and fears about a divisive multiculturalism led to a reassertion of the importance of a commitment to British values, particularly liberal democracy. This chapter shows how the practices of temporal othering that emerged in 1989 played out through democracy promotion and Democracy Promotion at a time when a Muslim other once again became highly visible.

It makes three related points. First, the incipiently violent othering practices and teleological narrative of history that emerged in 1989 can still be traced in media and political discourse. Second, however, these othering representations have become the focus of political struggle on the part of British Muslims. As such, there have been attempts to disrupt some of the narratives that suggest Muslims are somehow foreign, by producing new representations. The example I give here is a photography exhibition, *The Art*

148 *The art of integration*

of Integration (Sanders 2008, 2009), which was financially supported by the Foreign and Commonwealth Office (FCO). The representations in it attempt to redraw the boundary between British and foreign, with Muslims firmly on the inside. However, I suggest that this struggle has been conservative in its effects by tacitly putting forward the view that the everyday practices of liberal democratic governmentality and capitalism are the *remedy* for violence and not a matter for contestation.

Third, I go on to demonstrate that despite the well-intentioned efforts of the FCO to frame othering practices that *include* British Muslims, there has been no thoroughgoing attempt to dismantle the civilising stories we tell about ourselves, about the perfection of our institutions, about the savage and about the barbarian. Consequently, violence is still deeply implicated in the everyday ethical practices of British democratic lives. As ever, this is never more so than when interrogating the division of the public and private spheres and the related terrain of gender relations. I show this using Chris Morris's (2010) subversive film, *Four Lions*. Throughout, I will read these visual statements in the way suggested by Ariella Azoulay in the epigraph above: as always drawing on one another in a regime of statements.

They do not represent British Muslims

Some of the most shocking images of the bombers were those that suggested they were thoroughly British in all sorts of recognisable ways. The *Sun* newspaper printed copies of their birth certificates and there was great shock at hearing the bombers' voices – on pre-recorded videos – with their recognisably broad Yorkshire accents. Once again, the northern mill towns were in the spotlight. Perhaps most shocking of all, though, was the image of Mohammed Sidique Khan in his caring role as a professional classroom assistant. It seemed difficult to reconcile these young men, who appeared thoroughly ordinary, with a threat to the national security and the democratic values that constituted British life. If the foreign is identical to a particular barbarian ideology, how was it to be recognised? If the border could not be policed using passport checks, how might it be managed instead?

Democracy promotion continued to be used as a way of managing this kind of epistemological uncertainty. It was widely accepted that not all Muslims were terrorists, but if not, how might we tell the barbarian from the democrat (or the savage)? A broad set of representations imply that it is through ordinary practices of thought, the minutiae of daily life, through which the border between the self and the other can be distinguished. These representations are not *describing* the border but performatively producing and reproducing it.

On 9 July 2005, before it became known that the four bombers were all British citizens, the *Sun* published five pictures of people whom they implied may be suspects, including Osama bin Laden. All five are identified as Muslims, an identity which in four out of five pictures is inscribed physically by beards, a skullcap and other kinds of headgear. They are also identified by name and as not British. Nevertheless, the accompanying article suggests "fears that more and more young Muslims are being brainwashed to hate Britain – and target their adopted country with terror strikes" (Hughes and Kay, 2005: 8). This implies not only a dichotomy between Muslims and Britain but also an association between Muslims (British or not) and terrorists. This sits alongside the implication that even if they are born in the UK, Muslims are in some way still "foreign", that Britain may only ever be "adopted". Such a condition of difference is underlined by the proximity of the article to the pictures of "known" foreign terrorists. Underlined in the way that an Islamic identity may be inscribed onto bodies by modes of dress and appearance is the implication that people who look like this might be foreign, suspicious, dangerous.

The supposed dichotomy between Muslims and Britons is echoed on the day the announcement is made that the bombers were British; whilst the *Sun*'s leading article itself insists that the bombers "do not represent Britain's Muslim community" (*The Sun*, 2005: 8), the opposite page is half covered by a large headline which states: "200 more Brits are ready to blow themselves up." Anxiety resides in the uncertainty as to whether the bombers do represent a form of Britishness or not. It is not clear, when observing any given individual Muslim's practices, whether they are British or whether they are displaying worrying signs of terrorism and a foreign, barbarian ideology.

The most poignant of representations of British Muslims at the time of the bombings is that of Shahara Akhter Islam, a young Muslim woman of 20 who was killed in the bus bombing on Tavistock Square. Shahara Islam is regularly invoked by the press as an exemplar of a British Muslim who manages to embrace both "sides" of this identity, and in a particularly telling article in the *Sun*, she is contrasted with Hasib Hussain, the bomber who killed her. The photograph of her, presented here side by side with an impassive Hussain, and which is reproduced numerous times in a wide variety of newspapers, shows her smiling, wearing make-up, earrings, a *shalwar kameez* and light *dupatta* covering her shoulders but not her head. Thus, unthreatening in her femininity, recognisably Muslim, she is said to have "straddled two cultures effortlessly" whilst "Hussain struggled with both" (Hendry, 2005: 8). She is an idealised representation of a "truly modern Muslim" (note the now-familiar invocation of temporality) and her participation in consumerist practices typical of economically developed societies, particularly a love of fashion, is everywhere cited as proof of her "Britishness": "[she] loved her Burberry handbag as much as the shalwar kameez she occasionally wore at home" (ibid.; see also Kurki, 2013 for a detailed discussion of the inextricable intersection of certain forms of liberal democracy with capitalist economic formations).

This is in marked contrast with Hussain, who "began dressing in traditional Muslim clothes and growing a beard" (Hendry, 2005: 8). Britishness may not be incompatible with wearing clothes that are "traditional" or "Muslim", but the physical, *visible* inscription of identity and the way it

150 *The art of integration*

represents a set of everyday and ordinary practices are important and can constitute grounds not only for approval but also for fear and suspicion. This is a point that was doubtless not lost on many Muslims in an atmosphere of ongoing fear of a "backlash" (Dodd et al., 2005), and in which passengers on London public transport were encouraged to police one another, keeping their eyes open for "something suspicious" (Closs Stephens, 2008: 70).

If these representations of "good" and "bad" (Mamdani, 2002) "civilised" and "barbarous" Muslims appear to reinforce the binary formulation of self and other – domestic and foreign – they are also the point at which it begins to collapse. After all, Shahara Islam and Hasib Hussain both occupy a liminal space in which they enact the practices and conduct both of being British and of being Muslim; they represent the possibility, and inevitability, of postcolonial ways of being in which the domestic and the foreign are indivisible and inextricable. Nevertheless, the presentation of their identities serves to discipline performances of being a "Muslim": such images establish an embodied norm of commitment to British identity in the shape of Shahara Islam.

These kinds of representations do not stay in the tabloids, but are recombined and rearticulated in political speeches: Kim Howells, at the time a Foreign Office minister, invokes Shahara Islam's memory by stating that "she symbolises the multiculturalism that is so evident in London and in the UK". His speech goes on to articulate the attack that killed her as "an attack on all of us who espouse the cause of openness and democracy" (Howells, 2005). The binary oppositions of the barbarous and the civilised, backwardness and modernity, violence and democracy are played out in inscriptions of the gendered bodies of Shahara Islam and the bombers, enacting and embodying the borders of the nation, rendering visible acceptable and unacceptable practices and performances of being British.

As Andrew Gimson in the *Daily Telegraph* remarks at the strange sight of Tony Blair and other government ministers becoming the unlikely interpreters of the Islamic faith, "Mr Blair and his followers may claim to be saying something about the true nature of Islam, but what they are actually doing is laying down the conditions on which Muslims will be allowed to live in Britain" (Gimson, 2005). British Muslims are repeatedly encouraged by such foreign policy representations to conform to the practices of Britishness in their thoughts, values and "ideology" as well as in the minute details of their everyday lives – what they wear, how often they shave – in order to demonstrate a commitment to civilisation and embody its limits, including to liberal capitalist democracy.

The art of integration

The *Art of Integration* exhibition explicitly sets out to disrupt tabloid images of British Muslims and to deny that there is any incompatibility between Britishness and Islam. The preface of the book that accompanies the exhibition (Sanders, 2008), and the website (Sanders, 2009)[1] in English, Urdu and

Arabic which is funded by the FCO (2011), states unambivalently that it aims to make an intervention "[c]ontrary to the headlines and editorialising" (Sanders, 2008: 6). It is deeply involved with both disrupting and reproducing temporal narratives of Britishness.

There are photographs that focus on the detailed practices of the everyday lives of British Muslims: "lives without fanfare, controversy or violence" (Sanders, 2008: 7). We are presented with a variety of people whose lives are generally to be understood by virtue of the *work* that they do – they can be understood by means of the normal practices of production and consumption in a liberal democratic, capitalist society. Here we have pictures of Muslims who are fashion designers and businesspeople, bankers and scientists, (veiled) beauticians and taxi drivers, shop assistants and rock stars. There is no incompatibility, these pictures suggest, between the ordinary practices of everyday modernity and development, and the practice of Islam as it is pictured through the wearing (in some but not all cases) of the veil or beards, skull caps or traditional robes, and through everyday religious practices such as communal prayer.

Perhaps most striking is the picture that was used to publicise the exhibition: a picture of a white woman with bright blue eyes wearing a Union Flag as an Islamic veil. The accompanying caption states that she is: "British, actress, mother and Muslim" (Sanders, 2008: 10). This picture intersects with and contests a whole web of images that had been in circulation since 1989 portraying the gender relations mandated by some versions of Islam as incompatible with democratic British values. On the contrary, proclaims this picture, Islam is not what you think it is. It can – though it does not need to – be white, it can be passionately committed to Britain and its flag, it can be beautiful and luminescent, it can be feminine, it can subject itself to visibility and yet – by subtly disrupting conventional modes of representation – it will not be found wanting in its congruence with Britishness.

Britishness in these photos is likewise performed through a commitment to and participation in liberal democratic governmentality. This includes employment in state and governmental institutions such as the police force, state schools, the National Health Service, the legal system, the army and London Underground. There are, furthermore, a number of photographs of those all-important functionaries of liberal democratic governmentality: journalists, newsreaders, film-makers.

Even more importantly, however, British Muslims are shown in a variety of pictures that directly imply a commitment to the specific modes of governance employed in the UK. For instance, Salma Yaqoob, the local councillor and then vice-chair of the Respect Party is pictured wearing the veil; Lord Patel, Baroness Uddin and Lord Ahmad are shown meeting in the House of Lords; various people (some wearing the veil) are depicted celebrating Ramadan in a party sponsored by the erstwhile London Mayor Ken Livingstone; and heir to the throne Prince Charles is photographed talking to two very young, veiled girls at an Islamic school.

152   *The art of integration*

The wearing of a Union Flag as a veil is symbolic, then, of a much more detailed participation in Britishness which is involved in mundane practices, ordinary work and the everyday business of liberal democratic politics in which Muslims can be and are represented by other Muslims in a parliamentary democracy and constitutional monarchy.

Historical narratives of Britishness are likewise represented here, as the photographs present a narrative of a British history that is fully intertwined with Islam. The exhibition subtly disrupts the story we tell about ourselves by implying that Islam has been part of Britain for almost as long as democracy. The very subtitle of the exhibition, "Islam in our green and pleasant land", is a reference to William Blake's poem "Jerusalem", also a well-known hymn. It thereby invokes an imagined history that brings together the joint Islamic and Christian heritage of the Holy Land and the figure of Jesus, and a Romantic, literary vision of Englishness that encompasses not only a rural idyll but also the "dark Satanic mills" so familiar to many British Muslims. No satanic mills are pictured, although we see plenty of textiles in the exhibition. However, the intimate connections between Islam and Britain's industrial and colonial past are underlined not least by a picture of a majestic-looking mosque built in familiar local stone and blending seamlessly into its surroundings in Bradford.

Meanwhile, in one of the most scenic and striking pictures (as also suggested by some of the exhibition's visitors in the evaluation they provided for the FCO, 2011: annex B), ancient Llanbadrig Church on Anglesey is pictured perched on a recognisably British stretch of coastline beside its little graveyard dotted with Christian stone crosses. It is necessary to read the caption to work out what this picture has to do with British Islam, but it – along with accompanying pictures of Islamic-patterned stained glass and tiles – reveals the church to have been restored and refurbished by a Muslim convert, Lord Stanley of Alderley, in 1870. This sits alongside pictures of Muslims worshipping in an old converted convent and examples of nineteenth-century Islamic architecture in London, demonstrating the imbrication of British and Muslim histories and faiths.

Finally, an image that draws on the most traditional brand of foreign policy – the depiction of Britain as superior to France – shows three French Muslim women wearing veils, with the British Houses of Parliament in the background. The caption – "French Muslims – happy to be in London! In Britain's multicultural capital, few people take notice of what you wear" – is a clever intervention: it strategically defends the multiculturalism that establishes the dress code as a matter of personal choice to be made in the private sphere and exteriorises threats to this as foreign. The backdrop of Parliament reminds the spectator that what is to be defended here is a particularly British brand of liberalism and toleration that is rooted in the country's journey through time towards liberal democracy. However, it also invokes the broader civilisational story that legitimates a particular set of gender relations and the division of a public/private sphere as the end of history.

The art of integration 153

These pictures do not disrupt the civilising story of Britain and its inexorable progress to a liberal democratic end of history. They do, however, co-opt it and demand inclusion, in order to legitimate contemporary democratic participation, multiculturalism and acceptance.

In the context of the – at best ambivalent – representations of British Muslims in the mainstream media, it is not surprising that a photographer and his subjects would attempt to claim inclusion for Muslims in the British polity in this way. What is more intriguing is the fact that the FCO saw a Foreign Policy opportunity in these photographs, and provided funding for them to be viewed both as a physical exhibition – often physically sited in British Embassies and High Commissions (FCO, 2011) – and as a website. I attempted to obtain more information about FCO support for the exhibition through the Freedom of Information Act, but unfortunately many of the paper records relating to this exhibition cannot be sourced at present. Staff at the FCO were therefore generous enough to offer me a short meeting in July 2012 in which they gave me as much information as they could remember or surmise about why this exhibition had been funded and what the FCO were hoping to achieve.[2]

Officials stressed that this exhibition was not part of the Prevent strand of the Counter-Terrorism strategy, as it is not their intention to "securitise" the work they do to promote "cohesion and integration". Nevertheless, they agreed that the timing of the project was not coincidental. Many of the photographs had been taken shortly before the London bombings, but the FCO's interest in them occurred as a result of increased interest in Islam, integration and cohesion triggered by these events. Indeed, in a speech that launched the exhibition's tour, Baroness Scotland made explicit reference to the London bombings (Scotland, 2007).

The FCO officials confirmed that the exhibition's aim was to "challenge stereotypes" about the daily lives of British Muslims, which might include notions that Muslims are persecuted, forced to assimilate or – expressed with a genuine embarrassment that such a stereotype might exist – "that we think they're all terrorists". The point here is not to criticise the FCO for linking the exhibition with the attacks, but rather to note that the photographs are already embedded in a whole regime of statements and images that preceded the London bombings but which were transformed and reconfigured by them. The invocation of the attacks is unavoidable, given that what is at stake is the set of modes of belonging and exclusion that exceed any particular state institution, which enabled the bombers to be understood as "foreign" and which thereby intensified the precarious liminality of British Muslims.

The officials claimed that the value of the exhibition was to "demystify British Islam": that it made something visible which had hitherto not been grasped, particularly by an overseas audience. The power of the exhibition, they claimed, was in the moment when a visitor said: "Oh, I didn't realise!" However, I suggest that this exhibition does not straightforwardly render visible to a conventional Foreign Policy audience the objective fact that the

154   *The art of integration*

UK's community is not constituted in the way that stereotypes might suggest. On the contrary, both this exhibition and the FCO's involvement with it themselves attempt to *reconstitute* the community and its boundaries, *enacting* the possibility that Muslims can and should be included. Insofar as the exhibition disrupted preconceived notions and stereotypes – including the artificial divide between the putative "we" of those who conduct foreign policy and "they" who are Muslims – its logic was to be actively involved in changing bordering practices and to establish British Muslims as firmly on the "inside".

With this in mind, it is important to note just how "domestic" this example of foreign policy was. The FCO officials noted explicitly that "the overseas and domestic reinforced each other". When Baroness Scotland launched the exhibition, it was in her role as a Home Office minister, and the officials mentioned that their aim was to involve the Pakistani diaspora in conversations about foreign policy because "democratically [they] have a say". Peter Sanders and his subjects are conceived in this way as "UK people in an ambassadorial role". The aspiration here is not only to provide a narrative about Britishness and its liberal democracy that includes the "Muslim MPs, Muslim members of the House of Lords and over 200 Muslim municipal councillors" who are mentioned in the speech at the exhibition's launch (Scotland, 2007) Also important is that Muslims are *democratically* included in formulating and reformulating that narrative. The project is to be sure not securitising in the narrow sense that it is expected directly to prevent further terrorism, therefore, but I suggest that it does function to secure a British identity understood through a commitment to and participation in liberal democracy.

The epistemological uncertainty intensified by the London bombings is therefore addressed by providing in some detail – and with the full democratic participation of British Muslims – a set of scripts, practices and narratives that establish the sorts of practices that constitute belonging. The FCO are actively intervening in building commitment to the nation by negotiating the ways in which a particular form of Muslim identity can not only be represented, but can *represent itself* and be interwoven with the familiar narrative – without changing the narrative itself very much. This is democracy promotion. The promotion of these democratic identities by making them visible overseas is much less significant than the constitution and legitimation of those identities *as domestic* in the first place.

The art of domestication

The democratisation of foreign policy and the well-meaning desire, on the part of the FCO, Peter Sanders and the many Muslims in these photographs, to make British identity more inclusive is a genuine improvement on the spectacular and violent othering that we saw in the previous chapter and, to a lesser extent, in the tabloid representations from 2005 that we saw above.

The art of integration   155

However, they come at a cost. It is now more than half a century since Roland Barthes's famous critique in *Mythologies* of a photograph on the cover of *Paris-Match* of a North African soldier saluting the French national flag, which – he proposes – suggests that "there is no better answer to the detractors of colonialism, than the zeal of this Negro to serve his supposed oppressors" (Barthes, 2009: 139). Nevertheless, such images continue to be reformulated. One consequence of portraying Islam in a patriotic veil is that critique of liberal democracy and its articulation with Britishness is arrested by a demonstration of commitment to British values by those who had appeared marginal. By explicitly proclaiming that Islam can be identical to Britishness, this image concedes to the flows of power that ask us to be "for or against". It therefore conceals the limitations of the liberal democratic values that constitute Britishness, particularly the way they still enact a violent othering.

It is important to note, then, that the exhibition not only makes Islamic identities *domestic*, but also *domesticates*. This can be understood by looking in more detail at the photographs themselves, in which there is a profound conservatism. Thinking particularly about the depictions of governmental institutions in this exhibition, there are many more photographs that show a commitment to the unelected House of Lords and the monarchy than there are even of the elected institutions. Not a single Muslim member of Parliament is pictured, whereas we see three Lords, two members of the Royal Family and a portrait of Hafiz Abdal Karim, servant to Queen Victoria. The accompanying book also contains a preface by Prince Charles. This sits alongside a broader social conservatism, in which the Islam practised at elite Eton College – far beyond the financial means of the overwhelming majority of British Muslims – is celebrated in five pictures, whereas only one photograph shows a state school (in which, perhaps somewhat unusually for a British state school, all but one of the children seem to be white). The possible critique that Muslims might offer of the highly racialised inequalities of British life (in which a Muslim can, for instance, be servant to a Queen but never an elected head of state) is subordinated here to a commitment to British institutions as they are.

Even such critique as can be discerned in these pictures is muted. In one picture we see a huge pile of cast-off clothes – the waste generated by an affluent consumer society – being patiently sorted by volunteers for Islamic Relief. The havoc wreaked on local textile markets by Western cast-offs (Rivoli, 2014), the environmental catastrophe of fast fashion (Siegle, 2011) and the global inequalities (and their history) that led many Muslim majority countries like Pakistan to a reliance on aid and development, is less visible in this picture than the benign opportunity for depoliticised charitable giving.

Meanwhile, the very real grievance about British Foreign Policy that has driven Muslim demands to be more involved in its formulation (UK Cabinet Office, 2008: 26) – which is to say, British involvement in the wars in Iraq and Afghanistan – is alluded to only obliquely as local councillor Salma Yaqoob

156   *The art of integration*

and singer Yusuf Islam (formerly Cat Stevens) are both captioned as campaigners for peace. In the latter case, this caption appears to be as much a tacit disavowal of the violence of the Salman Rushdie protests as it is a reference to violence perpetrated by the British state: Yusuf Islam gained notoriety in 1989 by appearing to make a death threat against Salman Rushdie on live television (BBC, 2009).

Meanwhile, Yaqoob's well-known opposition to the invasion of Iraq is rendered unthreatening by her feminisation in this smiling portrait, which labels her as a "mother of three", as well as by her participation in electoral politics. This is not to criticise Yaqoob for pursuing her political objectives through the institutional means at her disposal, but rather to show that this exhibition is fully implicated in legitimating and promoting liberal democracy (and its associated gender relations, including the importance of providing care) as the incontestable mode through which politics can be pursued, rather than disrupting or even approaching its limits. Even more importantly, whilst liberal democracy is quite clearly fully implicated in violence in these wars, the fact that Yaqoob's struggle for peace is understood to be taking place through the very same institutions reiterates the familiar idea that liberal democracy is a *remedy* for violence. As we will see again, it is not.

However, it is particularly important for this exhibition to make explicit Muslims' commitment to peace because the representations of the foreign, barbarian enemy that these pictures are implicitly dissociating from British Islam are those of the London bombers and their violence. It is therefore especially useful to look in detail at the one picture in the exhibition that directly addresses the events of July 2005.

The photograph is of Muhammad Jamil, a bearded (and therefore visibly observant Muslim) employee of London Underground, tending his garden at Edgware Road Station with a Tube train in the background. It is only the caption that makes this picture fully intelligible: "When a bomb exploded at his station on 7th July 2005, he was among the first to rush into the tunnel to help the victims." This is a moving and memorable image, in which the sheer ordinariness of Mr Jamil's appearance seems to belie the great bravery of his actions that day. Indeed, perhaps viewers cannot help but be prompted to wonder whether they would have been able to respond in the same way, given their own ordinariness.

It is this sympathetic move that perhaps enables us to wonder how we might have felt had a Muslim employee understandably, humanly, run away or frozen in terror or otherwise failed to act heroically on that appalling day. When Muslims in particular are called upon to demonstrate and embody commitment to the nation in their daily lives and practices – and are particularly scrutinised whilst they do so – we may set up a worryingly high standard for them to live up to. That Mr Jamil is extraordinary and courageous is not in doubt, but this picture also reminds us that British Muslims occupy a particularly precarious position in which their commitment to Britishness and democracy *is* implicitly in doubt, posing to them a constant question that

The art of integration   157

must be answered not only in their ordinary practices, but sometimes in extraordinary ones too.

In Chapter 2, we noted the shift first identified by Foucault between the spectacular violence of sovereign power and the everyday policing and internalisation of the most minute norms of everyday behaviour characteristic of discipline and the freely choosing subject of liberal governmentality. At a more modest level, a similar shift can be seen to be taking place between this and the previous chapter. Whereas during the Salman Rushdie affair we had seen the borders of the nation seemingly both challenged and reasserted with spectacular and polarising violence, in the *Art of Integration*, and in images of Shahara Islam, there is rather an internalisation of the norms of Britishness on the part of British Muslims.

Whereas previously we have seen examples of white men protecting brown women from brown men, in this chapter we see Mr Jamil. There is no need for a civilising mission if brown men too can be relied upon to join with white men in protecting brown women like Shahara Islam from brown men like Mohammed Siddique Khan, because they have now entered history and become civilised. In this exhibition, we see in minute detail just what is required for the entrance of the savage into history under conditions of late liberal governmentality.

An exhibition that initially seemed to be disrupting our expectations about where the borders of the nation lie, turns out to reproduce the status quo in a variety of ways.

Uncertain boundaries: misrecognition and violence in *Four Lions*

I argued above that these visible representations of British Muslims are a means of trying to manage uncertainty in a situation where the national border is apparently uncertain and unknowable. The photographs in the exhibition attempt to redraw the border to solve this epistemological problem, so that British Muslims can unproblematically be understood to be included, and they do so by making visible the sorts of freely chosen practices that secure a liberal democratic, civilised identity.

It is important to note that this attempt to manage uncertainty is not particularly successful on its own terms. Shahara Islam would by no means look out of place in *The Art of Integration*. Neither, though, it should be noted, would Mohammed Sidique Khan in his role as a classroom assistant in the years before the attack. The public, visible practices of freely choosing Muslim subjects are not reliable guides to their identities, interests and ideologies, fully formed in the separate private sphere away from government intrusion.

Chris Morris's satirical and meticulously researched feature film of 2010, *Four Lions* (Morris, 2010), which won him an award from the British Academy of Film and Television Arts, engages directly with the problems raised for liberal democratic governmentality by the British Muslim suicide bomber. The film's main character – Omar, the leader of the bombers – would also

158   *The art of integration*

have looked at home in *The Art of Integration* with his ordinary job and life and his friendships and manly banter with his white colleagues. He might, however, have had to cede his place to his wife, Sofia – a Lady Macbeth figure, although rather less troubled by conscience – who is beautiful, veiled and feminine, a mother and a nurse. She offers endless emotional and caring support to Omar in the private space of their modern, comfortable, ordinary home in encouraging him to blow himself up and assume leadership of his friends to do the same. From the visible everyday practices of their lives (secretive bomb making notwithstanding), there is nothing to suggest that they are not exactly what they are: British.

Is it – as Tony Blair suggested – in their "ideology" that they mark themselves as foreign, then? A detailed textual analysis of this film suggests that, on the contrary, the difficulty in knowing where the border lies is precisely located in the difficulty of separating a liberal democratic, British, set of values from the violent ideology of the bombings. Once again, the values of liberal democratic governmentality, with its sharply delineated and gendered private sphere, turn out to be so fully implicated in violence that the ideology animating the actions of the bombers appears to be almost entirely domestic.

Morris's film has by and large been discussed mainly in terms of its portrayal of suicide bombers themselves and whether or not it is appropriate to laugh at this subject matter, as ridiculed by the bungling and general idiocy of the bombers themselves (French, 2010; Doggart, 2010). However, its target is much broader (Basham and Vaughan-Williams, 2012) and demonstrates some of the profound epistemological problems emerging from the difficulties of establishing and policing the border between Britain and the outside, democracy and violence.

The usual institutions of liberal democratic governmentality, then, appear helpless in the face of the difficulty of recognising who is British, who is a pious Muslim, who is a terrorist, and how these categories might intersect. For example, Malcolm Storge, the local MP, shares a platform with Barry, white Muslim convert and would-be suicide bomber, at a community meeting of the type that reminds us of the way particular faith identities were constituted by liberal governmentality in the 1980s (see Chapter 6). A banner proclaims that the meeting is about "Islam: Moderation and Progress", reminding us of the ordinary teleologies that characterise understandings of democratic life. The elected representative mouths platitudes that echo Tony Blair and also *The Art of Integration*: "Most British Muslims don't want to be abroad, fighting UK Foreign Policy. They want to be getting on peacefully with their daily lives." This familiar othering of political opponents – which equates an opposition of British Foreign Policy with violence and being "abroad" and its rhetorical opposition to the ordinary practices of "daily life" – fails to instigate any kind of democratic conversation, but rather an antagonistic response from Barry. Nevertheless, it is not clear that Barry speaks for or represents anyone at all – even his "jihadist" friends, led by Omar, with whom he is in constant conflict.

The art of integration   159

Meanwhile, Has, a young man in the audience, stands up and threatens to set off a suicide bomb, leading to mayhem in which the MP is particularly terrified, only to reveal that he is armed with just streamers. The appearance of harmless and callow idiocy is itself undermined, however, when he is recruited to the "gang" after the meeting by Barry – though perhaps he was never a real danger as he is killed by Barry just after attempting to give himself up to the police in a telling exchange. The policeman asks Has: "You've got a bomb but it's not going to go off? How do I *know* that?" "Look!" says Has, and as Barry activates the bomb, he promptly explodes. In other words, this is a film that abounds with situations that simply cannot be read off from appearances. The answer to the question, "How do I know?" is constantly in doubt and the answer is never unproblematically available just by looking.

The very title of the film demonstrates epistemological anxiety about the meaning of Britishness and how this might relate to Muslims. It refers to the three lions emblazoned on the England football team's emblem. This invocation seems to be a subtle reference to the "Tebbit test": Norman Tebbit's rather gendered view that the test of whether someone was "really British" depended upon their allegiance to the country's national sports teams. The bombers seem quite likely to pass the Tebbit test, but are they British? They are planning a suicide attack, so they must be the enemy, yet their unremarkable appearance, everyday lives and accents, their taste in English pop music (which they clearly prefer to "Songs of Arabic Struggle"), their preoccupation with small debts, their failure to enact ordinary religious practice, such as praying or going to the mosque, and the almost heartbreakingly ordinary family life and job of Omar and his wife mean that they hardly appear very different from anyone else in British society.

Small wonder, perhaps, that white neighbours and friends remain oblivious to the danger, despite seeing the men acting in what can only be thought of as a suspicious manner, buying industrial quantities of bleach from the same shop in inept "disguises", running with great care with bags full of explosives, screaming in terror when one of these is thrown at them or occupying a flat full of bottles of bleach and boxes of wires and nails. These episodes in the film patently deride the poster campaigns that endlessly exhort citizens to police one another, keeping their eyes open for "something suspicious" and report potential radicalisation (Closs Stephens, 2008: 70; Basham and Vaughan-Williams, 2012: 1), as if it could ever be clear what these things might look like. What is left is only a profound confusion about what sorts of practices are really culpable. Can someone be both so British as Omar appears and yet so opposed to democracy, and therefore foreign, as to perpetrate a suicide bombing?

Omar's white friend, Matt, states at the end of the film, after the former has demonstrably blown himself up causing death and destruction:

> Omar had nothing to do with this. Because I *knew* him [...] When we talk about a so-called terrorist attack on the London marathon just remember one thing. Most loud bangs are not bombs. They're scooters backfiring.

160 *The art of integration*

No one escapes ridicule in this biting film, but Matt's defence of his friend in the face of all the evidence is nevertheless rather touching. It echoes a certain type of anti-racist discourse and underlines the ways in which the pieties of political speech about "the vast majority of Muslims" intersect with the everyday experiences of having Muslim neighbours. In the face of a seeming contradiction between Omar's deep familiarity, his ordinary lifestyle, his engagement in the bantering mores of male friendship, and yet the foreignness that makes him a suicide bomber, Matt can only deny the reality of what has happened.

Even more seriously, the police too are in the grip of epistemological confusion. This turns out to be deeply dangerous, as – in a comically virtuoso moment – they shoot and kill the wrong man because of confusion about his costume at the London marathon ("Is a wookie a bear, Control?"), echoing the tragic death of innocent Juan Charles de Menezes at the hands of police on 22 July 2005 (Vaughan-Williams, 2008).

There is, moreover, a moment when the film sets up an expectation that Omar's house and gang will be raided just the night before they bomb the marathon. Any viewer who had followed, for instance, the police raid on the home of Mohammed Abdulkahar and Abul Koyair on 2 June 2006 – the former being shot and injured and both receiving an apology when no charges were brought against them (BBC, 2006a) – might be unsurprised when, in the film, the wrong house is raided.

What is particularly noteworthy is that the house that is raided is occupied by people who *appear* to be rather foreign. Ahmed – unlike Omar, who is his brother – is a pious and observant Muslim and *that is why* he firmly believes that violence is wrong. He has a distinctly Pakistani accent, wears *shalwar kameez* and a long beard (like Abdulkahar and Koyair), attends the mosque and prayer meetings, and irritates everyone with his saintly expression. He also refuses to enter a room when Sofia is in it and his own female relatives are heavily veiled and confined to a separate small room that used to be a toilet. *Here* appearances would suggest that what we have is an alien ideology, most particularly in the gender relations that are always at stake in establishing what is domestic and what is foreign.

This is perhaps why Ahmed's innocence can do little to save him: his position when we last see him seems hopeless. "We *know* more than you think we do", says a police interrogator to him – a formulation that by now causes the heart to sink – as he inexplicably brandishes a Weetabix (breakfast cereal).

Minding your own business: the British private sphere

Here, as ever, it is useful to note how the particular (very dangerous) delineation of public and private spheres functions. A certain tendency to mind their own business – the sense that what goes on in private is not a matter for undue interference – pervades the attitudes of the white characters. Matt asks Omar about one of the gang's preparatory misadventures: "It's not jihad,

The art of integration   161

though, is it? Blowing up a crow?" Omar replies, "No. It's a cultural thing". Matt shows no further curiosity and this is taken to be a satisfactory answer. Meanwhile, Alice – a neighbour – not only does not view it as appropriate to ask any questions about the explosive material lying around, but also misunderstands why the men want her to leave their flat in a hurry, taking them to mean that they intend to indulge in sex together. She happens to disapprove (traditional masculinity being more vigorously policed than exploding crows), but removes herself anyway.

Culture and sexuality, then, along with what is contained in the private space of a man's flat or his bag, are not readily understood to be of public concern and are therefore of interest only insofar as they extrude into the public sphere in outward bodily practices. Meanwhile, although public spaces are relentlessly policed by endless surveillance cameras – some watched by Omar in his job in the shopping centre along with the hapless Matt – there is little sense that anyone knows quite what they are looking for. Thus, Ahmed's refusal of violence and criminality, his sincere attempts to persuade Omar of the error of his ways, these are not enough to make him British; but his outward, public appearance (and that of his wife) visibly bespeaks a foreign ideology and constitutes him as a risk. Publicly visible manifestations are taken to make a fully formed private identity legible in ways that reveal themselves as perilous.

Liberal democratic governmentality and violence

The difficulty with knowing the difference between British democratic rationality and foreign despotic violence, is that they are not separate in practice and do not map onto each other. Indeed, it is Britishness and liberal democracy that is more complicit in violence than any portrayal of what is "foreign".

Victoria Basham and Nick Vaughan-Williams are right to suggest that one of the principal dangers to which this film calls our attention is that of "blundering, inept police officers, armed with live ammunition pointed at large crowds of people" (Basham and Vaughan-Williams, 2012: 14): government institutions are implicated in violence and terror as police shootings of the innocent and the apparent "rendition" of Ahmed make apparent. It is perhaps unsurprising that a panicked policeman would say, "He must be the target; I've shot him". Possibly more worrying, though, is when Malcolm Storge MP states: "The report makes crystal clear that the police shot the *right* man, but as far as I'm aware the wrong man exploded". This parodies the fact that, following his calamitous death, Jean-Charles de Menezes's family called in vain upon "the public and their representatives" to instigate a "public discussion" in order that "lessons should be learned and officers held to account" (Jean Charles de Menezes Family Campaign, 2009). The democratic institutions that are meant to make violence unnecessary because of their ability to manage conflict between diverse interests not only fail utterly,

162   *The art of integration*

but are actually involved in perpetrating violence and then denying it and covering it up.

However, there is a violence associated with British everyday life that is far more diffuse and widespread than that practised by the state authorities. It is precisely in the ordinary rituals of British private life that violence can readily be discerned in the film. Omar and his gang are painfully inept at articulating the scripts of their "jihadi video" and their political and spiritual position on why they are blowing themselves up in the first place is riven with contradictions (Basham and Vaughan-Williams, 2012: 13–14). What comes through much more coherently, though, is the way they are indebted to violent films and video games. "Look at me, I'm Paki Rambo!" shouts Waj, filming himself on his mobile phone whilst firing a large gun. This is a scene that causes horror amongst the Pakistanis running the training camp he is attending in Swat, and identifies Waj and Omar as utterly British: nothing less than an archetypal "Mr Bean".

Furthermore, the men's repetition that they are "four lions" re-invokes not only the (sometimes violent) masculinity and national allegiance of the football crowd but also the still-familiar number-one song (twice: in 1996 and 1998) *Three Lions*, by The Lightning Seeds along with comedians David Baddiel and Frank Skinner whose television collaboration was an early epitome of "laddish" behaviour on British screens (*The Independent*, 1999). The bombers appear to demonstrate their Britishness in their adherence to prevailing forms of masculinity, with their laddish humour, underlying desire to "bang white girls" (also referred to as "slags", not an especially Islamic word), macho initiation rites – and violent fantasies (Basham and Vaughan-Williams, 2012: 13). Violent narratives weave themselves into the conventional British masculinity of the men. Violent games form the basis of conversations and analogies: jihad will be "just like" *Mortal Kombat* or Xbox *Counter-Strike*. This narrative brutalisation is a process that obviously begins in early childhood. It may seem a little odd that Omar's young son talks openly about people blowing themselves up to get to heaven – why has no one in his (primary) school noticed this? – but there is nothing strange in playing with toy guns at home or in watching Disney film *The Lion King*, whose story only has to be tweaked a little to be perfectly suited to explain the complexities of "jihad" to a young boy at bedtime.

I want to emphasise that I am *not* here advocating more surveillance of the private sphere, more searches of homes or sports bags, more suspicion of British Pakistani neighbours, more reporting of primary school children to the authorities under the Prevent agenda. The logic of my argument should make it abundantly clear what the consequences would be, given the broader configurations of power that currently exist: Omar and his family would probably escape attention because they look so British, whereas foreign-sounding Ahmed and his wife would be searched and humiliated, yielding such suspicious material as the Holy Qu'ran and its message – as he takes it, anyway – of non-violence. Rather, any meaningful response will need to involve new

The art of integration   163

narratives and practices of what it means to be British, including a transformed relationship with time and history. It is best to be cautious about spelling out alternatives, which cannot emerge from the patterns of thought they aim to transcend. Nevertheless, in the final pages of this book, I begin to elaborate on ideas hinted at by *Four Lions* about how things could be different.

Time for intimate knowledge?

The only people who suspect what Omar is planning are the ones who love him: not just his wife and son, but also his brother. It is the latter who is well aware that blowing up a crow is not "a cultural thing". However, this is not something that it would be beyond Matt's ability to learn. An understanding of and imbrication in one another's stories, a curiosity about cultural practices, based not on suspicion and violence, but genuine relationships and negotiation grounded in love and mutual concern might give us cautious grounds for optimism.

We see two moments in the film when death and destruction might genuinely have been avoided. One is the desperate last-minute attempt that Omar makes to save his friend, Waj. This ends in death and more confusion thanks to the gung-ho actions of the police, but Omar still warns Matt – with genuine affection – to stay away when he does finally explode. The other is when Omar approaches his brother for advice. In the latter case, it is just a shame that Ahmed has such an irritatingly pious face.

There are no transcendent virtues in which we can ground a politics. Sofia's love of Omar (and superior face) is what persuades him to blow himself up. Nevertheless, this comic film has a touching and poignant ending because of the love between Omar and Waj: a love that ends up being tragically militarised in the service of incoherent violence. The only moments of possible redemption – although always compromised and riven with power – are the ones where people get to know, and care for, one another.

This film is a fiction, of course, so the good end unhappily and the bad end up in heaven. Nevertheless, it is hardly far-fetched to suggest that ways of living in which we pay genuine attention to one another's stories and care about one another's lives might be a remedy to violence. Anecdotally, Maajid Nawaz (2012) provides a telling story about his life as an "Islamist radical" in which he was instrumental in setting up "terror cells" and ended up in an Egyptian prison. He states that whilst violence had initially seemed a response to constant police harassment and racist violence, his eventual refusal of terrorism came down to Amnesty International's letter writers, who took him on as a "prisoner of conscience". This provoked a realisation of the humanity of the other, which made continued violence seem an impossible option. These kind of caring practices, then, offer possibilities for remaking the world and they do not have to be as dramatic as Nawaz's story.

More broadly, we will only be able to imagine different ways to live if we are fully cognisant of the ways that our stories, films, photographs, games and

164 *The art of integration*

songs *produce* our practices and identities as part of a web of power relations that saturate our lives and cut across the artificial divide between public and private, domestic and foreign. Insofar as we accept these divides and understand others' private practices to be none of our business, we are ignoring this crucial dimension of productive power and thereby enabling it to flourish as it is. As long as democracy is viewed as the liberal business of voting in representatives and maintaining the freedom of the press, the flows of power that constitute the identities and interests that end up being represented in legislatures and in newspapers will remain invisible.

Yet only by making them visible can we hope to change them. In my detailed readings of the photographs that are used to promote democracy, I have shown one way of doing this. Chris Morris's *Four Lions* is yet another kind of intervention. He demonstrates the way that chaos, uncertainty and casual brutality pervade our everyday lives. He shows that the categories of domestic versus foreign, private versus public, secure versus dangerous, democratic versus violent, Islamic misogyny versus Western women's rights, barbarism/savagery versus civilisation are always on the verge of collapse and therefore require constant policing and reproduction. He suggests the ways in which disaster might have been averted and, crucially, these are all ways that involve love and intimate involvement, ways that take *time*. In doing so, he enables us also to see glimpses of how life might be different.

Notes

1   All the pictures and captions from the exhibition are still available on this website at the time of writing.
2   I took detailed notes during this meeting and the statements made form the basis of my analysis below, unless otherwise referenced. Words in quotation marks are direct quotes as I noted them at the time.

Conclusion
Democracy promotion, time and the "radical ordinary"

This book started with the puzzles and problems I encountered in my life as a professional development manager and "Democracy Promoter". It has taken me a long time to understand what I was involved in in that other life. We began with the bombings in London on 7 July 2005. The narrative we have become used to hearing is the one offered by Tony Blair and the other G8 leaders that these bombers were opposed to democratic values, civilisation, development, progress and women's rights. Although they were British, they had espoused a foreign, violent, barbaric ideology characterised by its hyper-masculine refusal of women's rights and which advocated a return to a medieval past. This version of the terrorist ideology re-emerged in responses to the then Archbishop of Canterbury's lecture on *shari'ah* law. The mainstream media turned on the Archbishop in fury because in defending *shari'ah* law, they believed he was an apologist for this very anti-democratic, out-dated and terrorist ideology.

The bombers themselves were no strangers to a version of this narrative about ideology. Mohammed Sidique Khan, whose very exploding body came so violently to symbolise the limits of British identity, left a videotaped message explaining his motives for perpetrating the London bombings, in which he suggests that the government wishes "to scare the masses into conforming to their power and wealth-obsessed agenda" and contrasts his own "driving motivation [which] doesn't come from tangible commodities". He furthermore explicitly defines himself against "[y]our democratically elected governments" (BBC, 2005b). Mohammed Sidique Khan was *a product of the same discourses and practices* as the political leaders of the UK, and by taking the very categories of democracy and economic development and positioning himself *against* them, was availing himself of the same discursive resources later used by Tony Blair.

The problem of considering why this young man – who had a job, a family and seemingly everything to live for – decided that there was no space for his voice to be heard within the institutional setting of the democracy in which he grew up is difficult and there are no simple answers, however we may wish to condemn him as simply "uncivilised". There is a grave danger at the heart of the insidious cruel choice that asks us to opt for either a domesticated liberal

166   *Conclusion*

democracy or an alien despotism, either civilisation or barbarism, either women's rights or violent masculinity, either development or backwardness, either the future or the past. We can only hope that the answer never again comes back, as it did from Mohammed Sidique Khan: "This is a war and I am a soldier" (BBC, 2005b).

I have been less interested in these pages in the spectacular violence of suicide bombing, than the everyday dispiriting violence that is enacted in the name of liberal democracy. When the Archbishop of Canterbury was pilloried, it was done in the most personal and belittling of tones. He is called the "Great Mufti" (White, 2008) or the "Ayatollah" (Hitchens, 2008) of Canterbury as well as "a dangerous threat to the nation" and a "silly old goat" (*The Sun*, 2008). The point is not that a senior public figure should be immune to criticism, but that the bullying name calling is unlikely to stop there. As a young Muslim woman put it when interviewed by a newspaper in the middle of the controversy, "once again it is us being demonised" (Doward et al., 2008). Positing a choice between a liberal democratic, modern secularism and a despotic, backward, religious authority invites demonisation and puts faithful Muslims into a painfully difficult and vulnerable position.

Furthermore, the separation into public and private spheres – as we have seen in accounts of domestic violence, racist crime and epistemic exclusion – makes some acts of violence more visible than others. Book burning in Bradford and suicide bombing in London are decried and condemned, but violence in the private sphere is often difficult to see and absent from democratic debate. From Partition to the corner shop, from suicide bombing and rendition to the daily miseries of "Paki-bashing" and racist insults, liberal democracy is not a remedy for violence, then, but is fully complicit in its practice. This is not only because of its structure, but also because of the exclusionary practices of thought, the teleological narratives, through which we come to know who belongs, who counts as democratic, what sorts of arguments we are allowed to make – about faith, about community, about belonging, about violence – in the first place.

Meanwhile, in his much-awaited speech in Munich in February 2011 (Cameron, 2011), in which he first addressed the subject of terrorism and security, Prime Minister David Cameron spelled out the now accustomed view that what is to be combated when we think about terrorism is a particular "ideology". This ideology is defined as "a real hostility to western democracy and liberal values". The solution to the problem of terrorism and insecurity, therefore, alongside surveillance and intelligence gathering, is – he proposes – a "muscular liberalism": "[a] genuinely liberal country [...] believes in certain values and actively promotes them." Lest there be any doubt, he spells out what these values are: "Freedom of speech. Freedom of worship. Democracy. The rule of law. Equal rights regardless of race, sex or sexuality [...] To belong here is to believe in these things." So far so familiar.

Alarmingly, Cameron also makes explicit what Blair had only hinted at. He argues that "non-violent extremists" need to be combated, thus making it absolutely clear that modes of belonging are premised entirely on practices of

Conclusion 167

thought and belief related to a commitment and loyalty to a highly specified set of liberal institutions, *not* on whether or not a particular violent crime has been committed, or even advocated, by an individual (Basham and Vaughan-Williams, 2012). This is the logic that runs through the controversial Prevent agenda which defines the "extremism" that is to be monitored, disciplined and ideally eradicated as "opposition to British values, including democracy, the rule of law, individual liberty and mutual tolerance and respect" (HM Government, 2015: 12).

Intriguingly, though, David Cameron attempts in this speech to distance himself from the "war on terror" discourse by denying that Democracy Promotion or development overseas are viable solutions to the problem of terrorism. He points out quite correctly that "extremists" can emerge in liberal democratic societies and that people convicted of terrorist offences are often middle class, thus denying any causal link between "poor governance", lack of development and terrorism. He also avoids drawing explicitly on a particular narrative of history, eschewing the civilisational narrative favoured by Tony Blair. There are no doubt good political reasons for this, as Cameron can hereby distance himself from the politically unpopular invasions of Afghanistan and Iraq (which he and his party supported at the time) by avoiding both the explicit civilisational discourse and the logic of Democracy Promotion that implicitly underwrote them.

However, like any subject of a discourse, Cameron is not in control of its terms and therefore cannot entirely avoid its logic. He is obliged to say: "Yes – we must tackle poverty." He cannot avoid supporting "[h]undreds of thousands of people demanding the universal right to free elections and democracy [in Cairo and Tunis]", particularly given that the value of these things must be taken for granted for his policies to be legitimate. His interventions within conventionally understood UK borders involve promoting "a common culture and curriculum", which inevitably reminds us of the familiar narrative of British institutions and their ineluctable, democratic evolution. Thus, in response to the so-called "Trojan Horse" scandal, in which Birmingham schools were said to be promoting "radical" and "un-British" ideas to pupils, Cameron responded that British values must henceforth be promoted in schools. How might this be put into practice?

> We are bringing proper narrative history back to the curriculum, so our children really learn our island's story – and where our freedoms and things like our Parliament and constitutional monarchy came from.
>
> (Cameron, 2014)

As the ongoing so-called "history wars" attest (Evans, 2013; Robinson, 2012: 100–109; Cannadine et al., 2011; Bowen et al., 2012), stories about national identity that draw on narrative history, continue to play a particularly important role in this ongoing reproduction of the nation under Cameron's government.

168 *Conclusion*

Meanwhile, under the Coalition government, the Department for International Development (DFID) was spending around £30 million per year on "government and civil society" (DFID, 2014) in Pakistan. The rationale for this was as follows:

> The UK has deep family, historic and business ties with Pakistan. That's why we are committed to Pakistan for the long term, to help millions of people lift themselves out of poverty, and to help Pakistan become the stable, prosperous, democratic country it has the potential to be.
>
> (DFID, 2012b)

The work that we have done so far in understanding the genealogy of Democracy Promotion makes these two sentences easy to read. The "stability" of Pakistan is important because Pakistan and the UK are deeply imbricated: "what happens in Pakistan matters on the streets of Britain" (Blair, 2007b). The family ties of people like Mohammed Sidique Khan mean that danger in Pakistan can spill over into danger to Britain's very identity.

Not only this, of course – family and historic ties quite rightly mean that many British citizens care particularly about Pakistan, and may be outraged by the poverty and undemocratic rule to which its people are subjected. Moreover, the only legitimate future that can be envisioned for Pakistan is underwritten by a notion that its trajectory needs to mirror the past of countries like Britain. It is hard, then, within prevailing discourses, to imagine alternatives to poverty and military rule that do not include economic development, liberalism and elections. This gives the government something to do, as democratically mandated by its own population, not least the Pakistani diaspora: a whole range of projects continue to attempt to know and domesticate Pakistan by supporting the institutions of liberal democratic governmentality (DFID, 2012a). There is a clear endpoint in mind, underwritten by pictures on the website of people (mainly women) voting, and as implied by the word "potential", which bears with it the teleological reading of history that always assumes that a better future will imply liberal democratic institutions and the capitalist economic development that is assumed to come with them.

Although the language of the "war on terror" is no longer *de rigueur*, the elision of these words does not mean that a new politics has been crafted. As Louise Amoore (2008) has eloquently argued, a forgetting of the "war on terror" and its discourses permits us to accept the categories and modes of othering it has bequeathed us as if they were natural and inevitable, rather than the result of long histories that could have been different. If we are going to be able to grasp the logic of democracy promotion, and the policy discourse that goes with it, then an understanding of its history is as urgent as ever. That is why the history of the modes of othering that I have uncovered in this book and their relation to the promotion of highly specific democratic identities remain crucially important.

It is by understanding the *function* of narratives about democracy that we are able to discern the logic of the democracy promotion that is constantly

Conclusion 169

re-inscribed in temporal modes of othering. Stories about history, teleology, development and the inevitable spread of liberal democracy are reiterated in newspapers, in Cameron's "common curriculum and culture", in political speeches, on television and in our daily lives in ways that seem so automatic, we can sometimes find it hard to see them. However good our intentions, they can make it difficult to recognise that our contemporary liberal democratic practices may not be the endpoint of history, nor yet the best we can do. The ability to recognise these narratives, to understand where they came from and to contest them is particularly important if we value democracy and perhaps want more of it.

Democratic temporalities and the "radical ordinary"

Is democracy something we value and want more of? A report (Wind-Cowie and Gregory, 2011), by the think tank Demos, on Britishness and a sense of belonging, patriotism and pride in the nation – based on qualitative focus-group research with a representative sample of over 2,000 British people – suggests that despite the best democracy promotion efforts by politicians, the media and photographers that we have seen in the preceding chapters, a commitment to the institutions of British liberal democracy is not a pre-eminent source of identification for British people. They argue that loyalty to Britain does not flow *from* allegiance to democratic values, the specific institutions of British governance (such as the monarchy or Parliament) or a progressive narrative about British history. Rather:

> [f]or most people, patriotism is an equation that travels in the opposite direction – they begin with a sense of pride in their country, which pre-disposes them to identifying things about their country, its history and institutions which reinforce that pride.
>
> (Wind-Cowie and Gregory, 2011: 75)

This makes sense when considering the preceding pages. There would be little need for the never-ending reinforcement of democracy promotion practices if a sense of belonging based on liberal democracy were fixed and stable. Rather, a relatively inchoate desire for belonging is both incited and given form by democracy promotion practices.

More intriguingly, the authors argue that a sense of Britishness "is founded in a profound emotional connection to the everyday acts, manners and kind-nesses that British people see in themselves" (Wind-Cowie and Gregory, 2011: 112). One of the quotations from their focus groups that they offer to support this conclusion is worth quoting in full:

> I think of being British as being about littler things, more boring, I sup-pose. Like doing your bit and manners and helping out. The thing about British people is that we do things for each other, you know? Being

170   *Conclusion*

> British is more about the way we are than things like Buckingham Palace
> or Parliament.
>
> (quoted in Wind-Cowie and Gregory, 2011: 22)

Somewhat similarly, another participant – aware of the logic that British identity is only possible insofar as it is marked by difference from others – remarked:

> You said about democracy and the law in your examples, but they're not just British are they? If you asked an American what was good about America they'd say the same thing, and the French.
>
> (quoted in Wind-Cowie and Gregory, 2011: 23)

A form of foreign policy with such a serious flaw that it cannot distinguish Britain from France, the notion of democracy as a universal value appears not to have caught contemporary imaginations. Locally rooted, everyday relational and caring practices, perhaps located in the private or domestic sphere, appear to offer forms of belonging that are more compelling than the familiar institutions of liberal democracy. In all their imperfections and possibilities, perhaps they remind us of the Edmund Burke we encountered in Chapter 4, the practices of the *biraderi* we saw in Chapter 5, the solidaristic attempts to defend friends and neighbours against violence in Chapter 6, the potentially life-saving (if ultimately, in this instance, tragically thwarted) love between Omar and Matt, Ahmed and Waj, or the Archbishop of Canterbury's careful exposition of how different forms of law and belonging might be talked about, accommodated, compromised upon. It reminds me of the young Muslim woman interviewed by a newspaper in a market in East London who said of the Archbishop, "Rowan Williams was trying to be kind" (Doward et al., 2008).

The relational forms of belonging alluded to by the focus group participants do not imply a rejection of democracy – at most, they demonstrate a vague indifference to the symbols and rituals of liberal democracy. However, must we read this research as a worrying sign that British everyday lives are not as democratic as we thought? Are we bored of democracy? I suggest that this would only be the right analysis if we were to accept that liberal democracy is the only form of democracy.

For political theorist Romand Coles, however, this would be the wrong approach. In his work, the "radical ordinary" – the everyday practices of caring, listening, sharing a meal, ceding one's place in a queue, sitting talking on a porch – *is* a form of democracy (Hauerwas and Coles, 2012). Rejecting as "too obvious" democracy as "the sheer existence of 'representative' institutions that incant a virtually unquestionable 'yes' to 'democracy'" (ibid.: 113), he instead asks us to consider it as a complex relational set of practices.

Importantly, by their very nature, such practices require a temporality that is not progressive or teleological, but rather privileges the present over the future. They are going to take *time* and to require us to take our time. This is

Conclusion 171

a slow, pulsing time in which a democratic ethics may play out, always with difficulty, always involving negotiation, always ungraspable in its entirety, costing not less than everything:

> a sense of the world as immanently shot through with fugitive democratic possibilities, gifts, scattered shards of light calling us to receive, gather, and carefully engage each other in relationships that slip beyond the oblivion of anti-democratic cages to initiate better things.
>
> (Hauerwas and Coles, 2012: 115)

This is a democracy that cannot be achieved quickly, that will not be reached inevitably or through an ineluctable, unconscious evolution. Rather, it requires never-ending *work* that takes place not so much in statements in academic books or political speeches about how the world *should* be, but rather in patient engagement in the everyday practices of how the world now *is*: the dense fabric of our radically ordinary lives, the constant opportunities to enact kindness, manners, hospitality that already exist in the subjectivities in which we manoeuvre.

A radically ordinary democracy requires a temporality that is a "complicated ever-changing pulse" rather than a "flow" (Hauerwas and Coles, 2012: 85). It is incompatible with democracy understood as a shortcut to knowledge or a linear forward march straight to the future. This is because the intimacies of a radically ordinary democracy *take time*: not long historical time, but the everyday rhythmic and recursive time of listening and caring, strolling and wondering, teaching and telling stories, relearning and re-remembering, refictioning our histories and our modes of belonging. The radical ordinary can accept no separate public and private sphere, but instead insists that democracy exists and can be practised in all locations of our lives together. It must inevitably refuse the injunction to leave our emotions, our relational commitments, our religious faith, our passion, our anger, our care for others at the door when we enter the public sphere. Instead of wishing these things away, it takes these arenas of life – riven with power and oppression and the desire to exclude others as they may be – as the starting point of a democratic engagement which must always deal with them.

We should be careful. Radical ordinary democracy does not banish power and does not pretend, in all its messiness, that the world could be made perfect. There is a chauvinism, for instance, in proposing that British people are uniquely able practitioners of such things as good manners. Unspoken but familiar notions of a quintessentially British "fair play" appear to underwrite some of the modes of belonging identified in the Demos focus groups; these require a whole genealogy themselves. Then there is the whole set of modes of exclusion underwritten by the focus group participant who describes a worry about lack of integration by immigrants in the following terms:

172 *Conclusion*

> They don't queue up – some of them – like in the Post Office; they just march up to the counter. And it makes me think, what is this country becoming? When there are people who live here but don't know, or can't be bothered with, normal manners?
>
> (Wind-Cowie and Gregory, 2011: 32)

Ordinariness can be depressingly non-radical, as we have seen throughout this book. Ordinary life is generally the locale where othering practices are performed and they can be as exclusionary in their insistence on good manners as they are in their emphasis on voting. Any model of democracy we might like to imagine will always carry with it the limits of our discourses, the power relations that have crafted our own subjectivities, the possibilities of multiple practices of exclusion in the execution.

Nevertheless, in his explanation of democracy as an ongoing ethics that makes no distinction between theory and practice and which values the intimate temporalities of faith, friendship, love, emotion and relationships, Coles offers us a way forward in re-thinking democratic time. Thus, we can perhaps be attentive to the spaces, or moments, that open up when democratic subjectivities are caught between conflicting loyalties to the rational public sphere of voting and reason giving, and to passionate emotional commitment to the practices of good manners and kindness; or when the speedy, quantifying logic of the election comes into confrontation with deliberative practices and relationships that require more time and patience; or when an encounter with some other time or some other subject teaches us that our contemporary practices are not as non-violent or rational or neutral as we had thought. These are the intersections that offer us glimpses of other ways to live, that collapse the familiar distinctions between the future and the past, self and other, teacher and student, rationality and violence, civilisation and barbarism, so that we must make them anew and, in doing so, change them.

Each time the practices of democracy promotion are contested or called into question, each time we redirect our gaze onto the invisible violence – physical or epistemic – that had gone unnoticed, each teacher who provides an alternative narrative in a history lesson, each film-maker or photographer who reminds us that things are more uncertain than they look, each novelist who crafts chaos out of order, each veil worn in defiance of Page Three, each Archbishop who dares to question the secular neutrality of the law, each little act of hospitality to a foreigner, each patient smile at an errant immigrant queue jumper, each time we question what democracy is and try to locate it at the level of the radical ordinary – each of these acts and practices enables a certain work at the borders of democracy, these sets of borders that mutually reinforce one another in their articulation, and each attempts to remake them all.

Nor are any of these actions parochial endeavours. As we have seen, the Foreign Policy that mandates Democracy Promotion is simply a manifestation of the foreign policy that establishes certain practices as foreign, dangerous and alien in the first place, and attempts to control, contain and domesticate them. Thus, re-making the borders that establish what democratic practices are at a local level *inevitably* disrupts the practices of Democracy Promotion.

If democracy could be thought of as a relational, everyday practice located in the radical ordinary that denies the existence of separable public and private spheres, then three consequences would follow. First, the actual practices that are recommended and enacted in Democracy Promotion would no longer seem so self-evident, but rather politically motivated, historically constituted and therefore changeable. Second, the relational ethic that could be seen to constitute democracy itself would disrupt the teacher-pupil relationship such that it might seem possible to ask questions about how the imperfect yet, in principle, alterable deliberative practices of the *jirga* might enhance lives not only in the North West Frontier Province but also in Bradford. This curiosity and the radically ordinary relationships that might develop over slow, pulsing time might also enable a conversation about some of the abuses, violence and exclusions committed by *jirgas* and by *biraderis* and by *shari'ah* courts. This in turn might enable changes in subjectivity more profound than would be effected simply by banning or ignoring these deeply rooted institutions. Third, the very practices of state sovereignty that rely on the distinction between the domestic and the foreign would themselves be called into question. The limits to this unravelling would be set only by how far we might call the limits of our individualised and totalised subjectivities into question.

Genealogy as democratic ethics

The photograph from the *Art of Integration* exhibition that I cannot stop thinking about is the picture of Mr Jamil. Not the caption with its extraordinary story of heroism and courage; just the radically ordinary picture.

Mr Jamil is a figure who appears to participate fully in the ordinary flows of productive power that make life possible. He wears his uniform and his high-visibility jacket ready to participate in the modern, capitalist, developed economy that London Underground keeps running whilst it keeps the Tube trains running in turn. Meanwhile, his beard quietly denotes his private, religious identity, fully formed in some separate private sphere. Yet his back is turned to the train that powers London forward into the future and instead he is tending a garden. An Englishman's garden – that most private and domestic of symbols of everyday life – springs up there with irrepressible exuberance into the public sphere and is nurtured and cared for by this public servant for the benefit of London's public transport users in all their strangeness and diversity. The rural invades the urban here, transforming both. Perhaps even more extraordinary than the spectacular, lightning-fast act of saving a stranger's life, is the radically ordinary, slow, everyday practice of growing flowers for the enjoyment of the people he might tangentially encounter each day. Could the ethics of these two acts even be connected, as Mr Jamil lives a radically ordinary, democratic ethic of caring and kindness in

174 *Conclusion*

his everyday life that trains and forms his subjectivity, ready to do the right thing in an extraordinary moment? Could anything other than this photograph more beautifully illustrate the way that the boundary between the public and private is more or less impossible to police, so many are the temporal and spatial locations at which it incipiently threatens to collapse, leaving us with our passionate emotions, our religious devotion, our manners and kindnesses and care for one another, all painfully and vulnerably exposed in a public gaze that is all-encompassing?

This is a reading of a photograph that differs from the one put forward in the caption and from the one encouraged by the photographs that surround it and the context in which they have been displayed. A reading of a photograph is never fully determined by the photographer or the subject or the spectator (Azoulay, 2008). As with any meaning-making practice, it eludes attempts to fix its meaning and offers the possibility for multiple interpretations. Reading a photograph in this alternative way is itself a political intervention, which seeks to question the narratives that first present themselves. Narratives about history are likewise indeterminate. The stories we tell of ourselves can always be re-told: they are never fixed but always contestable.

In this book, I have discussed an influential story that has been told about Britain and Pakistan in lots of different places for quite a long time. Britain, the story goes, is a country that through a 1,000-year process of history has evolved civilised democratic institutions like elections and the freedom of the press which enable the community to manage and reconcile conflicting opinions rationally and without violence, to know and foster life in its whole population, to distribute power neutrally in the form of a ballot paper, and to provide women and minorities with important rights.

The story, as it goes on, is a little more unfortunate for Pakistan. The same civilising process that brings democracy was inhibited for a long time by British colonial power. However, by providing electoral institutions in colonial times and by supporting development and Democracy Promotion ever since decolonisation, Britain has been attempting to aid Pakistan to make its entrance into the same history that Britain has been through. By 1989 – the end of history – it became obvious that democracy was the one best way of governing and that this should ultimately motivate British support for Pakistan, despite the temptations of military dictators, who offer the main imaginable alternative mode of governance to liberal democracy.

This same history, the story continues, has brought us repeatedly up against others, at home and overseas, who attack democracy, burn books and people, bomb Britain and its capital city. These enemies have had to be civilised or contained. If they choose democracy and its accompanying narratives and institutions, we can help them to civilise. If not, they are foreigners, barbarians, enemies, who must be contained and destroyed.

Against this smooth narrative of history, I have provided some detailed fragments that contest everything about it. I have shown that this teleology is not a description of the driving force of history, but is rather a discourse that

Conclusion 175

enables a messy historicity to be managed: teleology does not produce history; rather, history produces teleology. I have shown that it is possible to disrupt the authoritative story that British people tell about themselves: that as a postcoloniser, the UK too is a postcolonial country. I have shown that the clear choice between democratic rationality and despotic violence, violent masculinity and women's rights, liberal delineation of the public and private sphere versus irrational chaos is not only cruel, but false. I have discerned violence, misogyny and also glimpses of radical ordinariness in Britain's liberal democracy. I have demonstrated that the borders and oppositions we might have taken for granted collapse at every turn, that democracy may not be quite what we think it is, that the ways we know democracy – and the ways we use democracy to know – are not neutral, but entangled with deeply troubling flows of power.

In doing this, I have used aesthetic productions by artists, novelists and film-makers to show the scattered shards of possibilities of other ways to live. I have not described history in a valid, reliable or objective way, but I have attempted to make a radically ordinary, deeply political, passionately committed intervention into its telling. That is what I mean when I say that genealogy is a way of practising radically ordinary democratic ethics.

Bibliography

All newspaper articles were accessed using the Nexis database, unless a page reference is given in the text, in which case the print edition was consulted.

Abrahamsen, Rita (2000) *Disciplining Democracy: Development Discourse and Good Governance in Africa*, London: Zed Books Ltd.

Abu-Lughod, Lila (2002) "Do Muslim women really need saving: Anthropological reflections on cultural relativism and its others", *American Anthropologist*, 104(3): 783–790.

Ahmed, Leila (2011) *A Quiet Revolution: The Veil's Resurgence, from the Middle East to America* (Kindle edition), London: Yale University Press.

Alibhai-Brown, Yasmin (2008) "What he wishes on us is an abomination", *The Independent*, 9 February.

Amoore, Louise (2007) "Vigilant visualities: The watchful politics of the war on terror", *Security Dialogue*, 38(2): 215–232.

Amoore, Louise (2008) "Response before the event: On forgetting the war on terror" in *Terrorism and the Politics of Response: London in a Time of Terror* (eds Closs Stephens, Angharad & Vaughan-Williams, Nick), Abingdon: Routledge.

Anderson, Benedict (2006) *Imagined Communities: Reflections on the Origin and Spread of Nationalism*, London: Verso Books.

Asad, Talal (2003) *Formations of the Secular: Christianity, Islam, Modernity*, Stanford, CA: Stanford University Press.

Asad, Talal et al. (2009) *Is Critique Secular? Blasphemy, Injury and Free Speech*, Berkeley: University of California Press.

Ayers, Alison (2006) "Demystifying democratisation: The global constitution of (neo)liberal polities in Africa", *Third World Quarterly*, 27(2): 321–338.

Azoulay, Ariella (2008) *The Civil Contract of Photography*, New York: Zone Books.

Baig, Anila (2008) "They don't live in a Muslim country", *The Sun*, 8 February.

Baker, Aryn (2007) "Pakistan's reluctant hero", *Time Magazine*, 14 June, www.time.com/time/magazine/article/0,9171,1632743,00.html (accessed 5 October 2009).

Barrington, Sir Nicholas (1989a) "FCO TelNo 076 to Kuwait: 'Satanic Verses'", March 1989, FOI Disclosure 0496-0412, received on 24 May 2012.

Barrington, Sir Nicholas (1989b) "FCO TelNo 114 to Cairo 'Satanic Verses'", March 1989, FOI Disclosure 0496-0412, received on 24 May 2012.

Barro, Robert J. (1999) "Determinants of democracy", *Journal of Political Economy*, 107(6): 158–183.

Bibliography   177

Bartelson, Jens (1995) *A Genealogy of Sovereignty*, Cambridge: Cambridge University Press.

Barthes, Roland (2009) *Mythologies*, London: Vintage Classics.

Basham, Victoria M. & Vaughan-Williams, Nick (2012) "Gender, race and border security practices: A profane reading of 'muscular liberalism'", *British Journal of Politics and International Relations*, 15(4): 509–527.

BBC (2005a) "Blair says hope can fight terror", news.bbc.co.uk/1/hi/uk_politics/4664391.stm (accessed 14 January 2012).

BBC (2005b) "London bomber: Text in full", news.bbc.co.uk/1/hi/uk/4206800.stm http://news.bbc.co.uk/1/hi/uk/4206800.stm (accessed 30 September 2009).

BBC (2006a) "Raid police apologise for 'hurt'", news.bbc.co.uk/1/hi/5077198.stm (14 June) (accessed 30 July 2012).

BBC (2006b) "The bombers", news.bbc.co.uk/1/shared/spl/hi/uk/05/london_blasts/investigation/html/bombers.stm (accessed 29 September 2009).

BBC (2006c) "UK and Pakistan forge terror pact", news.bbc.co.uk/1/hi/world/south_asia/6161500.stm (accessed 6 January 2012).

BBC (2007) "In pictures: Pakistan protests", news.bbc.co.uk/1/hi/in_pictures/6458503.stm (accessed 5 October 2009).

BBC (2009) "The Satanic Verses affair", broadcast on BBC2 Saturday 7 March at 21:00.

BBC (2015a) "Paris attacks: What happened on the night?", www.bbc.co.uk/news/world-europe-34818994 (accessed 21 April 2016).

BBC (2015b) "Andrew Neil's message to those who attacked Paris", www.bbc.co.uk/news/uk-politics-34877683 (accessed 21 April 2016).

Beattie, Hugh (2011) "Negotiations with the tribes of Waziristan 1849–1914 – The British experience", *The Journal of Imperial and Commonwealth History*, 39(4): 571–587.

Bellamy, Richard (2007) *Political Constitutionalism: A Republican Defence of the Constitutionality of Democracy*, Cambridge: Cambridge University Press.

Berg, Maggie and Seeber, Barbara (2016) *Slow Professor: Challenging the Culture of Speed in the Academy*, Toronto: University of Toronto Press.

Berman, Sheri (2012) "The past and future of social democracy and the consequences for democracy promotion" in *The Conceptual Politics of Democracy Promotion* (eds Hobson, Christopher & Kurki, Milja), Abingdon: Routledge.

Bernstein, R.J. (1992) *The New Constellation: The Ethical-Political Horizons of Modernity/Postmodernity*, Cambridge, MA: MIT Press.

Bevir, Mark & Rhodes, Rod (2004) "Interpreting British governance", *British Journal of Politics and International Relations*, 6(2): 130–136.

Bhabha, Homi (2004) *The Location of Culture*, London: Routledge.

Biccum, April (2005) "Development and the 'new' imperialism: A reinvention of colonial discourse in DFID promotional literature", *Third World Quarterly*, 26(5).

Biccum, April (2007) "Marketing development: Live 8 and the production of the global citizen", *Development and Change*, 38(6): 1005–1020.

Bigo, Didier (2000) "When two become one: Internal and external securitisations in Europe" in *International Relations Theory and the Politics of European Integration, Power, Security and Community* (eds Kelstrup, Morten & Williams, Michael C.), London: Routledge.

Blair, Tony (2005a) "PM's statement on London explosions: Full text", speech given on 7 July 2005 at G8 Summit in Gleneagles, www.number10.gov.uk/Page7853 (accessed 20 September 2009).

Blair, Tony (2005b) "We will hold true to the British way of life", *The Guardian*, 8 July.

178 *Bibliography*

Blair, Tony (2006) "Not a clash between civilisations, but a clash about civilisation", speech given on 21 March 2006 at Foreign Policy Centre, fpc.org.uk/events/past/clash-about-civilisation (accessed 20 September 2009).

Blair, Tony (2007a) "A battle for global values", *Foreign Affairs*, 86(1).

Blair, Tony (2007b) "What I've learned", *The Economist*, 31 May.

Bleiker, Roland (2001) "The aesthetic turn in international political theory", *Millennium: Journal of International Studies*, 30(3): 509–533.

Bohman, James (1998) "Survey article: The coming of age of deliberative democracy", *Journal of Political Philosophy*, 6(4): 400–425.

Bohman, James (2000) *Public Deliberation: Pluralism, Complexity and Democracy*, Cambridge, MA: MIT Press.

Bowden, Brett (2009) *The Empire of Civilization: The Evolution of an Imperial Idea*, Chicago, IL: University of Chicago Press.

Bowen, Lloyd et al. (2012) "History in the UK National Curriculum: A discussion", *Cultural and Social History*, 9(1): 125–143.

Bridoux, Jeff and Russell, Malcolm (2012) "Liberal democracy promotion in Iraq: A model for the Middle East and North Africa?" *Foreign Policy Analysis*, 9(3): 327–346.

Brigg, Morgan (2002) "Post-development, Foucault and the colonisation metaphor", *Third World Quarterly*, 23(3): 421–436.

Bromwich, David (2011) "The disappointed lover of the West", *The New York Review of Books*, 8 December.

Brown, Andrew (1989) "Faith and reason", *The Independent*, 19 August.

Bulley, Dan (2008) "'Foreign' terror? Resisting/responding to the London bombings" in *Terrorism and the Politics of Response: London in a Time of Terror* (eds Closs Stephens, Angharad & Vaughan-Williams, Nick), Abingdon: Routledge.

Bunting, Madeleine (2008) "A noble, reckless rebellion", *The Guardian*, 9 February.

Burchell, Graham (1991) "Peculiar interests: Civil society and governing 'the system of natural interests'" in *The Foucault Effect: Studies in Governmentality* (eds Burchell, Graham, Gordon, Colin & Miller, Peter), Chicago, IL: University of Chicago Press.

Burke, Edmund (1990) "Miscellaneous writings" in *Library of Economics and Liberty* (ed. Payne, E.J.), www.econlib.org/library/LFBooks/Burke/brkSWv4c5.html (accessed 3 May 2012).

Burke, Edmund (1991a) "Letter to the sheriffs of Bristol (1777)" in *Empire and Community: Edmund Burke's Writings and Speeches on International Relations* (eds Fidler, David P. & Welsh, Jennifer), Boulder, CO: Westview Press.

Burke, Edmund (1991b) "Speech on conciliation with America (1775)" in *Empire and Community: Edmund Burke's Writings and Speeches on International Relations* (eds Fidler, David P. & Welsh, Jennifer), Boulder, CO: Westview Press.

Burke, Edmund (1991c) "Speech on Fox's India Bill (1783)" in *Empire and Community: Edmund Burke's Writings and Speeches on International Relations* (eds Fidler, David P. & Welsh, Jennifer), Boulder, CO: Westview Press.

Burke, Edmund (1991d) "Speech on opening of impeachment (1788)" in *Empire and Community: Edmund Burke's Writings and Speeches on International Relations* (eds Fidler, David P. & Welsh, Jennifer), Boulder, CO: Westview Press.

Burnell, Peter (2000) *Democracy Assistance: International Co-operation for Democratization*, London: Routledge.

Butler, Judith (2004) *Precarious Life*, London: Verso.

Butler, Judith (2006) *Gender Trouble*, Abingdon: Routledge.

Butt, Riazat (2008) "Uproar as archbishop says sharia law inevitable in the UK", *The Guardian*, 8 February.

Butterfield, Herbert (1965) *The Whig Interpretation of History*, New York: W.W. Norton.

Cameron, David (2011) "Prime Minister's speech at Munich Security Conference", speech given on 5 February 2011 at Munich Security Conference, www.number10. gov.uk/news/speeches-and-transcripts/2011/02/pms-speech-at-munich-security-confer ence-60293 (accessed 11 February 2011).

Cameron, David (2014) "British values", www.gov.uk/government/news/british-va lues-article-by-david-cameron (accessed 13 January 2015).

Campbell, David (1990) "Global inscription: How foreign policy constitutes the United States", *Alternatives*, 15(3): 263–286.

Campbell, David (1998) *Writing Security: United States Foreign Policy and the Politics of Identity* (revised edition) (Kindle edition), Minneapolis: University of Minnesota Press.

Cannadine, David, Keating, Jenny & Sheldon, Nicola (2011) *The Right Kind of History: Teaching the Past in Twentieth Century England*, Basingstoke: Palgrave Macmillan.

Carabine, Jean (2000) "Constituting welfare subjects through poverty and sexuality" in *Rethinking Social Policy* (eds Lewis, Gail, Gewirtz, Sharon & Clarke, John), London: Sage Publications Ltd.

Carey, Lord George (2008) "No change to British law", *The News of the World*, 10 February.

Carothers, Thomas (2004) *Critical Mission: Essays on Democracy Promotion*, Washington, DC: Carnegie Endowment for International Peace.

Carothers, Thomas (2006) "The backlash against democracy promotion", *Foreign Affairs*, 85(2): 5–19.

Caufield, Catherine (1996) *Masters of Illusion: The World Bank and the Poverty of Nations*, London: Macmillan.

Chambers, Robert (1997) *Whose Reality Counts? Putting the First Last*, London: ITDG Publishing.

Chambers, Simone (2009) "Rhetoric and the public sphere: Has deliberative democracy abandoned mass democracy?", *Political Theory*, 37(3): 323–350.

Charman, Matt (2009) *The Observer*, London: Faber and Faber.

Chatterjee, Partha (2004) *The Politics of the Governed: Reflections on Popular Politics in Most of the World* (Kindle edition), New York: Columbia University Press.

Chirol, Valentine (1910) *Indian Unrest*, London: Macmillan and Co.

Chossudovsky, Michael (2003) *The Globalization of Poverty and the New World Order*, London: Zed Books.

Chua, Amy (2004) *World on Fire: How Exporting Free Market Democracy Breeds Ethnic Hatred and Global Instability*, London: Arrow Books.

Closs Stephens, Angharad (2008) "Seven million Londoners, one London: National and urban ideas of community" in *Terrorism and the Politics of Response: London in a Time of Terror* (eds Closs Stephens, Angharad & Vaughan-Williams, Nick), Abingdon: Routledge.

Closs Stephens, Angharad (2013) *The Persistence of Nationalism: From Imagined Communities to Urban Encounters*, London: Routledge.

Coffey International Development (2011) "Pakistan country governance analysis", FOI Disclosure F2011-2233, received on 6 September 2011.

180   *Bibliography*

Cohen, Stephen Philip (2004) *The Idea of Pakistan*, Washington, DC: Brookings Institution Press.

Cohn, Bernard (1996) *Colonialism and its Forms of Knowledge*, Princeton, NJ: Princeton University Press.

Coleman, Stephen (2013) *How Voters Feel*, Cambridge: Cambridge University Press.

Colley, Linda (2009) *Britons: Forging the Nation 1707–1837*, New Haven, CT: Yale University Press.

Collier, Paul (2008) *The Bottom Billion: Why the Poorest Countries are Failing and What Can Be Done About It*, Oxford: Oxford University Press.

Cook, Robin (1997a) "Britain's new approach to the world", speech given on 2 October at Labour Party Conference, Brighton.

Cook, Robin (1997b) "British foreign policy, speech at the launch of the Foreign Office mission statement", speech given on 12 May at Locarno Suite.

Corbo, Vittorio, Fischer, Stanley & Webb, Steven B. (1992) *Adjustment Lending Revisited, World Bank Symposium*, Washington, DC: World Bank.

Cornia, Giovanni A., Jolly, Richard & Stewart, Frances (1987) *Adjustment with a Human Face: Protecting the Vulnerable and Promoting Growth*, Oxford: Oxford University Press.

Cowen, M.P. & Shenton, Robert W. (1996) *Doctrines of Development*, London: Routledge.

Croft, Stuart (2006) *Culture, Crisis and America's War on Terror* (Kindle edition), Cambridge: Cambridge University Press.

Cupitt, Don (1989) "The decade (faith)", *The Guardian*, 16 December.

Daalder, Ivo & Lindsay, James (2007) "Democracies of the world unite", *Public Policy Research*, 14(1): 47–58.

Dahl, Robert (1977) *Polyarchy: Participation and Opposition*, New Haven, CT: Yale University Press.

Daily Mail (2008a) "Archbishop should tend to his own flock", *Daily Mail*, 8 February.

Daily Mail (2008b) "Equality before the law is not negotiable", *Daily Mail*, 9 February.

Daily Telegraph (2005) "If these terrorists thought they could intimidate the people of a great nation", *Daily Telegraph*, 10 July.

Dalrymple, William (2006) *The Last Mughal, The Fall of Delhi, 1857*, Delhi: Penguin.

Dalrymple, William (2008) "A new deal in Pakistan", *The New York Review of Books*, 3 April, www.nybooks.com/articles/archives/2008/apr/03/a-new-deal-in-pakistan/?pagination=false (accessed 22 February 2013).

d'Ancona, Matthew (2008) "Comment: Britain must reject this craven counsel of despair", *Sunday Telegraph*, 10 February.

Das, Mammath N. (1964) *India Under Morley and Minto*, London: Allen and Unwin.

Dean, Mitchell (2010) *Governmentality: Power and Rule in Modern Society*, London: Sage.

de Goede, Marieke (2005) *Virtue, Fortune, and Faith: A Genealogy of Finance*, Minneapolis: University of Minnesota Press.

Der Derian, James (1991) *On Diplomacy: A Genealogy of Western Estrangement*, Oxford: Blackwell.

DFID (2004) "Pakistan: Strengthening the capacity of political parties to engage in local governance", FOI Disclosure: F2010-2327, received on 17 January 2011.

DFID (2006a) "Programme memorandum: Support for elections 2007", FOI Disclosure F2010-2278, received on 1 October 2010.

Bibliography 181

DFID (2006b) "Programme memorandum: Support for elections 2007", FOI Disclosure: F2010-2278, received on 1 October 2010.

DFID (2006c) "Project concept note: Pakistan: DFID support to the Poverty Reduction Support Credit (PRSC)", FOI Disclosure: F2011-2048, received on 27 June 2011.

DFID (2006d) "Project memorandum: Pakistan: DFID Pakistan: Project memorandum for up to £85 millions for Poverty Reduction Budget Support", FOI Disclosure F2011-2048, received on 27 June 2011.

DFID (2006e) *White Paper 2006: Making Governance Work for the Poor*, www.dfid.gov.uk/about-dfid/quick-guide-to-dfid/how-we-do-it/2006-white-paper-making-governance-work-for-the-poor/ (accessed 15 April 2010).

DFID (2007a) "Country governance analysis: How to note", emailed to me personally by DFID Freedom of Information team.

DFID (2007b) *Governance, Development and Democratic Politics: DFID's Work in Building more Effective States*, www.dfid.gov.uk/pubs/files/governance.pdf (accessed 22 April 2009).

DFID (2007c) "Programme memorandum: Improving citizen engagement through devolution", FOI Disclosure: F2011-2019, received on 4 February 2011.

DFID (2008a) *Evaluation of DFID Country Programmes: Country Study: Pakistan*, www.dfid.gov.uk/Documents/publications1/evaluation/ev687.pdf (accessed 3 May 2010).

DFID (2008b) "How we fight poverty: What's the point of voting?" www.dfid.gov.uk/howwefightpoverty/government.asp (accessed 6 August 2008).

DFID (2010) "FOI disclosure F2010-2203", received on 2 August 2010.

DFID (2012a) "Summary of DFID's work in Pakistan 2011–2015", www.dfid.gov.uk/Documents/publications1/op/pakistan-2011-summary.pdf (accessed 14 August 2012).

DFID (2012b) "Where we work: Pakistan", www.dfid.gov.uk/where-we-work/asia-south/pakistan/ (accessed 14 August 2012).

DFID (2014) *Operational Plan 2011–2016, DFID Pakistan, Updated December 2014)*, www.gov.uk/government/uploads/system/uploads/attachment_data/file/389059/Pakistan.pdf (accessed 28 April 2016).

Diamond, Dominik (2008) "No need for law unto themselves", *Daily Star*, 9 February.

Diamond, Larry (2002) "Thinking about hybrid regimes", *Journal of Democracy*, 13(2): 21–35.

Diamond, Larry (2008) *The Spirit of Democracy: The Struggle to Build Free Societies Throughout the World*, New York: Times Books.

Diamond, Larry, Linz, Juan J. & Lipset, Seymour Martin (1988) "Introduction" in *Democracy in Developing Areas*, London: Adamtine Press.

Dillon, Michael & Reid, Julian (2001) "Global liberal governance: Biopolitics, security and war", *Millennium: Journal of International Studies*, 30(1): 41–66.

Dodd, Vikram, Taylor, Matthew & Branigan, Tania (2005) "Attack on London: Backlash", *The Guardian*, 8 July.

Doggart, Sebastian (2010) "Chris Morris in the lion's den", *The Daily Telegraph*, 10 February.

Dooley, Mark (2008) "Why can't these clerics see that God and politics will never mix?", *Daily Mail*, 11 February.

Douzinas, Costas (2008) "2 July, 7 July and metaphysics" in *Terrorism and the Politics of Response: London in a Time of Terror* (eds Closs Stephens, Angharad & Vaughan-Williams, Nick), Abingdon: Routledge.

182 *Bibliography*

Dovi, Suzanne (2011) "Political representation" in *The Stanford Encyclopedia of Philosophy* (winter 2011 edition) (ed. Zalta, Edward N.), plato.stanford.edu/archives/win2011/entries/political-representation/ (accessed 3 February 2012).

Doward, Jamie et al. (2008) "Sharia row: How law and faith row swept the UK", *The Observer*, 10 February.

Dryzek, John S. (2000) *Deliberative Democracy and Beyond: Liberals, Critics, Contestations*, Oxford: Oxford University Press.

Dryzek, John S. & Niemeyer, Simon (2008) "Discursive representation", *American Political Science Review*, 102(4): 481–493.

Duffield, Mark (2007) *Development, Security and Unending War: Governing the World of Peoples*, Cambridge: Polity.

Dyer, Clare (2008) "Sharia row", *The Guardian*, 9 February.

Easterly, William (2006) *The White Man's Burden: Why the West's Efforts to Aid the Rest Have Done So Much Ill and So Little Good*, Oxford: Oxford University Press.

The Economist (2011) "The world in figures: Countries: Pakistan", *The Economist*, 17 November.

Edkins, Jenny (2003) *Trauma and the Memory of Politics*, Cambridge: Cambridge University Press.

Elliott, Cathy (2009) "The day democracy died: The depoliticising effects of democratic development", *Alternatives*, 34(3): 249–274.

Escobar, Arturo (1994) *Encountering Development: The Making and Unmaking of the Third World*, Princeton, NJ: Princeton University Press.

Esteva, Gustavo (1992) "'Development'" in *The Development Dictionary: A Guide to Knowledge as Power* (ed. Sachs, Wolfgang), London: Zed.

Evans, Richard (2013) "Michael Gove's history wars", *The Guardian*, 13 July, www.theguardian.com/books/2013/jul/13/michael-gove-teaching-history-wars (accessed 1 December 2015).

FCO (2006) *White Paper 2006: Active Diplomacy for a Changing World: The UK's International Priorities*, Norwich: HMSO.

FCO (2011) "Freedom of information request 0911-0911", received on 13 October.

FCO (2012) "Freedom of information request 0496-0412", received on 24 May.

Ferguson, James (1990) *The Anti-politics Machine: "Development", Depoliticization, and Bureaucratic Power in Lesotho*, Cambridge: Cambridge University Press.

Fidler, David P. & Welsh, Jennifer (1991) *Empire and Community: Edmund Burke's Writings and Speeches on International Relations*, Boulder, CO: Westview Press.

Fineman, Martha Albertson (2004) *The Autonomy Myth: A Theory of Dependency*, New York: The New Press.

Flyvbjerg, Bent (1998) "Habermas and Foucault: Thinkers for civil society?", *British Journal of Sociology*, 49(2): 210–233.

Foucault, Michel (1981) *The History of Sexuality*, Harmondsworth: Penguin.

Foucault, Michel (1982) "'Afterword: The subject and power'" in *Michel Foucault: Beyond Structuralism and Hermeneutics* (eds Dreyfus, Hubert L. & Rabinow, Paul), Brighton: Harvester.

Foucault, Michel (1988) "Practicing criticism" in *Politics, Philosophy, Culture: Interviews and Other Writings 1977–1984* (ed. Kritzman, Lawrence D.), London: Routledge.

Foucault, Michel (1990) *The History of Sexuality: The Care of the Self*, London: Penguin.

Bibliography   183

Foucault, Michel (1991a) "Nietzsche, genealogy, history" in *The Foucault Reader* (ed. Rabinow, Paul), Harmondsworth: Penguin.

Foucault, Michel (1991b) "On the genealogy of ethics: An overview of work in progress" in *The Foucault Reader* (ed. Rabinow, Paul), Harmondsworth: Penguin.

Foucault, Michel (1991c) "Space, knowledge and power" in *The Foucault Reader* (ed. Rabinow, Paul), Harmondsworth: Penguin.

Foucault, Michel (1991d) "Truth and power" in *The Foucault Reader* (ed. Rabinow, Paul), Harmondsworth: Penguin.

Foucault, Michel (1991e) "What is the Enlightenment?" in *The Foucault Reader* (ed. Rabinow, Paul), Harmondsworth: Penguin.

Foucault, Michel (1991f) *Discipline and Punish: The Birth of the Prison*, Harmondsworth: Penguin.

Foucault, Michel (1992) *The History of Sexuality: The Use of Pleasure*, London: Penguin.

Foucault, Michel (2002) *Archaeology of Knowledge*, London: Routledge.

Foucault, Michel (2005a) *The Hermeneutics of the Subject: Lectures at the Collège de France, 1981–1982*, London: Picador.

Foucault, Michel (2005b) *Society Must be Defended: Lectures at the Collège de France, 1975–76*, Harmondsworth: Penguin.

Foucault, Michel (2007) *Security, Territory, Population: Lectures at the Collège de France 1977–1978*, New York: Picador USA.

Foucault, Michel (2008) *The Birth of Biopolitics: Lectures at the Collège de France, 1978–1979*, New York: Palgrave Macmillan.

Foucault, Michel & Gordon, Colin (1980) *Power/Knowledge: Selected Interviews and Other Writings, 1972–1977*, Brighton: Harvester.

Franck, Thomas M. (1992) "The emerging right to democratic governance", *American Journal of International Law*, 86(1): 46–91.

French, Philip (2010) "Four Lions", *The Observer*, 9 May.

Fukuyama, Francis (1989) "The end of history?", *The National Interest*, 16 (Summer).

Fukuyama, Francis (1993) *The End of History and the Last Man*, London: Harper Perennial.

G8 Leaders (2005) "Statement from world leaders: Terrorist attacks on London, 7 July 2005", www.number10.gov.uk/Page7855 (accessed 20 September 2009).

Gadher, Dipesh, Taher, Abdul & Christopher, Morgan (2008) "An unholy mix of law and religion", *Sunday Times*, 10 February.

Gardner, Lyn (2010) "Blood and gifts: It's Afghanistan, Jim, but not as we know it, Guardian blog", www.guardian.co.uk/stage/theatreblog/2010/sep/20/blood-and-gifts-afghanistan (accessed 6 September 2012).

Garton Ash, Timothy (1989) "Death reads the newspaper", *The Independent*, 2 July.

Gasper, Des & Van Staveren, Irene (2003) "Development as freedom – and as what else?", *Feminist Economics*, 9(2–3): 137–161.

Geiser, Urs (2012) "Reading political contestation in Pakistan's Swat Valley – From deliberation to the 'political' and beyond", *Geoforum*, 43: 707–715.

Gillies, David (1993) "Human rights, democracy and good governance: Stretching the World Bank's policy frontiers" in *Essays on Human Rights and Democratic Development*, Montreal: International Centre for Human Rights and Democratic Development.

Gilligan, Carol (1990) *In a Different Voice: Psychological Theory and Women's Development*, Boston, MA: Harvard University Press.

184 *Bibliography*

Gilmartin, David (1998) "A magnificent gift: Muslim nationalism and the election process in colonial Punjab", *Comparative Studies in Society and History*, 40(3): 415–436.

Gilmore, Scott & Mosazai, Janan (2007) "Defence, development and diplomacy: The case of Afghanistan, 2001–2005" in *Exporting Good Governance: Temptations and Challenges in Canada's Aid Program* (eds Welsh, Jennifer & Woods, Ngaire), Waterloo, Ontario: Laurier (Wilfrid) University Press.

Gilmour, David (2007) *The Ruling Caste: Imperial Lives in the Victorian Raj*, London: Pimlico.

Gimson, Andrew (2005) "Blair welcomes converts to his version of Islam", *Daily Telegraph*, 14 July.

Golder, Ben (2011) "Foucault's critical (yet ambivalent) affirmation: Three figures of rights", *Social and Legal Studies*, 20(3): 283–312.

Goodin, Robert & Dryzek, John S. (2006) "Deliberative impacts: The macro-political uptake of mini-publics", *Politics and Society*, 34(2): 219–244.

Goodin, Robert & Niemeyer, Simon (2003) "When does deliberation begin? Internal reflection versus public discussion in deliberative democracy", *Political Studies*, 51(4): 627–649.

Gordon, Colin (1991) "Governmental rationality: An introduction" in *The Foucault Effect: Studies in Governmentality* (eds Burchell, Graham, Gordon, Colin & Miller, Peter), Chicago, IL: University of Chicago Press.

Gould, Jeremy (2005) "Poverty, politics and states of partnership" in *The New Conditionality: The Politics of Poverty Reduction Strategies* (ed. Gould, Jeremy), London: Zed Books Ltd.

Gregory, Derek (2004) *The Colonial Present: Afghanistan, Palestine, Iraq*, Oxford: Blackwell Publishing.

The Guardian (1989) "UK news in brief", *The Guardian*, 20 October.

The Guardian (2012) "Pakistan: A coup by other means", *The Guardian*, 11 January.

Gupta, Rahila (2003) *From Homebreakers to Jailbreakers: Southall Black Sisters*, London: Zed Books.

Gutting, Gary (2003) "Foucault and the history of madness" in *The Cambridge Companion to Foucault* (ed. Gutting, Gary), Cambridge: Cambridge University Press.

Habermas, Jurgen (1984) *The Theory of Communicative Action: Reason and the Rationalization of Society*, Boston, MA: Beacon Press.

Habermas, Jurgen (1987) *The Philosophical Discourse of Modernity*, Cambridge, MA: MIT Press.

Hacking, Ian (1991) "How should we do the history of statistics" in *The Foucault Effect: Studies in Governmentality* (eds Burchell, Graham, Gordon, Colin & Miller, Peter), Chicago, IL: University of Chicago Press.

Hadenius, Axel (1997) "Freedom and economic growth: A virtuous cycle?" in *Democracy's Victory and Crisis*, Cambridge: Cambridge University Press.

Hamid, Mohsin (2007) *The Reluctant Fundamentalist*, London: Penguin.

Hansard (1989a) "Business of the house", HC, *Deb*, 2 March, vol. 148.

Hansard (1989b) "Dr Siddiqi", HC, *Deb*, 26 October, vol. 158, cc619W.

Hansard (1989c) "Freedom of speech", HL, *Deb*, 15 November, vol. 512, cc1316–1318.

Hansard (1989d) "Hong Kong (Chinese people)", HC, *Deb*, 11 December, vol. 163, cc675–676.

Hansard (1989e) "Pakistan Bill", HL, *Deb*, 21 December, vol. 514, cc356–362.

Bibliography   185

Hansen, Lene (2006) *Security as Practice: Discourse Analysis and the Bosnian War*, Abingdon: Routledge.

Hartley-Brewer, Julia (2008) "Williams is just wrong", *Sunday Express*, 10 February.

Hauerwas, Stanley & Coles, Romand (2012) *Christianity, Democracy and the Radical Ordinary: Conversations between a Radical Democrat and a Christian*, Eugene, OR: Cascade Books.

Havel, Václav (1989) "I inhabit a system in which words can prove mightier than 10 military divisions", *The Independent*, 9 December.

Hawksley, Humphrey (2009) *Democracy Kills: What's So Good About Having the Vote?*, Basingstoke: Macmillan.

Held, David (1996) *Models of Democracy*, London: Polity Press.

Helliwell, John F. (1994) "Empirical linkages between democracy and economic growth", *British Journal of Political Science*, 24(2): 225–248.

Hendry, Sharon (2005) "Same religion but different worlds", *The Sun*, 15 July.

Hill, George (1989) "The Times Review of the Year", *The Times*, 27 December.

Hilton, Boyd (2006) *A Mad, Bad, and Dangerous People? England 1783–1846*, Oxford: Oxford University Press.

Hitchens, Peter (2008) "At least the Ayatollah of Canterbury is honest, Mr Brown", *Mail on Sunday*, 10 February.

HM Government (2015) *Revised Prevent Duty Guidance for England and Wales*, London: Crown Copyright, www.gov.uk/government/uploads/system/uploads/atta chment_data/file/445977/3799_Revised_Prevent_Duty_Guidance__England_Wales_ V2-Interactive.pdf (accessed 28 April 2016).

Hobson, Christopher (2008) "Democracy as civilisation", *Global Society*, 22(1): 75–95.

Hobson, Christopher & Kurki, Milja (2012) "Introduction: The conceptual politics of democracy promotion" in *The Conceptual Politics of Democracy Promotion* (eds Hobson, Christopher & Kurki, Milja), Abingdon: Routledge.

Home Office (2006) *Report of the Official Account of the Bombings in London on 7th July 2005: House of Commons Papers 2005–06, 1087*, London: Stationery Office.

Hope, Christopher (2015) "British lessons in primary schools will protect UK from terrorism, says Nicky Morgan", *Daily Telegraph*, 27 January, www.telegraph.co.uk/ news/politics/11373074/British-lessons-in-primary-schools-will-protect-UK-from-ter rorism-says-Nicky-Morgan.html (accessed 21 April 2016).

House of Commons Parliamentary Papers (1830a) *Report from the Select Committee of the House of Lords Appointed to Inquire into the Present State of Affairs of the East India Company, (646), (VI.1)*.

House of Commons Parliamentary Papers (1830b) *Second Report on from the Select Committee on the Affairs of the East India Company, (655), (V.675)*.

House of Commons Parliamentary Papers (1831a) *Appendix to the Report on the Affairs of the East India Company, (320E), VI.465*.

House of Commons Parliamentary Papers (1831b) *Minutes of Evidence Taken before the Select Committee on the Affairs of the East India Company, (65), (VI)*.

House of Commons Parliamentary Papers (1831c) *Report from the Select Committee on the Affairs of the East India Company, (320A), (V.225)*.

House of Commons Parliamentary Papers (1831d) *Report from the Select Committee on State of Affairs of East India Company Report, (734) (735-I) (735-II) (735-III) (735-IV) (735-V) (735-VI)*.

House of Commons Parliamentary Papers (1833) *The Government of India Act, 3 & 4 Will 4 c 85*.

186 Bibliography

House of Commons Parliamentary Papers (1892) *Indian Councils Act, 55 & 56 Vict c 14.*

House of Commons Parliamentary Papers (1909) *Indian Councils Act 9 Edw 7 c 4.*

House of Commons Parliamentary Papers (1918) *Indian Constitutional Reforms*, HL *Deb*, 23 October vol. 31, cc 773–824.

House of Commons Parliamentary Papers (1919) *Government of India Act, 9 & 10 Geo 5 c101.*

House of Commons Parliamentary Papers (1989) *Home Affairs Committee. First Report. Racial Attacks and Harassment, 1989/90 HC 17.*

Howells, Kim (2005) "Counter terrorism: The UK approach", speech given on 21 July 2005 at Kuala Lumpur, Malaysia, www.fco.gov.uk/en/newsroom/latest-news/?view= Speech&id=1893794 (accessed 20 September 2009).

Howse, Christopher (2008) "Where is the justice in sharia", *Daily Telegraph*, 9 February.

Huber, Daniela (2015) *Democracy Promotion and Foreign Policy: Identity and Interests in US, EU and Non-Western Democracies*, Basingstoke: Palgrave Macmillan.

Hughes, Simon & Kay, John (2005) "Hate Britain", *The Sun*, 9 July.

Huntington, Samuel (1968) *Political Order in Changing Societies*, New Haven, CT: Yale University Press.

Huntington, Samuel (1991) *The Third Wave: Democratization in the Late Twentieth Century*, Norman: University of Oklahoma Press.

Huntington, Samuel (1996) "Democracy's third wave" in *The Global Resurgence of Democracy* (eds Diamond, Larry & Plattner, Marc), Baltimore, MD: Johns Hopkins University Press.

Huntington, Samuel (2002) *The Clash of Civilizations: And the Remaking of World Order*, London: Free Press.

Hurd, Douglas (1989) "Race relations and the rule of law", speech given on 24 February 1989 at Birmingham Central Mosque, Parliamentary Archives: HINF/89/0233.

Hurd, Douglas (1990) "Promoting good government", *Crossbow*, Autumn.

Hutchings, Kimberley (2008) *Time and World Politics: Thinking the Present*, Manchester: Manchester University Press.

Hyde, Susan (2011) *The Pseudo-Democrat's Dilemma: Why Election Monitoring Became an International Norm*, Ithaca, NY: Cornell University Press.

Ibrahim, Anwar (2006) "Universal values and Muslim democracy", *Journal of Democracy*, 17(3): 5–12.

The Independent (1989) "Muslims call for Rushdie poem ban", *The Independent*, 28 August.

The Independent (1999) "Profile, Frank Skinner: A bloke for all seasons", *The Independent*, 29 August.

India Office (1833a) *Further Papers Respecting the East India Company's Charter Ordered, by the House of Commons, to be Printed, 10 June 1833*, British Library: India Office Records(A/2/19).

India Office (1833b) *Further Papers Respecting the East India Company's Charter Ordered, by the House of Commons, to be Printed, 27 March 1833*, British Library: India Office Records(A/2/19).

India Office (1833c) *Papers Respecting the East India Company's Charter*, British Library: India Office Records(A/2/19).

Jackson, Patrick Thaddeus (2006) *Civilizing the Enemy: German Reconstruction and the Invention of the West*, Ann Arbor, MI: University of Michigan Press.

Bibliography 187

Jackson, Richard (2005) *Writing the War on Terrorism: Language, Politics and Counter-terrorism*, Manchester: Manchester University Press.

Jahangir, A. (2009) "Pakistan: A path through danger", www.opendemocracy.net/article/pakistan-a-path-through-danger (accessed 5 October 2009).

Jalal, Ayesha (1994) *The Sole Spokesman: Jinnah, the Muslim League and the Demand for Pakistan*, Cambridge: Cambridge University Press.

Jalal, Ayesha (1995a) "Conjuring Pakistan: History as official imagining", *International Journal of Middle East Studies*, 27(1): 73–89.

Jalal, Ayesha (1995b) *Democracy and Authoritarianism in South Asia: A Comparative and Historical Perspective*, Cambridge: Cambridge University Press.

Jarvis, Lee (2009) *Times of Terror: Discourse, Temporality and the War on Terror*, Basingstoke: Palgrave Macmillan.

Jean Charles de Menezes Family Campaign (2009) "Statement on today's release of the coroner's rule 43 report, 4 March 2009", inquest.justice4jean.org (accessed 30 July 2012).

Jinnah, Mohammad Ali (1999) "Presidential address to the Constituent Assembly of Pakistan, 11 August 1947", reprinted in *Dawn, Independence Day Supplement*, 14 August.

Kagan, Robert (2008) *The Return of History and the End of Dreams*, Washington, DC: Atlantic Books.

Kaplan, Robert D. (2001) *The Coming Anarchy: Shattering the Dreams of the Post Cold War*, New York: Vintage Books USA.

Kapoor, Ilan (2008) *The Postcolonial Politics of Development*, London: Routledge.

Khalili, Laleh (2007) *Heroes and Martyrs of Palestine: The Politics of National Commemoration* (Kindle edition), Cambridge: Cambridge University Press.

Khan, Ayesha (2008a) "Sharia sensibilities", *The Guardian*, 11 February.

Khan, Saira (2008b) "If you live in Britain you must live by British laws", *The Mirror*, 9 February.

Khan, Yasmin (2008c) *The Great Partition: The Making of India and Pakistan*, London: Yale University Press.

Kiersey, Nicholas & Weidner, Jason (2009) "Michel Foucault: New directions in theorising world politics", *Global Society*, 23(4): 353–361.

Kolsky, Elizabeth (2005) "Codification and the rule of colonial difference: Criminal procedure in British India", *Law and History Review*, 23(3): 631–683.

Kothari, Uma (ed.) (2005) *A Radical History of Development Studies: Individuals, Institutions and Ideologies*, London: Zed Books.

Kureishi, Hanif (1995) *The Black Album*, London: Faber and Faber.

Kureishi, Hanif (2009) *The Buddha of Suburbia*, London: Faber and Faber.

Kurki, Milja (2010) "Democracy and conceptual contestability: Reconsidering conceptions of democracy in democracy promotion", *International Studies Review*, 12(3): 363–386.

Kurki, Milja (2011) "Governmentality and EU democracy promotion: The European instrument for democracy and human rights and the construction of democratic civil societies", *International Political Sociology*, 5(4): 349–366.

Kurki, Milja (2013) *Democratic Futures: Revisioning Democracy Promotion*, London: Routledge.

Laclau, Ernesto (2005) *On Populist Reason*, London: Verso Books.

Laclau, Ernesto & Mouffe, Chantal (2001) *Hegemony and Socialist Strategy: Towards a Radical Democratic Politics*, London: Verso.

188 *Bibliography*

Laffey, Mark & Weldes, Jutta (2004) "Methodological reflections on discourse analysis", *Qualitative Methods* (Spring): 28–30.

Langford, Paul (1991) *Public Life and the Propertied Englishman, 1689–1798*, Oxford: Oxford University Press.

Lawrence, Jon (2009) *Electing Our Masters: The Hustings in British Politics from Hogarth to Blair*, Oxford: Oxford University Press.

Lijphart, Arend (2004) "Constitutional design for divided societies", *Journal of Democracy*, 15(2): 96–109.

Ling, L.H.M. (1999) "Sex machine: Global hypermasculinity and images of Asian women in modernity", *Positions*, 7(2): 277–306.

Lipset, Seymour Martin (1960) *Political Man: The Social Bases of Politics*, London: Heinemann.

Lister, David (1989) "Rushdie friends try to sustain public interest", *The Independent*, 23 November.

Lundborg, Tom (2012) *Politics of the Event: Time, Movement, Becoming*, London: Routledge.

Macaulay, Thomas (1833) "Speech in the House of Commons", *Hansard*, Deb 10 July, vol. 19, cc479–550.

Macaulay, Thomas (1835) "Minute on education", www.mssu.edu/projectsouthasia/history/primarydocs/education/Macaulay001.htm (accessed 18 May 2012).

Macdonald Hull, Fiona (1989) "Outrage on our streets", *The Sun*, 17 February.

MacKenzie, Kelvin (2008) "Sharia? Then no coffee breaks for you, girls", *The Sun*, 14 February.

Mahmood, Saba (2005) *Politics of Piety: The Islamic Revival and the Feminist Subject*, London: Princeton University Press.

Majeed, Javed (1992) *Ungoverned Imaginings: James Mill's The History of British India and Orientalism*, Oxford: Clarendon Press.

Malik, Kenan (2009) *From Fatwa to Jihad: The Rushdie Affair and its Legacy* (Kindle edition), London: Atlantic Books.

Malik, Zaiba (2010) *We are a Muslim, Please*, London: Heinemann.

Mamdani, Mahmood (2002) "Good Muslim, bad Muslim: A political perspective on culture and terrorism", *American Anthropologist*, 104(3): 766–775.

Mandaville, Alicia Phillips & Mandaville, Peter P. (2007) "Rethinking democratization and democracy assistance", *Development*, 50(1): 5–13.

Marriage, Zoe (2006) "Defining morality: DFID and the Great Lakes", *Third World Quarterly*, 27(3): 477–490.

Marrin, Minette (2008) "Archbishop, you've committed treason", *Sunday Times*, 10 February.

Masood, Salman & Rosenberg, Matthew (2011) "Rumors buzz, but Pakistan's military denies talk of a coup", *The New York Times*, 23 December.

McFaul, Michael (2004) "Democracy promotion as a world value", *Washington Quarterly*, 28(1): 147–163.

Miliband, David (2008) "Dilemmas of democracy: Work in progress in Afghanistan, Pakistan", speech given on 21 May 2008 at Center for Strategic and International Studies, Washington.

Miliband, David (2009) "Our shared future: Building coalitions and winning consent", speech given on 21 May 2009 at Oxford Centre for Islamic Studies, www.fco.gov.uk/en/news/latest-news/?view=Speech&id=18709688 (accessed 4 April 2010).

Miliken, Jennifer (1999) "The study of discourse in international relations: A critique of research and methods", *European Journal of International Relations*, 5(2): 225–254.

Mill, James (1858) *The History of British India, edited with comments by Horace Hayman Wilson, 10 vols* (fifth edition), London: Piper, Stephenson and Spence.

Milne, Seumas (2008) "We need to listen the man from special branch", *The Guardian*, 14 February.

Mishra, Pankaj (2011) "Pakistan's writers: Living in a minefield", *New York Review of Books*, 13 October.

Mohan, C. Raja (2007) "Balancing interests and values: India's struggle with democracy promotion", *Washington Quarterly*, 30(3): 99–115.

Moore, Mick & Unsworth, Sue (2006) "Britain's new White Paper: Making governance work for the poor", *Development Policy Review*, 24(6): 707–715.

Morris, Chris (2010) *Four Lions* (film), London: Optimum Releasing.

Mosley, Paul, Harrigan, Jane & Toye, John (1991) *Aid and Power: The World Bank and Policy-based Lending*, London: Routledge.

Mouffe, Chantal (1999) "Deliberative democracy or agonistic pluralism?", *Social Research*, 66(3): 745–758.

Mouffe, Chantal (2000) *The Democratic Paradox*, London: Verso.

Mouffe, Chantal (2004) "Cosmopolitan democracy of multipolar world order?" *Soundings*, 28 (Winter).

Moyo, Dambisa (2010) *Dead Aid: Why Aid is Not Working and How there is Another Way for Africa*, London: Penguin.

Murray, James & Giannangeli, Marco (2008) "You're wrong but don't quit, our poll tells archbishop", *Sunday Express*, 10 February.

Murray Li, Tania (2007) *The Will to Improve: Governmentality, Development and the Practice of Politics*, London: Duke University Press.

Nash, David (2007) *Blasphemy in the Christian World: A History* (Kindle edition), Oxford: Oxford University Press.

Nawaz, Maajid (2012) *Radical: My Journey from Islamist Extremism to Democratic Awakening*, London: W.H. Allen.

Nelson, Matthew (2011) *In the Shadow of the Shari'ah: Islam, Islamic Law, and Democracy in Pakistan* (Kindle edition), New York: Columbia University Press.

Neuberger, Julia (1989) "Showing Islam's more gentle face", *The Sunday Times*, 8 October.

New Statesman (2010) "Pakistan: Inside the world's most dangerous country", *New Statesman*, 23 August.

New Statesman (2011) "Pakistan's dirty secret", *New Statesman*, 16 May.

The News of the World (1989a) "A welcome in Britain", *The News of the World*, 3 September.

The News of the World (1989b) "Live by the law", *The News of the World*, 29 October.

The News of the World (1989c) "Race madness in our schools", *The News of the World*, 17 September.

Nichols, Mike (2010) *Charlie Wilson's War* (film), Hollywood, CA: Universal Studios.

Norval, Aletta (2007) *Aversive Democracy: Inheritance and Originality in the Democratic Tradition*, Cambridge: Cambridge University Press.

Nustad, Knut (2001) "Development: The devil we know?", *Third World Quarterly*, 22(4): 479–489.

O'Gorman, Frank (1989) *Voters, Patrons and Parties: The Unreformed Electorate of Hanoverian England, 1734–1832*, Oxford: Clarendon Press.

190   *Bibliography*

O'Hagan, Jacinta (2007) "Discourses of civilizational identity" in *The Constitutive Politics of Civilizational Identity: The Production and Reproduction of "Civilizations" in International Relations* (eds Hall, Martin & Jacksonr, Patrick Thaddeus), Basingstoke: Palgrave Macmillan.

Okin, Susan Moller (1999) *Is Multiculturalism Bad for Women?*, Princeton, NJ: Princeton University Press.

O'Neil, Maureen (2007) "Foreword" in *Exporting Good Governance: Temptations and Challenges in Canada's Aid Program* (eds Welsh, Jennifer & Woods, Ngaire), Waterloo, Ontario: Laurier (Wilfrid) University Press.

Owen, John (1994) "How liberalism produces democratic peace", *International Security*, 19 (Fall): 87–125.

Parker, Noel & Vaughan-Williams, Nick (2009) "Lines in the sand: Towards an agenda for critical border studies", *Geopolitics*, 14(3): 582–587.

Parris, Matthew (2008) "Williams is dangerous", *The Times*, 9 February.

Pascoe-Watson, George (2008) "What a burkha", *The Sun*, 8 February.

Pateman, Carole (1975) *Participation and Democratic Theory*, Cambridge: Cambridge University Press.

Patten, John (1989) "The Muslim community in Britain", *The Times*, 5 July.

Petre, Jonathan & Porter, Andrew (2008) "'Adopt sharia law in Britain': Archbishop's call provokes political and religious backlash", *Daily Telegraph*, 8 February.

Phillips, Anne (1993) *Democracy and Difference*, London: Polity Press.

Phillips, Melanie (2008) "The Church should have the guts to sack the archbishop", *Daily Mail*, 11 February.

Philo, Chris (2007) "'Bellicose history' and 'local discursivities': An archaeological reading of Foucault's society must be defended" in *Space, Knowledge and Power: Foucault and Geography* (eds Crampton, Jeremy W. & Eldenr, Stuart), Farnham: Ashgate Publishing.

Pitkin, Hanna F. (1967) *The Concept of Representation*, Berkeley: University of California Press.

Pitts, Jennifer (2005) *A Turn to Empire: The Rise of Imperial Liberalism in Britain and France*, Princeton, NJ: Princeton University Press.

Porter, Henry (2005) "Review section", *Sunday Telegraph*, 10 July.

Prior, Katherine (2004) "Tucker, Henry St George (1771/2–1851)" in *Oxford Dictionary of National Biography*, Oxford: Oxford University Press.

Przeworski, Adam (1999) "Minimalist conception of democracy: A defence" in *Democracy's Value* (eds Shapiro, Ian & Hacker-Cordón, Casiano), Cambridge: Cambridge University Press.

Przeworski, Adam & Limongi, Fernando (1993) "Political regimes and economic growth", *Journal of Economic Perspectives*, 7(3): 51–69.

Przeworski, Adam et al. (1996) "What makes democracies endure?", *Journal of Democracy*, 7(1): 39–55.

Puar, Jasbir (2007) *Terrorist Assemblages: Homonationalism in Queer Times*, Durham, NC: Duke University Press.

Quadir, Fahimul (2007) "Assisting civil society through aid: The case of Bangladesh" in *Exporting Good Governance: Temptations and Challenges in Canada's Aid Program* (eds Welsh, Jennifer & Woods, Ngaire), Waterloo, Ontario: Laurier (Wilfrid) University Press.

Raja, S. (2007) "Pakistan: Inside the storm", www.opendemocracy.net/article/conflicts/pakistan_inside_the_storm (accessed 5 October 2009).

Rancière, Jacques (2007) *Hatred of Democracy*, London: Verso Books.

Rashid, Ahmed (2005) "Pakistan wakes up to the hatred within", *Daily Telegraph*, 14 July.

Rashid, Ahmed (2008) *Taliban* (third edition), London: I.B. Tauris and Co.

Razack, Sherene (2004) "Imperilled Muslim women, dangerous Muslim men and civilised Europeans: Legal and social responses to forced marriages", *Feminist Legal Studies*, 12(2): 129–174.

Rickards, Robert (1829) *India; or Facts Submitted to Illustrate the Character and Condition of the Native Inhabitants, with Suggestions for Reforming the Present System of Government, vol. 1* (downloaded from Google Books), London: Smith, Elder and Co.

Rist, Gilbert (1997) *The History of Development: From Western Origin to Global Faith*, London: Zed Books.

Rivoli, Pietra (2014) *The Travels of a T-Shirt in the Global Economy: An Economist Examines the Markets, Power and Politics of World Trade*, London: John Wiley and Sons.

Robinson, Emily (2012) *History, Heritage and Tradition in Contemporary British Politics: Past Politics and Present Histories*, Manchester: Manchester University Press.

Robinson, Fiona (2006) "Care, gender and global social justice: Rethinking 'ethical globalization'", *Journal of Global Ethics*, 2(1): 5–25.

Robinson, William I. (1996) *Promoting Polyarchy: Globalization, US Intervention, and Hegemony*, Cambridge: Cambridge University Press.

Rogers, J.T. (2010) *Blood and Gifts*, London: Faber and Faber.

Rose, David (1989) "Bitter questions of racial violence", *The Guardian*, 13 December.

Rosenthal, Tom (1989) "Why South Africa is a place for booksellers but not for cricketers", *The Independent*, 17 August.

Rostow, W.W. (1959) "The stages of economic growth", *The Economic History Review*, 12(1): 1–16.

Rothschild, Emma (2001) *Economic Sentiments: Adam Smith, Condorcet and the Enlightenment*, Boston, MA: Harvard University Press.

Roy, Amit (1989) "Muslim urges Rushdie killing", *The Sunday Times*, 22 October.

Roy, Ananya and Shaw Crane, Emma (eds) (2015) *Territories and Poverty: Rethinking North and South*, Athens, GA: University of Georgia Press.

Royal Statistical Society (n.d.) "History", www.rss.org.uk/site/cms/contentCategory View.asp?category=42 (accessed 20 May 2012).

Rushdie, Salman (1983) *Shame*, London: Jonathan Cape.

Russett, Bruce (1993) *Grasping the Democratic Peace: Principles for a Post-Cold War World*, Princeton, NJ: Princeton University Press.

Ruthven, Malise (1990) *A Satanic Affair: Salman Rushdie and the Rage of Islam*, London: Chatto and Windus.

Ruthven, Malise (2012) *Islam: A Very Short Introduction*, Oxford: Oxford University Press.

Said, Edward (1989) "The decade (Earthly powers)", *The Guardian*, 16 December.

Said, Edward (1994) *Representations of the Intellectual*, New York: Vintage.

Said, Edward (1995) *Orientalism*, London: Penguin.

Salter, Mark (2002) *Barbarians and Civilisation in International Relations*, London: Pluto Press.

192 Bibliography

Sammon, Robert Lane (2008) *Mullas and Maliks: Understanding the Roots of Conflict in Pakistan's Federally Administered Tribal Areas*, unpublished thesis, The Lauder Institute, University of Pennsylvania.

Sanders, Peter (2008) *The Art of Integration: Islam in Our Green and Pleasant Land*, Swansea: Awakening Publications.

Sanders, P. (2009) "The art of integration", www.artofintegration.co.uk/aoiEng/hom eEng.php (accessed 26 July 2012).

Sardar, Ziauddin & Wyn Davies, Merryl (1990) *Distorted Imagination: Lessons from the Rushdie Affair*, London: Grey Seal.

Saward, Michael (2006) "The representative claim", *Contemporary Political Theory*, 5(3): 297–318.

Sawyer, Stephen (2016) "Foucault 8/13 epilogue: Michel Foucault, neoliberalism and beyond", blogs.law.columbia.edu/foucault1313/2016/03/29/foucault-813-epilogue-m ichel-foucault-neoliberalism-and-beyond/ (accessed 28 April 2016).

Schmitter, Philippe C. & Karl, Terry L. (1996) "What democracy is. And is not" in *The Global Resurgence of Democracy* (eds Diamond, Larry & Plattner, Marc F.), London: Johns Hopkins University Press.

Schumpeter, Joseph A. (2010) *Capitalism, Socialism and Democracy*, Abingdon: Routledge Classics.

Scotland, Baroness (2007) "Speech at the launch of photographic exhibition: 'The Art of Integration: Islam in Britain's Green and Pleasant Land'", speech given on 20 February 2007 at British High Commission, Canada.

Seighart, Mary (2008) "Our British laws are there to protect Muslim women", *The Times*, 14 February.

Sen, Amartya (1999) "Democracy as a universal value", *Journal of Democracy*, 10(3): 3–17.

Sen, Amartya (2001) *Development as Freedom*, Oxford: Oxford University Press.

Sen, Amartya (2006) *The Argumentative Indian: Writings on Indian Culture, History and Identity*, London: Penguin.

Sending, Ole J. & Neumann, Iver (2006) "Governance to governmentality: Analysing NGOs, states and power", *International Studies Quarterly*, 50(3): 652–671.

Sethi, Najam (2012a) "GHQ must take joint ownership of US-PAK relations (Editorial)", *Friday Times*, 30 March.

Sethi, Najam (2012b) "Whither vs whether Pakistan", *Friday Times*, 25 April.

Seton, Craig (1989) "Hurd faces Muslim hostility on book", *The Times*, 25 February.

Shapiro, Michael (1988) *The Politics of Representation: Writing Practices in Biography, Photography and Policy Analysis*, Madison: University of Wisconsin Press.

Shapiro, Michael J. (1989) "Textualising global politics" in *International/Intertextual Relations: Postmodern Readings of World Politics* (eds Der Derian, James & Shapiro, Michael J.), Lexington, Massachusetts: Lexington Books.

Shepherd, Laura (2006) "Veiled references: Constructions of gender in the Bush Administration discourse on the attacks on Afghanistan post-9/11", *International Feminist Journal of Politics*, 8(1): 19–41.

Shipman, Tim (2005) "Now we must decide what values Britain has to defend", *Sunday Express*, 10 July.

Siegle, Lucy (2011) *To Die For: Is Fashion Wearing Out the World?* London: Harper Collins.

Singh, Ramjee & Sundaram, S. (1996) *Gandhi and the World Order*, New Delhi: APH Publishing Corporation.

Bibliography

Smillie, Ian (2007) "Boy Scouts and fearful angels: The evolution of Canada's good governance agenda" in *Exporting Good Governance: Temptations and Challenges in Canada's Aid Program* (eds Welsh, Jennifer & Woods, Ngaire), Waterloo, Ontario: Laurier (Wilfrid) University Press.

Smith, Adam (2010) *The Theory of Moral Sentiments*, Harmondsworth: Penguin.

Smith, Joan (2008) "British women are already suffering from Islamic law", *The Independent on Sunday*, 10 February.

Spivak, Gayatri Chakravorty (1987) "'Can the subaltern speak?'" in *Marxism and the Interpretation of Culture* (eds Nelson, Cary & Grossberg, Lawrence), Champaign, Illinois: University of Illinois Press.

Spivak, Gayatri Chakravorty (1995) "More on power/knowledge" in *The Spivak Reader* (eds Landry, Donna & Maclean, Gerald), London: Routledge.

Stephens, Angharad Closs & Vaughan-Williams, Nick (2008) *Terrorism and the Politics of Response: London in a Time of Terror*, London: Routledge.

Stewart, Frances (1991) "The many faces of adjustment", *World Development*, 19(12): 1847–1864.

Stokes, Eric (1959) *The English Utilitarians and India*, Oxford: Oxford University Press.

The Sun (1989a) "A crazy curry-on", *The Sun*, 13 December.

The Sun (1989b) "Cartoon on page 6", *The Sun*, 18 February.

The Sun (1989c) "Genius the satanic ayatollah wants dead", *The Sun*, 16 February.

The Sun (1989d) "The Sun says", *The Sun*, 20 February.

The Sun (1989e) "The Sun speaks its mind: We will blast back", *The Sun*, 18 February.

The Sun (1989f) "Your red hot sun rises in the east", *The Sun*, 8 December.

The Sun (2005) "Keep calm", *The Sun*, 13 July.

The Sun (2008) "Dangerous rant", *The Sun*, 8 February.

Swain, Ashok, Amer, Ramses & Öjendal, Joakim (2011) "The democratization project: Peace, conflict and development" in *The Democratization Project: Opportunities and Challenges* (eds Swain, Ashok, Amer, Ramses & Öjendal, Joakim), London: Anthem Press.

Sylvester, Christine (2008) *Art/Museums: International Relations Where We Least Expect It*, Boulder, CO: Paradigm Publishers.

Taheri, Amir (1989) "Exit communists and Khomeinists", *The Times*, 22 December.

Talbot, Ian (1980) "The 1946 Punjab elections", *Modern Asian Studies*, 14(1): 65–91.

Talbot, Ian & Singh, Gurharpal (2009) *The Partition of India*, Cambridge: Cambridge University Press.

Thacker, Andrew (1996) "Foucault and the writing of history" in *The Impact of Michel Foucault on the Social Sciences and Humanities* (eds Lloyd, Moya & Thacker, Andrew), Basingstoke: Palgrave Macmillan.

Thapar-Björkert, Suruchi & Shepherd, Laura (2010) "Religion" in *Gender Matters in Global Politics: A Feminist Introduction to International Relations* (Kindle edition), (ed. Shepherd, Laura J.), Abingdon: Routledge.

The Times (1989) "Yard seeks Muslim group; Rushdie controversy", *The Times*, 5 September.

The Times (2008) "Church in a state", *The Times*, 8 February.

Townsend, Mark (2006) "Leak reveals official story of London bombings", *The Observer*, 9 April.

Toynbee, Polly (2005) "Let the Olympics be a memorial", *The Guardian*, 8 July, www. guardian.co.uk/politics/2005/jul/08/london.july7 (accessed 23 September 2005).

194   *Bibliography*

Tripodi, Christian (2008) "Peacemaking through bribes or cultural empathy? The political officer and Britain's strategy towards the North-West Frontier, 1901–1945", *Journal of Strategic Studies*, 31(1): 123–151.

Tripodi, Christian (2009) "'Good for one but not the other': The "Sandeman System" of Pacification as applied to Baluchistan and the North-West Frontier, 1877–1947", *The Journal of Military History*, 73(3): 767–802.

Tucker, SirHenry (1833a) *Dissent dated 2 July 1833 in Papers Respecting the East India Company's Charter*, British Library: India Office Records(A/2/19).

Tucker, SirHenry (1833b) *Explanatory Remarks Referred to in Mr Tucker's Dissent in Papers Respecting the East India Company's Charter*, British Library: India Office Records(A/2/19).

Tudor, Maya (2013) "Explaining democracy's origins: Lessons from South Asia", *Comparative Politics*, 45(3): 253–272.

UK Cabinet Office (2008) *The National Security Strategy of the United Kingdom: Security in an Interdependent World*, www.cabinetoffice.gov.uk/security_and_intelligence/community/news/national_security_strategy.aspx.

UNDP (United Nations Development Programme) (2002) *Human Development Report 2002: Deepening Democracy in a Fragmented World*, New York: Oxford University Press.

Unsworth, Sue (2007) "Focusing aid on good governance: Can it work?" in *Exporting Good Governance: Temptations and Challenges in Canada's Aid Program* (eds Welsh, Jennifer & Woods, Ngaire), Waterloo, Ontario: Laurier (Wilfrid) University Press.

Valentine, S.R. (2006) "Muslims in Bradford, UK: Background paper for COMPAS, University of Oxford", www.compas.ox.ac.uk/fileadmin/files/Publications/Research_projects/Urban_change_settlement/Muslims_community_cohesion/Bradford%20Background%20Paper%200506b.pdf (accessed 7 July 2012).

Vallely, Paul (2008) "Williams is snared in a trap of his own making", *The Independent*, 8 February.

Vaughan-Williams, Nick (2008) "The shooting of Jean-Charles de Menezes: New border politics?" in *Terrorism and the Politics of Response: London in a Time of Terror* (eds Closs Stephens, Angharad & Vaughan-Williams, Nick), Abingdon: Routledge.

Vernon, Phil (2012) "Development is history looking forwards, 16 May", www.opendemocracy.net/phil-vernon/development-is-history-looking-forwards (accessed 4 September 2012).

Virdee, P. (2009) "Pakistan: Women's quest for entitlement", www.opendemocracy.net/article/pakistan-history-in-women-s-voices (accessed 5 October 2009).

von Tunzelmann, Alex (2008) *Indian Summer: The Secret History of the End of an Empire*, London: Pocket Books.

Vucetic, Srdjan (2011) "Genealogy as a research tool in international relations", *Review of International Studies*, 37(3): 1295–1312.

Wade, John (1832) *The Extraordinary Black Book: An Exposition of Abuses in Church and State, Courts of Law, Representation, Municipal and Corporate Bodies; with a Precis of the House of Commons, Past, Present, and to Come (A New Edition)*, London: Effingham Wilson, Royal Exchange.

Wahhab, Iqbal (1989a) "Muslims launch political party to contest elections", *The Independent*, 14 September.

Wahhab, Iqbal (1989b) "Muslims uphold death sentence of Salman Rushdie", *The Independent*, 16 December.

Walker, R.B.J. (1992) *Inside/Outside: International Relations as Political Theory*, Cambridge: Cambridge University Press.

Bibliography 195

Walker, R.B.J. (2011) *Before the Globe/After the World*, London: Routledge.

Wallis, Sara (2008) "Rowan faces a showdown", *The Mirror*, 11 February.

The Washington Post (2012) "Pakistan's three-way power struggle: A dispute with much at stake", *The Washington Post*, 27 January.

Weldon, Fay (1989) *Sacred Cows*, London: Chatto and Windus.

White, Roland (2008) "Great Mufti of Canterbury", *The Sunday Times*, 10 February.

Whitehead, Laurence (1986) "International aspects of democratization" in *Transitions from Authoritarian Rule: Comparative Perspectives: Prospects for Democracy: Volume 3* (eds O'Donnell, Guillermo, Schmitter, Philippe C. & Whitehead, Laurence), Baltimore, MD: Johns Hopkins University Press.

Whitehead, Laurence (2002) *Democratization: Theory and Experience*, Oxford: Oxford University Press.

Williams, R. (2008a) "Archbishop on Radio 4 World at One – UK law needs to find accommodation with religious law codes", www.archbishopofcanterbury.org/articles. php/707/archbishop-on-radio-4-uk-law-needs-to-find-accommodation-with-religious-law-codes (accessed 30 August 2012).

Williams, Rowan (2008b) "Archbishop's lecture – Civil and religious law in England: A religious perspective", speech given on 7 February at Royal Courts of Justice, www.archbishopofcanterbury.org/articles.php/1137/archbishops-lecture-civil-and-religious-law-in-england-a-religious-perspective (accessed 30 August 2012).

Wilson, Graeme & Pascoe-Watson, George (2008) "Archbishop says UK must accept sharia law", *The Sun*, 8 February.

Wilson, Jon E. (2008) *The Domination of Strangers: Modern Governance in Eastern India, 1780–1835*, Basingstoke: Palgrave Macmillan.

Wind-Cowie, Max & Gregory, Thomas (2011) *A Place for Pride*, London: Demos.

Winder, Robert (1989) "Books of the decade: Moneyed and satanic", *The Independent*, 23 December.

Wintour, Patrick (1989) "MP in furore over 'Muslims Go Home'", *The Guardian*, 29 August.

Wolpert, Stanley (2006) *Shameful Flight: The Last Years of the British Empire in India*, Oxford: Oxford University Press.

Wooding, David & Clench, James (2008) "Arch enemy", *The Sun*, 9 February.

World Bank (1992) *Good Governance and Development*, Washington, DC: World Bank.

Wynne-Jones, Jonathan (2008) "Carey and cardinal unite to attack 'divisive' sharia law", *Sunday Telegraph*, 10 February.

Young, Hugo (1989) "Life, death and Mr Rushdie", *The Guardian*, 24 November.

Zelin, Aaron (2015) *Tunisia's Fragile Democratic Transition*, Testimony submitted to the House Committee on Foreign Affairs, Subcommittee on the Middle East and North Africa, 14 July, www.washingtoninstitute.org/uploads/Documents/testimony/ZelinTestimony20150714.pdf (accessed 21 April 2016).

Zerilli, Linda (1994) *Signifying Woman: Culture and Chaos in Rousseau, Burke and Mill*, Ithaca, NY: Cornell University Press.

Ziai, Aram (2007) "The ambivalence of post-development: Between reactionary populism and radical democracy" in *Exploring Post-Development: Theory and Practice, Problems and Perspectives* (ed. Ziai, Aram), London: Routledge.

Žižek, Slavoj (2008) *In Defense of Lost Causes*, London: Verso Books.

Zohar, Danah (1989) "A Wonderland without the wonder", *The Independent*, 19 December.

Index

Abrahamsen, Rita 66
absolute government 100
Afghan Taliban 65
Age of Reform 90
agonistic democracy 31
Akhtar, Shabbir 135–6
Amoore, Louise 168
Anderson, Benedict 49
Appignanesi, Lisa 140
Archbishop of Canterbury 7–9, 57, 165,
    166, 170
Art of Integration exhibition 150–4, 173–4
autonomous civil society 112–13

Babbage, Charles 104
ballots 22–3 *See also* elections; voting/
    voting systems
barbarians 6, 34, 67–8, 70, 148
barbaric terrorism 57
bargaining 48–9
Barthes, Roland 155
Basham, Victoria 161
Begums of Oudh 87
belonging, relational forms of 170
Bengal system 92
Bentham, Jeremy 96
Benthamite principles 109–10
Berman, Sheri 61
Bevir, Mark 53–4n1
Bhutto, Benazir 128
Biccum, April 36, 66
biraderi 113–15, 117–18, 120, 123, 139, 170
The Black Album (Kureishi) 126–7
black feminist identity 138
blackmail 75
Blair, Tony 6, 11, 25, 34, 59, 70, 71
blasphemous libel offence 147
blasphemy laws 135, 136
Blood and Gifts (play) 64

bombings of London transport system 1,
    3–6
book burning 130–3, 135–6, 166
boomerang effect 82, 100–1
bordering 33
borders, non-territorial dimension of 33
Bowden, Brett 58
Bradford Council of Mosques 135–6, 137
Bradford protestors 131–4
Bragg, Melvin 132
Brigg, Morgan 64
British development spending 24–5
British government, dissatisfaction with 1
British identity 36–7, 83, 95–6
British ideology 4–5
British Islam 149–50, 152, 154 *See also*
    Islam
British Muslims: conforming to Britishness
    practices 150; democratic process and
    135–8; demonstrating commitment to
    nation 156–7; disrupting relations of
    power 129; everyday lives of 151, 153;
    integration 150–4; protesting *Satanic
    Verses* 130; Salman Rushdie affair
    126–7. *See also* Muslims
British polity 85–90
British private sphere 160–1
Britishness: British Muslims conforming
    to 150, 156–7; democracy and 34;
    displaying 151–2; emotional connec-
    tion to 169–70; historical narratives of
    152; meaning of 5, 159; muscular lib-
    eralism 162, 166; patriotism and 169;
    struggle against anti-democratic
    others 11
Brown, Andrew 134–5
Bunglawala, Inayat 144
Burchell, Graham 49
Burke, Edmund 83–4, 85–6, 87–8, 170

Index 197

Burkean polity 88, 95
Burnell, Peter 28, 29, 36
Bush, George W. 58
Butler, Judith 9–10, 13

Cameron, David 25, 166–7, 169
Campbell, David 11–12, 33
Capriolo, Ettore 141
Carey, Lord 8
Carothers, Thomas 35–6, 46, 47, 62, 70
censorship, absence of 50
Chapman, Peter 130
Charman, Matt 22
Charter Act (India) 94–5, 98, 99–100
chivalry 87–9
citizenship: active 30; gendered config-
    uration of 74; happiness and 86; rights
    to 131–2; in schools 36
city-citizen matrix 83–4, 94–5, 97
civilisation 57–9, 67–8, 70–1, 83, 104
civilised identity 57
civilised nations 59
civilised practices, gender and 71–6
civilising histories 57–9
codified law 110–11
coding: Hindus 118–19; Pakistan 115–16;
    private sphere 111–13, 120–1; public
    sphere 111–13, 120–1
Cohn, Bernard 109
Cold War 15, 63–5
Coles, Romand 170–1, 172
colonial present 10
colonial Utilitarian 93
colonialism 15–16, 117–18, 138
colonisation 64, 100–1
communism 65
conservatism 155
contestation: of bordering practices 11;
    Cold War as era of 65; of dress code
    14, 75; freedom of speech and 48, 50,
    53; promoting democracy with 30–2;
    in public sphere 112, 120, 122–3
cosmopolitan democracy 31
country governance analyses 47, 123
Critical Border Studies 33
Croft, Stuart 10
Czechoslovakia 139–40

d'Ancona, Matthew 7
de Menezes, Juan Charles 160
deference in electoral practices 86
deliberative democracy 30–1
democracy: alternative theories of 29–30;
    barbarism and 34; Britishness and 34;

commitment to 4–5; as contested concept 30–2; defence against terrorism 8,
34; in developing countries 65; development and 63–4; as ideal system of
government 24; as means to distribute
power 22; models of 30; moral duty to
promote 66; non-electoral forms of 51;
opposite of violence 107; in Pakistan
3–7; practice vs. theory 29; radical
ordinary as form of 170–1; relational
173; remedy to violence 141; as solution to home-grown terrorism 3–6;
terrorism as opposite of 34; threats to
1; as universal value 62; Western
forms of 29; Western history and
61–2. *See also* liberal democracy
Democracy Promotion: critiques of
76–7; democracy promotion vs. 32–6;
disappointments of 63; history of 15,
61–3; as intrinsic element of
development 60; technologies of
22–3
democracy promotion: Democracy Promotion vs, 32–6; end of history and
143–5; limits of 136; meaning of
11–12; tattered genealogies of
79–80
democratic accountability 26–7
democratic engagement 99
democratic ethics 173–4
democratic law making 7–8, 12–13, 74
Democratic Peace Theory 107
democratic theorising, power and
28–30
democratisation 127–8, 154–7
Department for International Development (DFID): British development
spending 24–5, 168; election support
27; G8 summit on development 60;
on social hierarchy and power
structures 123–4; transparency of
media 50
despotism in India 91
development interventions 76
devolution 27
Diamond, Larry 28, 49–50, 62, 63, 65,
107
discipline, governmentality and 43
discontinuity 80
discources 52
discursive representation 51–3
docile bodies 42
domestication 154–7
Dooley, Mark 57

198 *Index*

East India Company: Burke on 85; cultural distance of 89–90; gender relations 87–8; General Court 95; governing in 90–1; as representative institution 102
elections: colonial 117; controlled by collective 123–4; defined 45; failure of 32, 45; free and fair 17, 26, 28, 30, 40, 47; governmental technology 46; international visibility of 47; neutrality of 46; observation 47; in Punjab 120–1; useful practices 116–17. *See also* voting/voting systems
electoral behaviour 46–7
electoral commissions 24, 28
electoral democracy 32, 44, 49, 80–1, 117
electoral practices 86, 118–19
electoralism 44
End of History 65–6, 126–8, 134, 143–6, 152–3, 174
epistemic violence 77
Escobar, Arturo 71, 76
established democracies 35–6
ethics 87, 145, 173–4
Ewart-Biggs, Baroness 128
Extraordinary Black Book (Wade) 100–1
extremism 167

feminist identity 138
Foreign and Commonwealth Office (FCO) 26, 60, 65, 70, 148, 153
Foreign Policy: foreign policy vs. 11–12; identity-based logic of 35
foreign policy: civilisation and 131–5; democratisation of 154–7; Foreign Policy vs. 11–12
Foucault, Michel: on boomerang effect 82; as historian of discontinuity 80; on history 77–9; on importance of thought 2–3; liberal governmentality 40–1; on liberalism 44; looking at history 15; other of civilisation 11; on prison's self-perpetuation 66; on repressive hypothesis 25; on the savage 68; on sovereignty 41–2
Four Lions (film) 157–60, 164
free and fair elections 17, 26, 28, 30, 40, 47
free expression 49–50
freedom of association 48–50
freedom of expression 129
freedom of speech 48–50, 128–31 *See also* speaking
freedom of the press 49–50
French Revolution 89
Fukuyama, Francis 55–6, 128

G8 summit in Gleneagles 5–6, 36, 59–60
gender equality 72–4, 123
gendered constitution of civilisational narratives 72
gendered private sphere 112
gender/gender relations: blackmail 75; civilised practices and 71–6; coding inheritance 113–15; cultivation rights 113–14; East India Company 87–8; equality/inequality 72–4, 123; ethics of 87; integration 151; in Pakistan 128; political relations 87–9; private property rights 114; segregation 75; uncivilised 68–9; violence and 121; violent masculinities 13–14, 68. *See also* women's rights
genealogy 79–80, 173–4
Gilmartin, David 117, 119
Gilmore, Scott 32, 74
Gimson, Andrew 150
good governance 24, 34–5, 60, 95–7
Gould, Jeremy 62
governance: citizenship 86; concept of 6, 53–4n1; at country level 25–6; defined 41; forms of 25–6, 31; as a machine 98–9; pastoral role of 84; poor 34; radicalisation and 34; role of 45; use of power and authority 25. *See also* good governance
governing 83–5, 90
government: absolute 100; abstraction of 91–2; body metaphor 98–9; chivalry and 87–9; defined 41; as a machine 98–9; machinery of 92–3; uncertainty of 90–2
Government of India Act 94–5
governmentality: defined 42; discipline and 43; as form of power 43; liberal democracy and 44–6; population and 42–3; as web of productive power 46
governmentality regime 43
Grant, Charles 95
Gregory, Derek 10

Hamid, Mohsin 55–6
happiness, Burke's conception of 86
happy citizen 86
Hastings, Warren 87–8
Havel, Václav 132
Held, David 30
hierarchy, in electoral practices 86
Hindus 108–11, 117–19
historical narratives, factual accuracy of 78–9

Index 199

historicity, as an obstacle 62–3
history: alternative versions of 2; discontinuity 80; preserving continuity 89–90; tattered genealogies of 79–80; teleological narrative of 2, 7, 174–5
History of British India (Mill) 93–4
history wars 167
Hobson, Christopher 66
home-grown terrorism 4, 34
Homo economicus 68–9
Howe, Geoffrey 134
Howells, Kim 150
Huber, Daniela 63
Huntington, Samuel 27, 58
Hurd, Douglas 66, 128–9, 144, 145
Husain, Liaqat 130
Hussain, Hasib 149
Hyde, Susan 47

identity 35–7, 56–7, 108–10, 137, 138, 149–50
Igarashi, Hitoshi 141
imperialism 64, 76–7, 82
India: abstract system of rules 91–2; Charter Act 94–5, 98, 99–100; codification in 95–7, 103; constitution for 94; despotism 91; electoral democracy 32; general election in 116–17; good government in 95; governing in 90–5; law 94; Macaulay on 93; modes of governing 83; nationalist movement 115–16; native councils 97; public and private coding 111–13; public sphere and 99–101; publicity in Parliament 100; representation in Parliament 100, 115; shepherd-flock configuration in 84, 94–5
Indian Councils Act 1892 116
Indian nationalist movement 115
indigenous peoples 58–9
individual rights 73
integration 150–4
internal colonisation 104
intervention beyond borders 4
Iraq 156
Islam: Britishness and 149–50, 152; Christianity vs. 139; gender relations 128; jihadist movement and 70; merits of 135; oppressiveness of 139–40; portrayal of 138–9, 155; practice of 151; religious identity 147; spreading 64–5; values associated with 141; violent masculinities 13; women's rights 138–9. *See also* British Muslims; *shari'ah* law

Islam, Shahara Akhter 149, 157
Islam, Yusuf 156
Islamic identity 146, 147, 149

Jackson, Richard 10
Jinnah, Mohammed Ali 118–19, 120
jirga, as form of local governance 31, 173

Khan, Mohammed Sidique 4, 34, 37, 148, 157, 165–6
Khan, Yasmin 121
Khomeini, Ayatollah 128, 134, 138, 140–1
Kolsky, Elizabeth 112
Kureishi, Hanif 126
Kurki, Milja 28, 30, 37n1, 63

Lawrence, John 109, 112
liberal democracy: alternative models of 31–2, 36; criticisms of 62; as form of othering 1; governmentality and 44–6; liberalism vs. 37n1; to organise government within liberalism 44; in Pakistan 136; producing knowledge 41–4; as protective against tyranny 99; between public and private spheres 39; as remedy for violence 107, 156; repressive hypothesis of power 29–30; Soviet communism vs. 65; state's role in 129; support for 27–8; values associated with 6; women's rights and 74
liberal democratic governmentality 145, 151, 158, 161–3
liberal democratic institutions 15, 26–7, 41, 62, 84, 106, 140, 143, 168
liberal democratic rationality 25
liberal democratic theory 29
liberal governmentality 40–1
liberalism 14, 37n1
local power networks 123
London transport system, bombing attack on 1, 3–6
Lyall, Alfred 113

Macaulay, Thomas 2, 84, 93, 98–9, 102
Mackenzie, Holt 98–9
Macnaghten, William Hay 92
Madden, Max 136
Make Poverty History campaign 5–6, 60
Malik, Kenan 130, 134, 137, 142, 146
Malthus, Thomas 104
Marlow, Tony 132
Marquis of Cornwallis 91
Mayer, Peter 141
McFaul, Michael 24

200 *Index*

media: free speech and association in 48–9; freedom of the press 49–50; transparency of media 50
media, role of 49–50
Mill, James 84, 93–4, 96, 103, 109
Millennium Development Goals (MDGs) 26–7
modernisation theory 60
modes of exclusion 134
modes of othering 120, 127, 133, 145, 168–9 *See also* othering
modes of thought 2–3
Morris, Chris 157, 164
Mosazai, Janan 32, 74
Mughal Empire 108
multiculturalism 136–7, 147, 152–3
multiple civilisations 58–9
muscular liberalism 162, 166
Muslim identity 108, 154
Muslim League 118–19, 120
Muslims: anxiety about protests 134; codifying identity 108–10; codifying law 110–11; in colonial system 117–18; demonstrating commitment to nation 156–7; dichotomy between Britons and 149; electoral practices 118–19; *fitna-i-jahiliyat* 119; religious identity 108; social antagonism 115; *see also* British Muslims

National Democratic Institute for International Affairs (NDI) 27
native councils 96–7
natural evolution to democratic maturity 15–16
Nawaz, Maajid 163
Nelson, Matthew 110, 114, 123, 136
Nesin, Aziz 141
neutrality, desire for 28
Norman Conquest 77–8
Nygaard, William 141

The Observer (play) 22, 32
O'Neil, Maureen 35
ordinariness 170–2
Orientalism 71
othering: bordering and 33–4; development in 10; forms of 9–10; internal colonisation effect 104; liberal democracy as form of 1; modes of 120, 127, 133, 145, 168–9; spatial 10–11; teleological form of 83
other/s: contemporary understandings of 1; humanity of 163; participation in

governmental order 70–1; "speaking for" 50–1
Oudh incident 87

Page Three girl 25, 75, 140
"Paki-bashing" 142
Pakistan: British support for 174; civilising process for 174; coding 115–16; Cold War struggle in 64–5; democracy in 40, 106–7; democracy promotion 103; DFID spending 24–5, 168; domesticated 128; gender inequality 123; gender relations 128; intervention in 3–7; liberal democracy in 136; as other in democracy promotion 37; political landscape of 40; Punjab system of government 109; reliance on aid and development 155; religious identity 108; represented in British media 38–9; as solution to contemporary problems 119; stability of 168; as symbol of unity 119; unknowability of 39
parliamentary system 45
Parris, Matthew 14
participatory democracy 30
Partition 80, 106–7, 115, 117, 121–2
permanent settlement principles 91–2
Phillips, Melanie 57
Philo, Chris 78
political contestation 110–11
political mobilisation 49
political relations 87, 91–2
polyarchy 29
population, biopolitics of 42–3
post-developmental 76
poststructural International Relations 33
poverty, alternatives to 168
power: alternate forms of 41–4; democracy as means to distribute 22; within democracy promotion policy 25; democratic theorising and 28–30; distribution of 25; governmentality as form of 43; repressive hypothesis of 25, 29–30, 46, 49; sovereignty as form of 41–2; with truth 53; unequal 40
power politics 39
power relations: DFID intervention and 73–4; freedom of expression and 129; hidden 15; in India 111; of kinship 110–11; of private domestic sphere 40, 124; between public and private spheres 163–4; strategic reversibility of 116; subaltern's subversive agency and

51–2; unequal 19; between West and developing countries 23, 36
press, role of 49–50
Prevent agenda 34, 153, 162, 167
private coding 111–13, 120–1
private property 112, 114
private sphere: blasphemy 134; British 160–1; culture 161; divide between public and 14, 111–12; dress code choices 152; liberal democratic governmentality 145; Muslim identity 120–1; relations of care 75; religious belief 75, 131; sexuality 161; ungoverned in public sphere 101; violence in 166
progress, ideas about 84–5
property law 110
public coding 111–13, 120–1
public debate 51
public sphere: of democratic engagement 14; divide between private and 14, 111–12; free of censorship 129; free speech and association in 48–9; inclusive institutions 99–100; India and 99–101; Muslim identity 120–1
public-private divide 101
Punjab system of government 109
Punjab Unionist Party 117, 118, 120

Quadir, Fahimul 49

race war 78
racist violence 141–3, 147
radical ordinary democracy 170–1
radicalisation, as poor governance 34
Ramesh K 141–2
rape 121
rationalism 140–3
Rattigan, W.H. 110
relations of power 32
religious identity 108, 147
The Reluctant Fundamentalist (Hamid) 55–6
representation 50–2, 96, 101–3, 106
representative institutions 98, 99, 102, 107
repressive hypothesis of power 25, 29–30, 46, 49
Rhodes, Rod 53–4n1
Rickards, Robert 96–7
Robinson, William 62, 65
Rogers, J.T. 64
Rostow, W. W. 60
Roy, Rammohan 111–13

Royal Commission 104
Royal Society of Statistics 103–4
Rumsfeld, Donald 5
rural indebtedness 114–15
Rushdie, Salman 128, 130–2, 135, 139–41
Ruthven, Malise 133, 138, 139

Said, Edward 71, 143
Salman Rushdie affair 126–7, 133, 134, 157
Sanders, Peter 154
Sardar, Ziauddin 131
The Satanic Verses (Rushdie) 128, 139
sati 111–12
savage: as ancestor of Western civilised man 67–8; discovery of 62; domesticated 69; as subject of modern governmentality 70–1
Scotland, Baroness 153, 154
segregation 75
self-rule 112–13
Sen, Amartya 32
Sethi, Najam 39
Shapiro, Michael 106
shari'ah law: alien nature of 7; backwardness of 9; incompatible with democratic ideas 8–9; terrorism and 8, 57, 165; as threat to British values 8; women's rights and 74–5
Smillie, Ian 63
Smith, Adam 89
social antagonism 115
social conservatism 155
Southall Black Sisters 138
sovereignty 41–2, 45, 64
Soviet communism 65
spatial othering 10–11
speaking, modes of 51–2
Spivak, Gayatri 13, 23–4, 50–1, 76
"The Stages of Economic Growth" (Rostow) 60
Stanley of Alderley, Lord 152
Stephen, James Fitzpatrick 103
Stoddart, Lord 132
Storge, Malcolm 158
subaltern woman 51–2
subjectivity, forms of 69–71
subversive agency 51–2
suffrage 85
suicide bombers 158, 166
Swain, Ashok 35

Taheri, Amir 144
Tanweer, Shehzad 4

202 *Index*

Tebbit, Norman 159
Tebbit test 159
temporal othering 9–10, 96, 132
terrorism: consequences of 70; existential
  threat of 8; home-grown 4, 34; as
  ideology 166; as opposite of democracy 34; positions on women 71–2;
  shari'ah law and 8. *See also* war on
  terror
Thatcher, Margaret 134
Theory of Moral Sentiments (Smith)
  89
thought, importance of children 2–3
time: as form of power 10; preserving
  continuity 89–90
Townend, John 133
transparency 50
Trojan Horse scandal 167
Tucker, Henry 97, 98

ul-Haq, Zia 64
United Nations Development
  Programme (UNDP) 24, 72
Unsworth, Sue 26, 29, 61, 62, 63
Utilitarian codes 93–4

Vaughan-Williams, Nick 161
Vernon, Phil 60

violence: condemnation of 140–3; liberal
  democratic governmentality and 161–3;
  Partition and 121–2; in private sphere
  166
violent masculinities 13–14, 68, 80, 162
Visions of Ecstasy (film) 135
voting population 46–7
voting/voting systems 22–3, 43, 107,
  116–17, 120, 123 *See also* elections

Wade, John 100–1
Walker, R.B.J. 33
war on terror 10, 16, 34, 57–8, 81, 168
  See also terrorism
Warsi, Baroness 8
Western history, as model of democracy
  61–2
Whitehead, Laurence 35
Williams, Rowan 7–9, 57, 165, 166, 170
Wilson, Jon E. 93
women 71–6
Women Against Fundamentalism 138
women's rights 13, 73–5, 88, 114, 138–40
  See also gender/gender relations
Writing Security (Campbell) 33
Wyn Davies, Merryl 131

Yaqoob, Salma 151, 155–6